Education in India after Independence

EDUCATION IN INDIA AFTER INDEPENDENCE

JAGDISH CHAND

Former Deputy Director of Education and
Executive Director of the Delhi Bureau of Textbooks,
Delhi Administration

ANSHAH

Anshah Publishing House

Preface

The book Development of Education System in India, published in 2004, provides comprehensive description and analysis of the development of education system from Vedic times to modern times. As per the requirement of market and demand of curriculum prescribed in various universities, the book covering a particular period is brought out in the present form for the students and educators. It is hoped that this volume Education in India after Independence will be welcomed and its advantage also taken by the pre-service and in-service teachers.

The volume derives its material from several original and secondary sources and the author is grateful to all the authors and their publishers.

Jagdish Chand

Contents

1

University Education Commission (1948-49)

APPOINTMENT OF THE UNIVERSITY EDUCATION COMMISSION

After independence, the first action of a great significance to be taken by the Government of India in the field of education was the appointment of the University Education Commission under the Chairmanship of Dr. S. Radhakrishnan, a distinguished scholar and former Vice-Chancellor of Banaras University, who r ose to become the second President of India. The report of the Commission is a document of great importance as it has guided the development of university education in India since independence. The Commission was appointed by the Government of India to report on Indian University Education and suggest improvements and extensions that may be desirable to suit present and future requirements of the country. The Commission was inaugurated on December 6, 1948. It submitted its report in August 1949.

Besides the Chairman, the Commission included 9 members including Dr. Tara Chand, Secretary and Educational Adviser to the Government of India, Prof. N.K. Sidhanta, Prof. of English and Dean, Faculty of Arts, University of Lucknow, the Secretary of the Commission.

Terms of Reference

The terms of reference of the Commission were to consider and make recommendations in regard to:

(1) The aims and objects of university education and research in India.

(2) The changes considered necessary and desirable in the Constitution, control, functions and jurisdiction of universities in India and their relations with Government, Central and Provincial.

(3) The finance of universities.

(4) The maintenance of the highest standards of teaching and examination in the universities and colleges under their control.

(5) The course of study in the universities with special reference to the maintenance of a sound balance between the humanities and the sciences and between pure science and technological training and the duration of such courses.

(6) The standards of admission to university courses of study with reference to the desirabilities of an independent university entrance examination and the avoidance of unfair discrimination which militate against Fundamental Right 23(2).

(7) The medium of instruction in the universities.

(8) The provision for advanced study in Indian culture, history, literatures, languages, philosophy and fine arts.

(9) The need for more universities on a regional or other basis.

(10) The organisation of advanced research in all branches of knowledge in the universities and institutions of higher research in a well-coordinated fashion avoiding waste of effort and resources.

(11) Religious instruction in the universities.

(12) The special problems of the Banaras Hindu University, the Aligarh Muslim University, the Delhi University and other institutions of an all-India character.

(13) The qualifications, conditions of service, salaries, privileges and functions of teachers and the encouragement of original research by teachers.

(14) The discipline of students, hostels and the organisation of tutorial work and any other matter which is germane and essential to a complete and comprehensive enquiry into all aspects of university education and advanced research in India.

MAJOR OBSERVATIONS AND RECOMMENDATIONS

I. Concept of a Civilised Society

The Commission observed, "The greatness of a country does not depend on the extent of its territory, the length of its communication or the amount of wealth, not even on widespread education or equitable distribution of wealth important as all these things are. If we wish to bring about a savage upheaval in our society, a *raksasa raj*, all that we need to do so is to give vocational and technical education and starve the spirit. We will have a number of scientists without conscience, technicians without taste who find a void within themselves, a moral vacuum and a desperate need to substitute something, anything, for their lost endeavour and purpose. Society will then get what it deserves. If we claim to be civilised we must develop thought for the poor and the suffering, chivalrous regard and respect for women, faith in human brotherhood regardless of race or colour, nation or religion, love of peace and freedom, abhorrence of cruelty and ceaseless devotion of the claims of the justice."

II. Aims of Education

(i) To teach that life has a meaning.

(ii) To awaken the innate ability to live the life of soul by developing wisdom.

(iii) To acquaint with the social philosophy which should govern all our institutions, educational as well as economic and political.
(iv) To train for democracy.
(v) To train for self-development.
(vi) To develop certain values like fearlessness of mind, strength of conscience and integrity of purpose.
(vii) To acquaint with cultural heritage for its regeneration.
(viii) To enable to know that education is a life—long process.
(ix) To develop understanding of the present as well as of the past.
(x) To impart vocational and professional training.

III. Functions of Universities

The Commission laid emphasis on the following in view of the economic and political changes in the wake of independence.

(1) *Creating individuals with a change of spirit.* It is for the universities to create knowledge and train minds of men who would bring together the two – material resources and human energies. If our living standards are to be raised radical change of spirit is essential.

(2) *Preparing individual who seek guidance from the past but give up fatal obsession of the perfection of the past.* The universities are the intellectual sanctuaries of the inner life of the nation. They must train intellectual pioneers, seeking guidance from the past but providing dynamism to realise new dreams.

(3) *Developing individuals who understand the significance of an integrated way of life.* The universities must develop the qualities of synthesing the knowledge – a '*Samanavaya*' of the different items of knowledge.

(4) *Developing men of wisdom.* Our ancient teachers tried to teach subjects and impart wisdom. Their ideal was wisdom (*irfan*) along with knowledge (*ilm*), *Jnanam vijnana sahitam.* We cannot be wise without some basis of knowledge though we may easily acquire knowledge and remain devoid of wisdom. To use the words of the *Upanishad*, we may be the knowers of texts (*mantravit*) and not knowers of self (*atmavit*). No amount of factual information would make ordinary men into educated or virtuous men unless something is awakened in them, an innate ability to live the life of the soul.

(5) *Developing individuals who understand the aims of the social order.* The universities must develop a concept of the social order in the students. They must develop values of democracy, justice and liberty, equality and fraternity – ideals of the Indian Society.

(6) *Producing students who can adjust to society and bring about new changes.* Education is a means by which society perpetuates itself. In 1852, Newman defined the function of the university thus, "If a practical end must be assigned to a university course, then I say it is training good members of society." No system of education could be directed to the weakening of the State that maintains it. But education is also an instrument for social change.

(7) *Preparing leaders*. Training for leadership in the professions and in public life is one of the central aims of university education, which is difficult to realise. President Truman remarks, "Our national policies must be administered by men of broad experience, mature outlook and sound judgement."

If it is the function of universities to train men and women for wise leadership, they must enable young men and women to read with insight.

(8) *Developing Men of Character*. We are building a civilisation, not a factory or a workshop. The quality of a civilisation depends not on the material, equipment or the political machinery but on the character of men. The major task of education is the improvement of character.

(9) *Developing Appreciation of Cultural Unity of India*. Indian culture is like a palimpsest in which new characters do not entirely efface the old. In a single social pattern fragments of different ages are brought together. It would be impossible to think of an India where no Mughals ruled, where no Taj was built, where no Macaulay wrote his Minute on education. Indian culture is like a living organism growing in richness and content. Primitive cultures are marked by extreme conservatism where social groups follow the same path of custom and convention with irrational persistence. Living cultures are dynamic and maintain their cultural pattern by a continuous effort of individual and social discipline.

(10) *Developing individuals capable of understanding the spiritnal heritage of the past*. The chief source of spiritual nourishment for any people must be its own past perpetually rediscovered and renewed. A society without a knowledge of the past which has made it would be lacking in depth and dignity.

We must be critical and selective and use the past to illuminate the present. We should not blindly give up the great values of our past nor should we cling to beliefs simply because they are ancient.

(11) *Developing skills for the needed personnel*. The universities must prepare personnel to meet the increasing demand for every type of activity, *i.e.*, administration, commerce, industry, politics.

(12) *Developing scientists and technological personnel*. The universities must enable the country to attain in as short a time as possible, freedom from want, disease and ignorance, by the application and development of scientific and technical knowledge. India is rich in natural resources and her people have intelligence and energy and are throbbing with renewed life and vigour. It is for the universities to prepare such personnel.

(13) *Developing individuals with values and skills of cultural cooperation*. The setting for the development of a world culture through the cross fertilisation of cultures is ready. The world has become, through the speed of transportation and communication and economic independence, a single body. We must secure recognition and acceptance of the oneness of the world in the thinking of the people. Growth in mutual understanding arises from the recognition

that the different cultures are dialects of the one language of the spirit.

IV. Discipline and Indiscipline

Concept of Good Discipline. It is important that good discipline be looked upon not as student conformity to arbitrary standards of conduct, but rather as individual responsibility for behaviour. Peace and order maintained by rigidly executed rules is totalitarian, not educative, in method.

Discipline is a Universal Problem. Human nature knows no national boundaries. The sun never sets upon problems of conduct. Some youth at home, in school and in college gravitate into patterns of conduct which create concern for parents and teachers. Surplus energy, not finding a legitimate outlet, misadventure, idleness and occasionally malice, all conspire to create mischief and irregularities of conduct. Problem cases and indiscipline peculiar to college life are inevitable, but there is a wide difference in the extent of these in different parts in India.

Causes of Indiscipline

Indiscipline Arises from World and Local Conditions. Some of the unrest in college groups now appear to start from world conditions. Ferment is international and continental, a condition that follows in wake of wars, and is more acute now than ever before. "We should not forget that we are living in a period of confusion and conflict. This is a world-wide phenomenon. This has an unsettling effect on the youth of every country." was one of the many similar expressions from our witnesses.

Some of the student disturbances in India today may be initiated by students who do feel a personal responsibility for their action, and yet do not show mature judgement in its evaluation. While such situations call for disciplinary action, they call more directly for educational action and attitudes. The causes for such disturbances are complex, and their solution will be achieved, not by punitive force, but by a process of educational development undertaken in an attitude of sympathy, understanding and mutual helpfulness between the staff and the students.

Some witnesses cited the period of the struggle for national independence, in which students and staff were called upon by political leaders to engage in agitation, as a general cause of indiscipline carried over to the present. Such action may have served a patriotic purpose in an all-out drive for national freedom, but such practices now have a reverse effect, they promote confusion and become a serious impediment to national solidarity and integration.

Anarchical Elements Exploit Students. Unfortunately, some political cliques and even anarchical elements are continuing to exploit college students for their purposes. During the visit of the Commission to Calcutta, a riot was started in which students were apparently used as pawns and which issued in bloodshed and lawlessness that continued for two or three days. This disorder was the work of anti-social and violent elements, and neither the university nor students could be held responsible.

Causes of Indiscipline are Varied. (Adapted from the Report)The sources of indiscipline are many, but among the most general though indirect causes often cited by our witnesses were:

(i) Meagre finances and consequent lack of amenities required for healthy college life;
(ii) Closely related to these elements is the economic distress of some of the institutions which lack the means to provide adequate hostels and comfortable living conditions, playgrounds and desirable corporate activities for students;
(iii) The masses of students;
(iv) The failure of parents at times to support the college authorities;
(v) The inability of the teachers to cope with confused thinking, admission of students without the intelligence or industry requisite for successful study;
(vi) Tensions over examinations which unfortunately dominate the educational system; and
(vii) Financial worry caused to poor students by the cost of university education.

All these contribute to the difficulties of maintaining the best conduct and welfare of students.

Constructive Approaches to the Solution of Disciplinary and Allied Problems. The Commission felt "The key to the successful handling of young people is not found nowadays in a multitude of restraints and reprimands or in the infliction of continuous penalties. These devices may have to be restored to in extreme cases but wholesome student attitude and life cannot be created by negative and repressive measures. The true sanction of discipline lies in the development of the social conscience of the undergraduate body as a whole rather than in punitive measures of precautionary vigilance. As in society so in the university laws are observed because they are approved by reason rather than because they are imposed by force. Indiscipline should be terminated by the good sense of the students."

Students should be given the opportunity to develop self-respect and self-reliance through an attitude of trust rather than live in an atmosphere of suspicion and fear of the proctorial system. Good student government integrates the college community, imparts a wholesome social atmosphere, fosters common ideals and loyal pride in an institution but most important provides training for good citizenship and social responsibility. It gives scope for the right types of student political activity, which helps to develop the capacity to play the role of citizens in a republican form of government and a democratic society. It replaces the undesirable tendencies toward undermining respect for constituted authority and leaving youth a prey to propaganda of conflicting ideologies.

Other Measures for Promotion of Good Discipline. The National Cadet Corps is the most useful form of developing discipline and orderly habits among students. Opportunities for recreation, athletic sports, amenities of social life, especially for students residing outside hostels (who are often neglected), all play their part in good discipline.

Universities Should be Divorced from Party Politics. Students should not be encouraged to engage in party politics though we think it desirable that they take a wholesome and proper interest in election and good government. If the staffs are enlarged, as they should be, there will be opportunity for effective mingling of teachers and students. The fact that many staff members were side tracked in the drive for freedom has weakened in some measure their assumption of active responsibility which all staff members are expected to discharge.

The Problem of Discipline Requires Cooperative Effort. But administrators and teachers cannot solve satisfactorily the problems of promoting good life and high ethical standards on campuses. They must have the cooperation of the parents, the political leaders, the public and the press. This is a cooperative task which deserves the support of all good citizens. The outcome is significant not only for higher education but for the sound growth of our country.

V. Standards of Teaching

The University Education Commission 1948-49 made the following recommendations which still hold good:

1. The standard of admission to the university courses should correspond to that of the present intermediate examination, *i.e.*, after the completion of 12 years of study at a school and an intermediate college; (This has been done by the introduction of 10+2+3 pattern).
2. In each province a large number of well-equipped and well-staffed intermediate colleges (with classes IX to XII or VI to XII) be established;
3. In order to divert students to different vocations after 10 to 12 years of schooling, a large number of occupational institutes be opened;
4. Refresher courses to be organised by the universities for high school and intermediate college teacher;
5. To avoid overcrowding at universities and colleges, the maximum number in the Arts and Science faculties of a teaching university be fixed at 3,000 and in an affiliated college at 1,500;
6. The number of working days be substantially increased to ensure a minimum of 180 in the year, exclusive of examination days; with three terms, each of about 11 weeks' duration;
7. Lectures be carefully planned and supplemented by tutorials, library work and written exercise;
8. There be no prescribed textbooks for any courses of study;
9. Attendance at lectures be compulsory for undergraduate students as a

present, and that private candidates of only certain categories be allowed to appear for public examinations. An experiment should, however, be made with evening colleges for working people;

10. Tutorial instruction be developed in all institutions imparting university education in the following manner:

(a) students should report to tutors in groups not exceeding 6 in number;
(b) tutorials should be made available to undergraduates both pass and honours;
(c) tutorials should stimulate the mental development of students and should not become mere coaching for examinations;
(d) if tutorials are to succeed, the teaching staff should be improved in quality;

11. University libraries be greatly improved by:

(a) larger annual grants;
(b) the introduction of the open access system;
(c) longer hours of work;
(d) better organisation; and
(e) a well trained staff which should include reference assistants; and

12. The laboratories be improved in buildings, fittings, equipment, workshops and technicians.

VI. Medium of Instruction

1. The Federal languages be developed through the assimilation of words from various sources and the retention of words which have already entered into Indian languages from different sources, thereby avoiding the dangers of exclusiveness.

2. International technical and scientific terminology be adopted, the borrowed words be properly assimilated, their pronunciation be adopted to the phonetic system of the Indian language and their spelling fixed in accordance with the sound symbols of Indian scripts.

3. For the medium of instruction for higher education, English be replaced as early as practicable by an Indian language which cannot be Sanskrit on account of vital difficulties.

4. (i) Pupils at the higher secondary and University stages be made conversant with three languages—the regional language, the Federal language and English (the last one in order to acquire the ability to read books in English); and (ii) Higher education be imparted through the instrumentality of the regional language with the option to use the Federal language as the medium of instruction either for some subjects or for all subjects.

5. For the Federal language one script, Devnagri, be employed and some of its defects be removed.

6. Immediate steps be taken for developing the Federal and Regional languages.

VII. Teacher's Emoluments

Recognising the importance of the teaching profession, the Commission recommended the following grades:

University Teachers

1.	Professor	Rs. 900-500-1350
2.	Reader	Rs. 600-300-900
3.	Lecturer	Rs. 300-25-600
4.	Fellows or Instructors	Rs. 250-25-600
5.	Research Fellows	Rs. 250-25-500

University teachers should give the community punctuality, efficiency and devotion to duty in relation to their teaching work, and new ideas and newer methods in relation to their research work.

Scales of Pay for Affiliated Colleges with Post-Graduate Classes

Principal	Rs.800-400-1000
Senior Lecturers (Two in each College)	Rs.500-25-800
Lecturer	Rs.200-15-310-20-400-25-500

Scales of Pay for Affiliated Colleges with no Post-Graduate Classes

Principal	Rs.600-45-800
Senior Lecturer (Two in Each College)	Rs.400-25-600
Lecturer	Rs.200-15-320-20-400

VIII. Courses of Study

Knowledge should be considered as a whole. While drawing up the courses, link between various aspects should not kept in view. There should be a connecting bond between the general, academic and vocational education. The principles and practices of general education must become an integral part of courses at the intermediate and degree stage.

Courses at the Degree Level

Apart from a course in general education, following courses are to be taken up by students:

(1) Federal language or if that happens to be mother-tongue, a classical or a modern Indian language.

(2) English.

(3) and (4). *For Arts students*, not less than two special subjects, preferably from each group.

Humanities	*Social Sciences*
(i) Classical or a Modern Indian language (ii) English, German or French, (iii) Philosophy, (iv) History, (v) Mathematics, (vi) Fine Arts, (vii) Political Science	(1) Economics, (2) Sociology, (3) Psychology, (4) Anthropology, (5) Geography, (6) Home Economics

(3) and (4) for *Science students*, not less than two special subjects from the following list:

(i) Mathematics; (ii) Physics; (iii) chemistry; (iv) Botany; (v) Zoology and (vi) Geology.

IX. Professional Education

(a) *Agriculture.* The study of agriculture at the primary, secondary and higher education be given high priority in national economic planning. So far as is feasible, agricultural education be given a rural setting.

(b) *Commerce.* A commerce student should be given opportunities for practical work in three or four different kinds of firms.

(c) *Education.* The course be remodelled and more time given to school practice and more weight given to practice in assessing the students' performances.

(d) *Engineering and Technology.* The number of engineering schools of different grades be increased particularly for training of grades 4 and 5 (foremen, craftsmen, draftsmen, overseers, etc.).

In establishing new engineering colleges or institutes there should be fresh, critical inquiry as to the types of engineering services needed in India. Uncritical reception and imitation of existing institutions here and abroad should be avoided.

(e) *Law*: A three-year degree course be offered in special legal subjects. Students pursuing degree courses in law shall not be permitted to carry other degree courses simultaneously except in a few instances where advanced students have proved their interest and are studying related subjects in law and some other fields.

(f) *Medicine*: The maximum number of admission to a medical college be 100, provided the staff and equipment for that number are available.

7. *Religious Education*: (a) All educational institutions should start work with a few minutes for silent meditation.

(b) In the first year lives of the great religious leaders like Gautama Buddha, Confucius, Zoroaster, Socrates, Jesus, Samkara, Ramanuja, Madhva, Mohammad, Kabir, Nanak, Gandhi be taught.

(c) In the second year some selections of a universalist character from the scriptures of the world be studied.

(d) In the third year, the central problems of the philosophy of religion be considered.

X. Examinations

(a) A university degree should not be required for Government administrative services. Special State examination for recruitment to the various services should be organised.

(b) No credit is given, at present for class-work in courses except sometimes in the case of practical work. Such credit should be given.

(c) Three years will be involved for the first degree,

(d) The standards for success at the examination should as far as possible, be uniform in the various universities and should be raised. We suggest that a candidate should get 70 per cent or more marks to secure a first class, 55 per cent to 69 per cent for a second and at least 40 per cent for a third.

XI. Students, their Activities and Welfare

(a) Two years of physical education be required for all students, men and women, except those who are physically unfit or who are in the National Cadet Corps.
(b) Hostels be constructed in blocks of not more than fifty students per block, with common rooms and dining halls for four or five blocks.
(c) University unions should be as free as possible from political activities.
(d) An Advisory Board of Student Welfare be organised in universities which do not have such a body.

XII. Women Education

On the importance of women education, the Commission observed, "There can't be an educated people without education of women. If general education had to be limited to man or women, then opportunity should be given to women, from them it would more surely be passed to the next generation." The Commission further observed, "It is time to realise that the finest family relations result from the association of a man and woman who have had much of their education in common, but each of the whom has developed according to his or her own nature, and not in imitation."

A woman should be made familiar with the problems of home management and the skills developed in meeting these. They should be provided 'laboratory experience' in a baby home and nursery school etc.

Special Courses of Study for Women. These are (1) Home Economics, (2) Nursing, (3) Teaching, (4) Fine Arts.

Women students in general should be helped to see their normal place in a normal society, both as citizens and as women, and to prepare for it. College programmes should be so designed that it will be possible for them to do so.

Standards of courtesy and social responsibility should be emphasised on the part of men in mixed colleges.

Constitution and Control

(a) University education be placed on the Concurrent List.
(b) The concern of the Central Government with the universities be with regard to finance, coordination of facilities in special subjects, adoption of national policies, ensuring minimum standards of efficient administration and liaison between universities and national research laboratories and scientific surveys, etc.

XIII. Finance

The Commission observed that on account of resource crunch, the universities are not able to implement appropriate reforms. In this regard it made the following recommendations:

(1) A University Grants Commission should be set up to allocate finances to the universities.

(2) The State Government should shoulder the major burden of the university education.

(3) Recurring and non-recurring grants should be given to non-government colleges. Specific rules should be framed for giving grants.

(4) Income tax concessions may be given to individuals and firms which give financial aids to universities.

XIV. Rural Universities

Special attention should be paid to the setting up and developing universities in the rural areas.

EVALUATION OF THE RECOMMENDATIONS OF THE REPORT OF THE UNIVERSITY EDUCATION COMMISSION

While evaluating the report of the University Education Commission (1947-48) it may be borne in mind that the report was drafted and published before the finalisation of the Constitution of India and its inauguration on 26th of January 1950. It is, therefore, natural that some of the important points and terms like Socialism, Secularism, National and Emotional Integration, and Fundamental Rights, etc. do not find mention and accordingly their implications in the report.

Merits of the Report

The report of the Commission is a document of great importance as it has guided the development of university education in India since independence.

In the first instance we take up the philosophical and sociological aspects of the recommendations. It accorded due attention to synthesise the knowledge and wisdom of the East and the West and of the ancient and modern. Accordingly it gave its recommendations on the contents of the curriculum.

Second, while stressing scientific thoughts, it warned us not to ignore moral and spiritual values in education. Overemphasis on the material aspects may lead to '*Raksasa Raj*' (Rule of the Demons). The modern slogan in education is 'Promotion of Value Education'. It duly finds its echo in the report of the Commission.

Third, take the present educational structure of 10+2+3 (First University degree after 15 years of schooling) that saw its beginning in 1975. It was recommended by the University Education Commission nearly three decades before it came into operation. This shows the words of wisdom of the framers of the report. It looks strange that we took so much time to understand the implications of the recommendations of the report.

Fourth, the Commission, very right and clearly brought out the significance of women education.

Fifth, its recommendation that a university degree should not be required for government administrative service is quite weighty. It recommended the organisation of state examination for recruitment to various services.

Sixth, it rightly recommended that so far as is feasible, agricultural education be given a rural setting and new universities should be opened preferably in the rural areas.

Seventh, it appreciated the significant role played by the teachers and recommended suitable grades and service conditions for them.

Eighth, since India is a religious country, the Commission recognised the necessity of introducing some kind of religious education (without religious dogmas and rituals).

Ninth, the Commission recommended a course in general education for all students pursuing different courses.

Lastly, the Commission's recommendations on the maintenance of discipline and curbing indiscipline in educational institutions are very relevant even today.

Demerits/Shortcomings of the Report

The report is too philosophical and ideal.

One fails to understand the rationale underlying the separate pay scales for teachers working in universities and affiliated colleges for the same type of work.

Likewise is the case with separate pay scales for teachers teaching in degree colleges and post-graduate colleges. Of course, one can find some justification for paying separate pay scales for teacher's teaching post-graduate classes. However, the Commission made no such recommendations.

Summing Up

Writing about the recommendations, our first President Rajendra Prasad, very aptly observed in 1955, "The value of the University Education Commission Report lies very largely in the fact that it recognises the necessity for a fundamental change in the set up of things in this country and proceeds to deal with its educational problems on that basis. It has, further the merit of not contemplating a complete break with the past but of conserving the best that is available."

Though more than half a century has elapsed since the publication of the Report, it is still quite relevant. In spite of its repetitive observations, it is undoubtedly weighty and full of wisdom and pragmatic action in several respects in the present scenario also.

2

Secondary Education Commission (1952-53)

APPOINTMENT OF THE SECONDARY EDUCATION COMMISSION

The Secondary Education Commission also sometimes known as the Mudaliar Commission, known after its Chairman was appointed on account of the following considerations:

1. With the attainment of independence, the political situation underwent a complete revolution. Education also needed a fresh outlook. This was appropriately voiced by Maulana Abul Kalam Azad, the then Education Minister in his presidential address to the Central Advisory Board of Education in 1948, "The scales in which the educational problems were weighed by this Board up till now have grown out of date. The dimensions of the national problems of the day cannot be judged by the same measurements. The new aspiration of new India will require fresh outlook and new measures to tackle its problems".

The Central Advisory Board of Education at its 14th meeting, held in January 1948 recommended the appointment of a Commission to examine the prevailing system of secondary education in the country and suggest measures for its reorganisation and improvement. The Board at its 18th meeting held in 1951 reiterated its former decision and pressed for early implementation of its recommendations.

2. There had been no comprehensive examination of the problems pertaining to secondary education, while the problems of elementary and university education had been surveyed and steps taken to improve.

3. It was the secondary school that supplied teachers to the primary schools and students to the universities. An inefficient system of secondary education was bound to affect adversely the quality of education at all stages. It was felt that one of the major defects of the prevailing system of secondary education was its unilinear and predominantly academic character. The need for the reorganisation of secondary education with diversified courses had become more urgent as a result of acceptance by the Government of Basic Education as the pattern of education at the elementary stage.

4. The Constitution of India had come into force on January 26, 1950. Educational needs had to be studied in this context.

In view of these considerations, the Government of India set up the Secondary Education Commission by Resolution dated 23 September, 1952. The Commission was inaugurated on 6 October, 1952. It submitted its Report in June, 1953.

Members of the Commission

The Commission consisted of 9 members including the Chairman, Dr. A. Lakshmanaswami Mudaliar, Vice-Chancellor, Madras University, A.N. Basu, Principal, Central Institute of Education, Delhi, was its Member-Secretary. Two foreign educators namely, Principal John Christie, Jesus College, Oxford (U.K.) and Dr. Kenneth Rast Williams, Associate Director, Southern Regional Educational Board, Atlanta (USA) were also members of the Commission.

Terms of Reference

Under the terms of reference, the Commission was asked:

"(a) to enquire into and report on the present position of Secondary Education in India in all its aspects; and

(b) suggest measures for its reorganisation and improvement with particular reference to:

- (i) the aims, organisation and content of Secondary education;
- (ii) its relationship to Primary, Basic and Higher education;
- (iii) the inter-relation of Secondary Schools of different types;
- (iv) other allied problems

so that a sound and reasonable uniform system of Secondary Education suited to our needs and resources may be provided for the whole country".

MAJOR RECOMMENDATIONS OF THE COMMISSION

I. *Needs, Aims and Objectives of Secondary Education.* The Commission took note of the changed political, social and economic conditions of the country and restated the objectives of education. According to it following are the main objectives of education:

1. Development of democratic citizenship.
2. Improvement of vocational efficiency.
3. Development of personality.
4. Development of qualities for leadership.

II. *Duration of Secondary Education.* Under the new organisational structure, education should commence after a four or five years' period of Primary or Junior Basic Education and should include: (a) the Middle or Senior Basic or Junior Secondary Stage of 3 years, and (b) Higher Secondary stage of 4 years.

III. *Multi-purpose Schools and Vocational Schools.* 1. Multi-purpose schools should be established wherever possible to provide varied courses of interest to students with diverse aims, aptitudes and abilities.

2. Those who have successfully completed such course should be given opportunities to take up higher specialized courses in polytechnics or technological institutions.

IV. *Diversified Curriculum*. It suggested seven groups out of which students could select anyone besides languages and core curriculum.

V. *Guidance and Counselling*. The Commission suggested a comprehensive programme for guidance and counselling at the secondary stage.

VI. *Technical Schools*. Technical Schools should be started in large numbers either separately or as a part of multi-purpose schools.

VII. *Agricultural Schools*. The Commission observed that as agriculture is the most important industry, it must receive its due attention.

VIII. *Other Types of Schools*. (1) Public schools should continue to exist for the present and the pattern of education given in them should be brought into reasonable conformity with the general pattern of national education.

(2)A number of residential schools should be established, more particularly in certain rural areas.

(3) A large number of schools should be established to meet the needs of handicapped children.

Co-education. (1) While no distinction need be made between education imparted to boys and girls, special facilities for the study of home science should be made available in all girls' schools and co-education of mixed schools.

(2) Efforts should be made by State Governments to open separate schools for girls wherever there is demand for them.

IX. *Textbooks*. (1) With a view to improving the quality of textbooks prescribed, a high power Textbooks Committee should be constituted.

(2) The Textbooks Committee should lay down clear criteria for the type of paper, illustration, printing and format of the books.

(3) A single textbook should not be prescribed for every subject of study, but a reasonable number of books which satisfy the standards laid down should be recommended leaving the choice to the schools concerned. In the case of languages, however, definite textbooks should be prescribed for each class to ensure proper gradation.

(4) No book prescribed as a textbook or as a book for general study should contain any passage or statement which might offend the religious or social susceptibilities of any section of the community or might indoctrinate the minds of the young students with particular political or religious ideologies.

(5) Frequent changes in textbooks and books prescribed for study should be discouraged.

X. *Dynamic Methods of Teaching*. (1) The methods of teaching in schools should aim not merely at imparting of knowledge in an efficient manner, but also at inculcating desirable values and proper attitudes and habits of work in the students.

(2) The emphasis in teaching should shift from verbalism and memorisation to learning through purposeful, concrete and realistic situation and, for this purpose, the principles of 'Activity Method' and 'Project Method' should be

assimilated in school practice.

(3) In the teaching of all subjects special stress should be placed on clear thinking and expression both in speech and writing.

(4) A well thought-out attempt should be made to adopt methods of instruction to the needs of individual students as much as possible so that dull, average and bright students may all have a chance to progress at their own pace.

(5) Students should be given adequate opportunity to work in groups and to carry out group projects so as to develop in them the qualities necessary for group life and cooperative work.

(6) Every Secondary School should have a well-equipped school library, class libraries and subject libraries should also be utilised.

XI. *Discipline.* (1) The education of character should be envisaged as the responsibility of all teachers.

(2) In order to promote discipline, personal contact between the teacher and the pupils should be strengthened; self-government in the form of house system with perfects or monitors and student councils, whose responsibility will be to draw up a code of conduct and enforce its observance, should be introduced in all schools.

XII. *Religious and Moral Instruction.* Religious instruction may be given in schools only on a voluntary basis outside the regular school hours, such instruction being confined to the children of the particular faith concerned and given with the consent of the parties and the managements.

XIII. *Extra-curricular Activities.* Extra-curricular activities should form an integral part of education imparted in the school and all teachers should devote a definite time to such activities.

XIV. *Guidance and Counselling in Secondary Schools.* Educational guidance should receive much greater attention on the part of the educational authorities. The services of trained guidance officers and career masters should be gradually made available to all schools.

XV. *Health Education.* A properly organised school medical service should be built up in all States. A thorough medical examination of all pupils and necessary follow-up treatment where necessary should be carried out in all schools.

XVI. *Physical Education.* (1) All teachers below the age of 40 actively participate in many of the physical activities of students and thus make them a lively part of the school programme.

(2) Full records of physical activities of the students must be maintained.

XVII. *A New Approach to Examination and Evaluation.* The number of examinations should be reduced and the element of subjectivity in the essay-type tests should be minimised by introducing objective tests. In the final assessment of the pupils due credit should be given to the internal tests and the school records of the pupils. The system of symbolic rather than numerical marking should be adopted. There should be only one public examination at the completion of the secondary school course.

XVIII. *Improvement of the Teaching Personnel.* (1) The normal period of probation for trained teachers should be one year.

(2) The teachers possessing the qualifications and performing the same type of work should be treated at par in the matter of grades of salary irrespective of the type of institution in which they are working.

(3) The system of triple benefit scheme, pension-cum-provident fund-cum-insurance should be introduced in all States.

(4) Arbitration Boards or Committees should be established to look into the appeals and grievances of teachers.

(5) The age of retirement in the case of physically fit and competent teachers may be extended to 60 with the approval of the Director of Education.

(6) The children of teachers should be given free education throughout the school stage.

(7) Through a system of cooperative house building societies teachers should be provided with quarters so as to enable them to live near the school.

(8) The practice of private tuitions by teachers should be abolished.

XIX. *Teacher Training.* (1) There should be only two types of institutions for teacher training:

(i) For those who have taken the School Leaving Certificate or Higher Secondary School Leaving Certificate, for whom the period of training should be two years; and

(ii) For graduates for whom the training may, for the present, be of one academic year, but extended as a long-term programme to two academic years.

(2) During the period of training all the student-teachers should be given suitable stipend by the State.

(3) All Training Colleges should provide adequate residential facilities.

XX. *Organisation and Administration.* (1) There should be a Board of Secondary Education consisting of not more than 25 members with the Director of Education as its Chairman to deal with all matters of education at the secondary stage and to lay down general policies. A Sub-Committee of the Board should deal with the conduct of examinations.

(2) State Advisory Boards should be constituted in each State to advise the Department of Education on all matters pertaining to education.

XXI. *Inspection of Schools.* (1) The true role of an Inspector should be to study the problems of school and view them comprehensively in the context of educational objectives, to formulate suggestion for improvement and help the teachers to carry out his advice and recommendations. The Commission prepared the term 'Educational Adviser'.

(2) In addition to direct recruitment, Inspectors should also be drawn from (i) teachers of ten years' experience, (ii) headmasters of High Schools, and

(iii) duly qualified staff of Training Colleges who may be allowed to work as such for a period of three to five years.

XXII. *Management of Schools.* (1) The Managing Boards of all schools should be registered and should consist of a limited number of persons with the Headmaster as an *ex-officio* member.

(2) No member of the Managing Board should directly or indirectly interfere with the internal administration of the school.

XXIII. *School Building and Equipment.* (1) The open spaces available in cities must be conserved to be utilised as playground by groups of schools.

(2) Normally, in designing buildings for schools, care should be taken to see that an area of not less than 10 sq. ft. is provided per student in the classroom.

(3) The optimum number of boys to be admitted to any class should be 30 and the maximum should not in any case exceed 40; the optimum number in the whole school should be 500 while the maximum should not exceed 750.

XXIV. *Hours of Working and Vacation.* (1) As a rule the total number of working days in a school should not be less than two hundred, the working hours per week should be at least thirty-five periods about forty-five minutes each; the schoo's should work regularly for six days in the week. One of the days being a half day when the teachers and students might meet informally and work together on various extra-curricular and social projects.

(2) Normally during the year there should be a summer vacation of two months and two breaks of ten to fifteen days at suitable periods during the year.

XXV. *Finance.* (1) A cess called the Industrial Education Cess be levied, the amount collected to be utilised for the furtherance of technical and vocational education at the secondary stage.

(2) The Centre should assume certain amount of direct responsibility for the contemplated reorganisation of secondary education and give financial aid for the purpose.

AIMS OF SECONDARY EDUCATION

Needs of a Nation as the Determining Factor in the Formulation of Aims of Education Including Secondary Education. While formulating the aims of secondary education, the Commission observed, "As political, social and economic conditions change and new problems arise, it becomes necessary to re-examine carefully and restate clearly the objectives which education at each stage, should keep in view. Moreover, this statement must take into account not only the facts of the existing situation but also the direction of its development and the nature and type of the social order that we envisage for the future to which education has to be geared."

The Secondary Education Commission pointed out the following needs of India:

(a) Transformation of India into a secular democratic republic.
(b) Improvement of productive efficiency.

(c) Stimulation of a cultural renaissance.

In the light of the above mentioned needs the Secondary Education Commission stated the following aims of secondary education:

1. Developing democratic citizenship.
2. Improvement of vocational efficiency.
3. Development of personality.
4. Development of qualities of leadership.

1. *Developing Democratic Citizenship.* Citizenship is a very exacting and challenging responsibility for which every citizen has to be carefully trained. For democratic citizenship, education should develop in them the following five qualities:

(i) *Capacity for clear thinking.* The first requisite in this connection is to develop capacity for clear thinking and receptivity to new ideas. This is the hall-mark of educated mind. A democratic citizen should be able to sift fact from fiction and reject what is bad.

(ii) *Clearness in speech and writing.* It is an essential pre-requisite for successful living in a democracy which is based not on force but on free discussion, persuasion and peaceful exchange of ideas.

(iii) *Education for living.* Education should initiate the students into the many-sided art of living in a community graciously. This art should be imbibed. Amongst the qualities which should be cultivated for this purpose are: (a) discipline, (b) co-operation, (c) social sensitiveness, and (d) tolerance.

(iv) *Sense of true patriotism.* The concept of patriotism is three fold: (a) a sincere appreciation of the social and cultural achievement of one's country, (b) a readiness to recognise its weaknesses frankly and work for its eradication, and (c) an earnest resolve to serve it to the best of one's ability. Education should develop these.

(v) *Sense of world citizenship.* Lastly, education must instil in an individual sense of one world and we must discharge our duties accordingly. 'My country — right or wrong' is a dangerous slogan these days. These are the days of internationalism.

2. *Improvement of Vocational Efficiency.* The second important aim is technical and vocational efficiency of our students. This includes (a) creating a new attitude that implies an appreciation of the dignity of all work, however, slowly; (b) making the students realise that self-fulfilment and national prosperity are only possible through work in which everyone must participate and a conviction that when our educated men take any piece of work in hand they will try to complete it as efficiently and artistically as their powers permit; (c) making attempts by all the teachers to ensure that such an attitude on the part of the students finds expression in every activity of the school; and (d) promotion of technical skill and efficiency at all stages of education so as to provide trained and efficient personnel to work out schemes of industrial and technological advancement.

3. *Development of Personality.* The third aim of education includes:

(i) to release the sources of creative energy in the students so that they may be able to appreciate their cultural heritage;

(ii) to cultivate rich interests.

4. *Development of Qualities of Leadership.* The special function of the secondary school in this context, is to train persons who will be able to assume the responsibility of leadership — in the social, political, industrial or cultural fields — in their own groups of community or locality.

SIGNIFICANCE AND STRUCTURE OF SECONDARY EDUCATION ACCORDING TO SECONDARY EDUCATION COMMISSION

Significance of Secondary Education. The Secondary Education Commission (1952-53) has pointed out the significance of secondary education 1952-53. "We have to bear in mind that secondary education is a complete unit in itself and not merely a preparatory stage; that at the end of this period, the student should be in a position, if he wishes, to enter on the responsibility of life and take up some useful vocation". It helps individuals to become useful members of a complex modern society. Since our needs are to transform the Indian State into a democratic, secular and socialist one, the secondary education being a terminal stage must discharge this function effectively. It is of interest to note that just 5 to 6 per cent of the college–age students, enter the portals of higher education. Thus a good quality of secondary education is very essential to meet the needs of the country.

Providing Teachers for Primary Schools. Secondary education provides teachers for the primary schools. Now the qualification for training in an elementary teacher training institute or school is the completion of the secondary schooling. Secondary education must fulfill this need adequately.

Preparing Mature Students for Higher Education. Secondary education leads to higher education. It is expected that students completing this stage should have the requisite maturity to pursue higher education.

According to the Secondary Education Commission, the secondary education is expected to enable the individual to meet the four-fold needs of the country which are: (i) Democratic citizenship, (ii) Vocational efficiency, (iii) Personality development, and (iv) Leadership qualities.

Structure of Secondary Education

Keeping in view the above factors, the Secondary Education Commission observed, "It is now generally recognised that the period of secondary education covers the age-group of about 11 to 17 years. Properly planned education, covering about 7 years should enable the school to give a thorough training in the courses of study taken up by the student and also help him to attain a reasonable degree of maturity in knowledge, understanding and judgement which would stand him in good stand in life.

(i) After four or five years of primary or junior basic education, a middle or junior secondary or senior basic stage covering a period of four years.

(ii) A higher secondary stage covering a period of four years.

(iii) The present intermediate stage should be replaced by the Higher Secondary stage which should be four years' duration, one-year of the present Intermediate being included in it.

(iv) As a consequence of the preceding recommendations the first degree course in the university should be of three years' duration.

(v) For those who pass out of the High School, there should be provision for a Pre-university course of one-year, during which period the scheme of studies should be planned with due regard to the needs of the degree or the professional course to be taken by the students and special emphasis should be placed on the quickening of intellectual interests, training in methods of study at college and the study of English so long as it continues to be the medium of instruction at the University.

(vi) Admission to professional colleges should be open to those who have completed the higher secondary course, or have taken the one-year's pre-university course.

(vii) In the professional colleges, a pre-professional course of one year should be provided for the students, preferably in the professional colleges themselves. As a transitory measure, they may be given in the degree colleges where facilities exist, till professional colleges are able to provide for such courses.

Conditions for the Conversion of High Schools into Higher Secondary Schools

The Commission felt that it would not be possible to convert all existing high schools into higher secondary schools in the near future. In the case of such schools, the problem would be to improve their efficiency within their present structure and the recommendations that we have made elsewhere to reconstruct the curriculum and methods of education will apply to them also. In other ways too, considerable improvements will be needed to make them more efficient and to enable them to be converted ultimately into Higher Secondary Schools. These improvements should include the provision of better qualified and more carefully selected personnel, better equipment, better laboratory and library facilities and better organisation of co-curricular activities. In addition, the scheme of diversified courses of study recommended by us elsewhere, should also be introduced as far as possible.

A number of schools will, however, be in a position to add the additional year to their course and convert themselves into Higher Secondary Schools. If these schools are to develop into efficient institutions capable of achieving the objectives in view, it is necessary that their recognition should be governed by carefully defined and strict conditions, which must be fulfilled scrupulously before such recognition is given.

These conditions should prescribe special criteria for:

1. Accommodation
2. Equipment
3. Qualifications of the staff
4. Salaries and Grades, and
5. Adequate finances to ensure that the institution will continue to function efficiently. Such assurance must be offered either by the management itself or be provided on the basis of help guaranteed by the State and Central Governments.

CURRICULUM AT THE SECONDARY STAGE OF EDUCATION ACCORDING TO THE SECONDARY EDUCATION COMMISSION

Meaning of the Curriculum. In the words of the Secondary Education Commission, "It must be clearly understood that according to the best modern educational thought; curriculum in this context does not mean only the academic subjects traditionally taught in the school but it includes the totality of experiences that a pupil receives through the manifold activities that go on in the school, in the class room, library, laboratory, workshop, playgrounds and in the numerous informal contacts between teachers and pupils. In this sense, the whole life of the school becomes the curriculum which can tough the life of the students at all points and help in the evolution of a balanced personality."

Defects in the Curriculum and Need for a Suitable Curriculum.

The Secondary Education Commission thoroughly studied the existing curriculum in the light of the needs of India and noticed the following criticism regarding school curriculum in India:

1. The present curriculum is narrowly conceived.
2. It is bookish and theoretical.
3. It is overcrowded, without providing rich and significant contents.
4. It makes inadequate provision for practical and other kinds of activities which should reasonably find room in it, if it is to educate the whole of the personality.
5. It does not cater to various needs and capacities of the adolescents.
6. It is dominated too much by examinations.
7. It does not include technical and vocational subjects which are so necessary for training the students to take part in the industrial and economic development of the country.

The Secondary Education Commission highlighted the following principles of Curriculum Construction:

1. Principle of totality of experience.
2. Principle of variety and elasticity.
3. Principle of core subjects.
4. Principle of linking with community life.
5. Principle for the use of leisure.
6. Interrelation of subjects.

Suggestive Curriculum

A. *Curriculum at the Middle Stage or Secondary Stage*

The Secondary Education Commission points out the function of the middle school curriculum is to introduce the pupil in 'a general way' to certain broad fields of human knowledge and interest. The middle school is not the place for specialisation but the stage when a general introduction to all the broad and significant fields of knowledge can and should be given. The purpose is two-fold:

(i) The child as the inheriter of the treasures of human civilisation has the right to know what its main components are.

(ii) As a result of acquiring the knowledge to choose at a later stage, the particular field in which he can, in his own way, contribute his share to this fund of human culture.

Keeping in view these considerations, the Commission suggested the broad outline of the middle school curriculum: (1) Languages, (2) Social Studies, (3) General Science, (4) Mathematics, (5) Art and Music, (6) Craft, and (7) Physical Education.

Languages include the mother-tongue, the natural medium of self-expression or the regional languages, and the official language of the Republic, *i.e.*, Hindi. Where Hindi is the mother-tongue the pupil may study another language. English is also to be provided for but not to be treated as a compulsory subject.

DIVERSIFICATION OF COURSES AT THE HIGH AND HIGHER SECONDARY STAGE

The Secondary Education Commission observed that by the end of the middle school stage, the special abilities and interests of the pupils would generally be taking definite form; at least, it will be so with most of the pupils. So the curriculum at the high school stage (both for high schools and higher secondary schools) should be, as far as possible, framed on the basis of there abilities and interests ... if a number of well thought programmes are offered the young people will be in a position to choose from among them in accordance with their own abilities and inclinations. So we have to provide varied courses in high schools and higher secondary schools with a fairly wide latitude for choice.

There is yet another criterion which will help us in deciding what would be the appropriate curriculum for any particular pupil. For the large majority of thee adolescents this will be all the education that they will receive. In a normally functioning educational system, not more than twenty-five to thirty per cent of the pupils in high schools are likely to go to the Universities and other institutions of higher learning such as technological and similar institutions. So most of them have to think of earning a living and the educational programme should give them some training in this direction—not, so much in terms of specific vocations as in training their practical aptitudes in preparation for definite vocational work later. The educational programme will not be narrowly vocational, but will have a definite vocational bias.

Any attempt to force uncongenial subjects and studies on children, unfit to take them up, is bound to lead to a sense of frustration and to hinder their normal development. There are, of course, certain broad areas of knowledge, skill and appreciation with which all children must come into contact and these must find a place in the curriculum.

This postulates that our secondary schools should no longer be "single-track" institutions but should offer a diversity of educational programmes circulated to meet varying aptitudes, interests and talents which come into prominence towards the end of the period of compulsory education. They should provide more comprehensive courses which will include both general and vocational subjects, and pupils should have an opportunity to choose from them according to their needs. It is necessary to point out clearly that this diversification of courses and the introduction of many practical subjects at the secondary stage does not mean that something called "general" or "cultural" education is to be provided for one group of students, while others are to be given a narrow "practical" or "vocational" or "technical" education. The whole modern approach to this question is based on the insight that the intellectual and cultural development of different individuals takes place best through a variety of media, that the book or the study of traditional academic subject is not the only door to the education of the personality and that, in the case of many—perhaps a majority—of the children, practical work intelligently organised can unlock their latent energies much more successfully than the traditional subjects which address themselves only to the mind or, worse still, the memory. If this principle is clearly understood by educationists, they will see to it that these various courses are accorded priority of esteem, and students are helped to select them with due regard to their natural interests and talents. In view of the fact that they have all to be trained in certain basic ideas, attitudes and appreciations, which are essential for playing the role of intelligent citizens in a democracy, there should be a certain core of subjects of general value and utility which all students may study.

General Considerations for the Construction of the Curriculum at the Higher Secondary Stage

The Commission thinks that the following considerations should be kept in mind while constructing the curriculum:

(i) The curriculum at the Higher Secondary Stage should be, as far as possible, framed on the basis of the abilities and interests of the students.

(ii) Varied courses with a fairly wide latitude for choice should be provided for.

(iii) The educational programme should not be narrowly vocational but should have a definite vocational bias.

(iv) The curriculum should provide for certain core subjects, common to all, and certain optional subjects.

Detailed Outline of the Curriculum

The curriculum as we envisage it will consist of the following:

1. Mother tongue or Regional language or a Composite course of the mother tongue and a Classical language.

2. One other language to be chosen from among the following:

(a) Hindi (for those whose mother-tongue is not Hindi).

(b) Elementary English (for those who have not studied it in the middle stage).

(c) Advanced English (for those who have studied English in the earlier stage).

(d) A modern Indian language (other than Hindi).

(e) A modern foreign language (other than English).

(f) A Classical language.

3. Social Studies—general course (for the first two years only).

4. General Science including Mathematics—general course (for the first two years only).

5. One Craft to be chosen from the following list (which may be added to according to local needs):

(a) Spinning and Weaving; (b) Wood-work; (c) Metal work; (d) Gardening; (e) Tailoring; (f) Typography; (g) Workshop Practice; (h) Sewing, Needlework and Embroidery; (i) Modelling.

6,7,8. Three subjects from one of the following groups:

Group 1. (*Humanities*)—(a) A classical language or a third language from (a) not already taken; (b) History; (c) Geography; (d) Elements of Economics and Civics; (e) Elements of Psychology and Logic; (f) Mathematics; (g) Music; (h) Domestic Science.

Group 2. (*Sciences*)—(a) Physics; (b) Chemistry; (c) Biology; (d) Geography; (e) Mathematics; (f) Elements of physiology and Hygiene (not to be taken with Biology).

Group 3. (*Technical*)—(a) Applied Mathematics and Geometrical Engineering; (b) Applied Science; (c) Elements of Mechanical Engineering; (d) Elements of Electrical Engineering.

Group 4. (*Commercial*)—(a) Commercial Practice; (b) Book-keeping; (c) Commercial Geography or Elements of Economics and Civics; (d) Shorthand and Typewriting.

Group 5. (*Agriculture*)—(a) General Agriculture; (b) Animal Husbandry; (c) Horticulture and Gardening; (d) Agricultural Chemistry and Botany.

Group 6. (*Fine Art*)—(a) History of Art; (b) Drawing and Designing; (c) Painting; (d) Modelling; (e) Music; (f) Dancing.

Group 7. (*Home Science*)—(a) Home Economics; (b) Nutrition and Cookery; (c) Mother Craft and Child Care; (d) Household Management and Home Nursing.

9. Besides the above a student may take at his option *one* additional subject from any of the above groups irrespective of whether or not he has chosen his other options from that particular group.

It will be seen that the Commission has recommended seven groups of optional courses. Other groups may, of course, be added to the list. Ordinarily, however, these seven groups would provide enough scope for full freedom of choice to pupils with different interest and aptitudes. The State Departments of Education should examine the position in the light of their experiences and modify or add to these groups.

Thus the curriculum consists of:

A. Three languages.

B. Two core subjects: (i) Social Studies, (ii) General Science for first two years.

C. One Craft

D. Three subjects

Total Subjects: 8 + One Craft.

MULTIPURPOSE OR MULTILATERAL SCHOOLS

Meaning of a Multipurpose School A multipurpose school seeks to provide varied types of courses for students with diverse aims, interests and abilities. It endeavours to provide for each individual pupil suitable opportunity to use and develop his natural aptitude and inclinations in the special course of studies chosen by him.

Main Advantages of Multipurpose Schools. The main advantages claimed for it are:

1. It removes all invidious distinctions between students preparing for different courses of studies, breaking down the sense of inferiority that is associated with vocational subjects and makes it possible to plan the educational system on a truly democratic basis.
2. It provides a greater variety of educational media and thereby facilitates proper educational guidance in the choice of studies.
3. It helps to solve the problem of the wrongly classified pupil, because transfer within the same school is easier to arrange than transfer from one school to another.

While the Commission advocated the starting of a certain number of multipurpose schools, it was not its intention to suggest that all should be of the same type. There will be room for unilateral schools also where intensive training will be provided in particular types of vocational courses according to the occupational needs of the community and the locality.

Study of Languages and Medium of Instruction

Languages at the Middle Stage. During the middle school stage, every child should be taught at least two languages. English and Hindi should be introduced at the end of the junior basic stage subject to the principal that no two languages should be introduced in the same year.

Languages at the High and Higher Secondary Stage. At the high and higher secondary stage, at least two languages should be studied, one of which being the mother-tongue or the regional language.

Medium of Instruction. The mother-tongue or the regional language should generally be the medium of instruction throughout the secondary school stage, subject to the provision that for linguistic minorities special facilities should be made available.

EVALUATION OF REPORT AND ITS IMPACT

Impact of the Report. A '*Discussion Paper*' of the Education Commission (1964-66), observed that the impact of the recommendations of the Secondary Education Commission (1952-53) during the period 1953 and 1964, had been very little and the progress in the implementation of the recommendations was hardly visible. It remarked, "In fact, it may be said that the major defects pointed out by the commission still persist in a majority of schools today. The education imparted in these institutions continues to be more or less isolated from life. The curriculum is still, generally speaking, narrow and one-sided and not designed to develop the full personality of adolescents. The methods of teaching are by and large dreary and unimaginative and do not aim at inculcating desirable values and proper attitudes and habits of work among the students."

It is observed that in 1963-66, out of nearly 22,600 Secondary Schools, there were only about 2000 multipurpose schools.

Merits

First. The Commission's suggestions regarding the levy of 'Industrial Educational Cess' was rightly conceived.

Second. The Commission rightly laid stress upon the need of providing higher secondary education according to 3 A's, *i.e.*, Age, Ability and Aptitude.

Third. The Commission underlined the need for providing educational and vocational guidance to students.

Fourth. The Commission's suggestion for laying emphasis on agricultural education was very valuable.

Fifth. The Commission fully realised the need for providing dynamic and progressive methods of education.

Sixth. The Commission's concept of curriculum including subjects, experiments and co-curricular activities is quite modern.

Seventh. The Commission made significant recommendations regarding the necessity of raising the economic and social status of teachers.

Eighth. Recommendations of the Commission on improving the system of examination were very valuable. Now objective types of tests have become an integral part of evaluation.

Cumulative records cards are increasingly being used.

Ninth. Several tax exemption were suggested for the promotion of educational facilities.

Tenth. Recommendations on the thorough medical check-up was quite timely.

Shortcomings and Drawbacks of the Report

Before discussing the shortcomings of the recommendations, a few words may be said regarding the composition of the Secondary Education Commission. The Commission was male-dominated. There was only one representative of women. No representation to agriculture/commerce and trade was given. The most glaring defect was the omission of any educator associated with the running of state-run or state-aided schools. Representation to any Education Board was also missing. Thus the Commission's composition was lop-sided and university/higher education dominated.

Following were the major shortcomings of the recommendations:

1. *No Programme of Action.* The Commission did not suggest either any long term or short term plan for the implementation of recommendations.

2. *No Estimate of Financial Estimates.* The Commission lamented on the non-implementation of the recommendations of the earlier Education Commission. It observed, It has been pointed out "... the recommendations of the previous Commissions have not been given effect to largely because the necessary financial resources could not be made available either by the State or by the Centre". It is an irony of fate that the recommendations of this Commission also met the same fate. The Secondary Education Commission itself did not give thought to the financial aspect of the various reforms.

3. *Vague Recommendations on the Structure of Secondary Education.* It has used several terms like primary school stage, middle school stage, high school stage, secondary school stage without defining each stage.

4. *No Clear-cut Duration of the School Course.* The Commission's recommendations use the term 'either' several times. While mentioning the duration of each stage. This led to a good deal of confusion.

5. *Post-Graduate Qualifications of Teachers.* The Commission suggested that the minimum qualification required for teaching in the last two years of the higher secondary school should be an M.A. degree or a first class B.A. degree with a degree in teaching. An adequate number of qualified post-graduate teachers were not readily available.

6. *Core Subjects.* The introduction of core-subjects like crafts and general science in the curriculum of the higher secondary school created further difficulties regarding staff requirements.

7. *Difficulties in Upgrading Higher Secondary Schools.* The serious

difficulties in the process of implementing the recommendations of establishing multipurpose schools could not be foreseen with the result that out of 22,581 higher secondary schools in 1963-64, there were only 2,000 multipurpose schools. Subsequently their number began to dwindle. Thus we find that schools remained as bookish and stereotype as at the time of the recommendations of the Secondary Education Commission.

8. *Unpopularity of Multipurpose Schools*. The multipurpose schools benefited neither the school leavers nor the seekers of higher education.

9. *Expansion without Quality*. A close scrutiny of the implementation of the recommendations of the Commission reveals that the quantitative expansion of secondary education had not been simultaneously accompanied by qualitative improvement.

10. *Vague Recommendations on Vocational Education*. The Commission did not suggest a clear-cut path of vocationalised education. In no way education facilitated the task of finding suitable manpower for various sectors of development of industries and other services.

11. *Lack of Coordination*. The Commission did not suggest methods of coordination between growth of economy, manpower needs, employment opportunities and the output of secondary schools.

12. *No Definite Guidelines for Conversion of Schools*. The selection of high schools for conversion into higher secondary schools was to be governed by strict and carefully defined conditions. The Commission's Report stated that only those schools would develop into efficient higher secondary institutions which satisfied definite criteria prescribed regarding accommodation, equipment, qualification of the staff, salaries and grades and adequate finances, and that such conditions had to be fulfilled scrupulously before the schools were recognised as higher secondary schools. The establishment of higher secondary schools in several areas unfortunately became a matter of prestige for the people concerned. Social and political pressures were sometimes used for getting the necessary conversion and recognition for their institutions. This resulted in the upgrading of a number of schools which did not satisfy the minimum criteria regarding accommodation, equipment, qualifications of staff etc.

3

Education Commission (1964-66)

INTRODUCTION

The Education Commission (1964-66), popularly known as the Kothari Commission after the name of its Chairman, Dr. D.S. Kothari, was the third Commission on Education since independence. However, it is still the only Commission that went into all aspects of education at all stages and made detailed recommendations on the reconstruction of education in India. It was appointed by the Government of India in July 1964 and it submitted its report in June 1966. The report of the Commission is entitled, '*Education and National Development*'. The title of the report indicates the significance of education in national development.

CIRCUMSTANCES LEADING TO THE APPOINTMENT OF THE COMMISSION, ITS COMPOSITION AND TERMS OF REFERENCE

After independence it was hoped that the traditional system of education would undergo a great change. But, in spite of a number of Committees and Commissions on education satisfactory progress could not be achieved. Very naturally, a comprehensive policy was needed. Hence, the Commission was appointed.

Secondly, in the post-Independence period, a good deal of expansion had taken place in the field of education, but all this was mostly at the expense of quality. This needed a detailed study.

Thirdly, the Commission was appointed to bring home to the people that they should also have a share in the reconstruction of the country through education, the government of course shouldering the main responsibility.

Fourthly, there was an explosion of knowledge, particularly in science and technology. The appointment of a Commission was consequently felt to meet this challenge.

Fifthly, in the past, several Commissions ana Committees had examined specific sectors and specific aspects of education. A Commission was needed to survey the entire field of educational development as the various parts of the educational system strongly interact with and influence one another. Education needed to be considered as a whole and not in fragments.

Sixthly, the system of education could not be strengthened without eliciting the cooperation of teachers. The teacher community had hitherto been neglected to a considerable extent. All these years, the teachers had been subjected to great economic hardships. A positive approach to the problems of the teacher was, therefore, urgently needed.

Composition of the Kothari Commission

The Commission included 16 members including the Chairman, Dr. O.S. Kothari, who was the Chairman of the University Grants Commission. Shri J.P. Naik, Head of the Department of Educational Planning Administration and Finance, Gokhale Institute of Politics and Economics, Poona, was the Member-Secretary of the Commission. The Commission included a few foreign experts also.

Terms of Reference

The Commission will advise the Government on national pattern of education and on the general principles and politics for the development of education at all stages and in all aspects. It needed not, however, examine the problems of medical or legal education, but such aspects of these problems as are necessary for its comprehensive enquiry may be looked into.

ESSENCE OF THE REPORT–NEEDED EDUCATIONAL REVOLUTION

Role of Education : Education and National Development. The report begins with these observations, "The destiny of India is now being shaped in her classrooms. This, we believe, is no more rhetoric. In a world based on science and technology, it is education that determines the level of prosperity, welfare and security of the people. On the quality and number of persons coming out of our schools and colleges will depend our success in the great enterprise of national reconstruction whose principal objective is to raise the standard of living of our people.

Need for the Educational Revolution. The Commission felt, "The present system of education, designed to meet the needs of an imperial administration within the limitations set by a feudal and traditional society, will need radical changes if it is to meet the purpose of a modernising democratic and socialistic society— changes in objectives, in content, in teaching methods, in programmes, in the size and composition of the student body, in the selection and professional preparation of teachers, and in organisation. In fact, what is needed is a revolution in education which in turn will set in motion the much desired social, economic and cultural revolution".

Relating Education to the Life, needs and Aspirations of the People. In this regard, the Commission said, "in our opinion, therefore, no reform is more important or more urgent than to transform education, to endeavour to relate it to the life, needs and aspirations of the people and thereby make it a powerful instrument of social, economic and cultural transformation necessary for the realisation of our national goals. This can be done if education:

- — is related to productivity;
- — strengthens social and national integration, consolidates democracy as a form of government and helps the country to adopt it as a way of life;
- — hastens the process of modernisation; and
- — strives to build character by cultivation of social, moral and spiritual values.

All these aspects are inter-related and in the complex process of social changes, we cannot achieve even one without striving for all."

MAJOR RECOMMENDATIONS OF THE KOTHARI COMMISSION

1. Important role of education in national development.
2. Stress on science and mathematics.
3. Introduction of work experience as an integral part of school curriculum.
4. Need for vocationalisation of education.
5. Introduction of common school system.
6. Educational structure – 12 years of schooling and 3 years degree course.
7. 234 instructional days with at least 1000 hours in schools and 216 in colleges.
8. Free textbooks at the primary stage.
9. Adequate number of scholarships.
10. Identification of gifted students and their nurture.
11. One residential school in each Community Development Block.
12. Provision of mid-day meals.
13. Facilities for learning while earning.
14. Promotion of the education of the handicapped.
15. Special measures for the education of the backward students.
16. Development plan for each district.
17. Enrolment between 300 and 450 in a secondary school.
18. Freedom to schools for experimentation in curricula.
19. Moral and religious education.
20. Continuous and objective evaluation.
21. Establishment of school complexes.
22. Neighbourhood Schools.
23. State Evaluation Organisation.
24. Correspondence courses.
25. Better pay scales and service conditions for teachers.
26. Passing of Education Acts.
27. Three Language Formula.
28. Delinking Degrees from jobs.
29. 6 per cent GNP to be spent on education
30. Scheme for expansion and improvement.
31. Constitution of Indian Education Service.

QUALITATIVE AND QUANTITATIVE PROGRAMME

Three Facets of Educational Revolution

The Commission identified three important facets of the big programme that would bring about the desired 'educational revolution'.

— Internal transformation so as to relate it to the life, needs and aspirations of the nation;

— Qualitative improvement so that the standard achieved are adequate, keep continually rising and, at least, in a few sectors become internationally comparable; and

— Expansion of education facilities broadly on the basis of manpower needs and with an accent on equalisation of educational opportunities.

I. Four-fold for Internal Transformation of the Educational System

Educational Programme. For the internal transformation of the system of education the following programmes urged high priority:

1. Work experience as an integral part of general education; vocationalisation of education at the secondary level; improvement of professional education and research, promoting national consciousness;
2. Introducing a common school system; making social and national service compulsory; developing all modern Indian languages;
3. Making science education an integral part of all school education and developing scientific research;
4. Inculcation of high values—social, moral and spiritual—at all stages of education.

II. Programmes for Improving the Quality of Education

The quality of education is crucial for national development and the nation must be prepared to pay for the quality. According to the Commission's recommendations, the major programmes for qualitative improvement include raising the economic, social and professional status of teachers and improving the quality and scope of teacher education and in-service programmes, radical reform especially in Science and Mathematics, vigorous improvement in the method of teaching and evaluation, and providing quality textbooks and other teaching material, search for introduction of a nation-wide programme of school and college improvement where each institute finds congenial condition to strive continually to achieve the best results of which it is capable, the establishment of 'quality' schools to act as pace-setters in their districts and the creation of 5 or 6 'major' universities; revitalising the system of supervision and reorganising the State departments and the reorganisation of the educational structure on the 10+2+3 pattern.

III. Expansion Programme

The Commission hoped that 5 per cent of the 3-5 and 50 per cent of the 5-6 age-groups would find places in nursery schools or classes by 1986. It recommended five years of good education for all children by 1975-76 and seven years of such education by 1985-86, and placed the highest priority for free and compulsory education up to the age of 14. The problems and policies of expansion at the Secondary stage would differ from those in primary education because on the one hand it would not be financially possible for several years to come to have universal secondary education and on the other hand it would be essential to enlist half the enrolment at the higher secondary stage in vocational education. It is an important recommendation that the expansion of higher secondary and collegiate education should be related to manpower needs and must be selective. The programme of equalisation of educational opportunities visualised by the Commission included the reduction of the regional imbalances to the minimum, increased provision of free education and scholarships, paying special attention to the education of girls, placing adequate emphasis on the spread of education among backward classes including the Scheduled Castes and the Scheduled Tribes. It was also recommended that nationwide campaign should be launched for complete liquidation of illiteracy within 20 years.

The Commission recommended that 6% of GNP should be spent on education.

EVALUATION OF THE COMMISSION IN GENERAL AND ITS RECOMMENDATIONS

Unique Commission

This was the sixth Commission in the history of Education Commissions in India. All the five earlier Commissions did not deal with education as a whole but focused attention on different levels of education. The first dealt with some aspects of primary, secondary and college education (excluding university education), the second, third and fourth with university education, and the fifth with secondary education. The unique feature of Education Commission (1964-66) was not to limit its enquiry to specific sectors or aspects of education, but to have a comprehensive review of the entire educational system. The Indian Education Commission (1882-83), the first in the series, was set up under the chairmanship of William Hunter to enquire into the manner in which effect had been given to the principles of the Despatch of 1854 with particular emphasis on elementary education. The second and the third Commissions, *viz.*, the Indian Universities Commission (1902) under the chairmanship of Mr. Releigh, a member of the Viceroy's Executive Council and the Calcutta University Commission (1917) under the chairmanship of M.E. Sadler, Vice-Chancellor of Leeds University, dealt with the problems and prospects of university education. The next three Commissions were appointed in post-Independence era. The University Education Commission (1948-49) set up under the chairmanship of Dr. Sarvepalli Radhakrishnan and the Secondary Education Commission (1952-53) appointed under the chairmanship of Dr. Lakshmanaswami Mudaliar were the fourth and the fifth respectively, in the series of Commissions on education. Mention may also be made of the Sanskrit Commission (1956-57) appointed to consider the state of Sanskrit education.

Another unique feature of the Commission was its conviction that education is the most powerful instrument of the national development. Educational and national reconstruction are intimately interlinked. The crucial role of education in national development appears in all its vividness on every page of the report.

Never before was education given such a niche of national honour, and never before was it conceived as a pivot of national honour, and never before was it conceived as a pivot of nation's progress and the prosperity as revealed in the pages of the Commission's Report.

The international composition of the Commission is also significant. Education in India must necessarily emerge from Indian experience, thought, culture and local conditions. But as education remains the common quest of mankind inhabiting a world closely knit together, it was found profitable to draw upon the experience and thinking of educationists and scientists from other countries and to take advantage of the latest developments in the educationally advanced countries. The Commission included seven Indian members and five others; one each from Japan, France, UK, USA and USSR. Besides, 20 consultants from different countries of the world were available.

The Commission made a detailed survey of all aspects of education and for this purpose constituted 12 Task Forces and 7 Working Groups purpose.

The Commission interviewed nearly 9,000 persons associated with education in one way or the other. It invited written evidence, memoranda, organised seminars and conferences, etc. to apprise its thoroughly with the educational problems so that an effective system of education could be evolved in India.

1. Favourable Comments on the Report

1. ... A unique report—Mr. M.C. Chagla, the then Union Education Minister.
2. ... Bold and pertinent—*The* Indian Express, 1 July, 1966.
3. ... A comprehensive, critical and constructive review of the education system prevailing in the country—*The Hindustan Times*, 1 July, 1966.
4. ... A good document—Mr. Chanchal Sarkar in *The Hindustan Times*, Calcutta, 14 July, 1966.
5. ... Bold, categorical and realistic—*The Hindustan Standard*, Calcutta, 12 July, 1966.

6. ... A historical document—*The Educational India*, Masulipatam, July 1966.
7. ... Revolutionary Recommendations—*Awaz-i-Ustand*, Chandigarh (Weekly), 7 July, 1966.
8. ... Revolution in Education—*National Solidarity* (Weekly), 7 July, 1966.
9. ... Original and Significant Contribution—Dr. D.S. Reddi, *Deccan Chronicle*, 17 July, 1966.

Critics of the Report

1. ... Death certificate of basic education—M.N. Acharya in *Blitz*, 9 July, 1966.
2. ... Intellectual discipline ignored. Sensible in parts but often platitudinous-*The Statesman,* 3 July, 1966.
3. ... Confusing—*Amrit Bazar Patrika*, 13 July, 1966.

Conclusion

Educational Commission's report is an achievement, a mine of information and wisdom. The report is a synoptic survey of the school preparation, a 7-8 year primary stage, a lower secondary stage of 2-3 years, higher secondary of two years, and higher education beginning with a three-year course, will no doubt be considered more scientific than the present system, but unless the proposals are uniformly applied, the existing confusion and imbalance as between States cannot be removed.

IMPLEMENTATION OF THE RECOMMENDATION OF THE EDUCATION COMMISSION

1. *National Policy Resolution (1968)*. Recommendations of the Education Commission 1964-66 were considered by various educational organisations and institutions. These were also discussed by educators all over the country. Many educational conferences were held to think over these recommendations. Meetings of Vice-Chancellors, State Education Secretaries, Directors of Education were convened. All these discussions and debates resulted in the adoption of a Resolution on the National Policy on Education in 1968.

2. *Introduction of the New Pattern of Education.* On the recommendations of the Education Commission and in accordance with the National Policy on Education (adopted by Parliament in 1968) the Central Advisory Board of Education adopted a resolution in its meeting held in November 1974 recommending the introduction of the 10+2+3 pattern of education all over India during the Fifth Plan. Now almost all States and Union Territories have adopted this pattern.

3. *Vocationalisation of Higher Secondary Education.* A Centrally-sponsored scheme for vocationalisation was formulated during 1976-77. Under it the

State Governments were provided with Central assistance during the Fifth Five-Year Plan period and thereafter the programme was run on a regular basis as a State scheme.

4. *Work Experience.* As recommended by the Education Commission, work experience has been made an integral part of the new scheme of studies under the pattern 10+2+3.

5. *Book Banks.* Book banks have been established in educational institutions which provide books to the students belonging to the weaker sections of the society.

6. *Two Levels of Courses.* Under the new pattern of education, provision made for the students to select courses in some subjects at two levels, *i.e.*, ordinary and advanced, depending upon their capacity to work and comprehend.

7. *Revised Pay Scale of Teachers.* The pay scale of teachers working in schools were revised almost in all the States as a result of the recommendations of the Education Commission.

8. *National Institute of Educational Planning and Administration, New Delhi.* The Working Party on Educational Planning, Administration and Evaluation in the Fourth Five-Year Plan set up by the Planning Commission reiterated the recommendation of the Kothari Commission for the setting up of the National Staff College. The Government of India accepted this recommendation. The National Staff College for Educational Planners and Administrators began to function on 1st January, 1971.

The Staff College was renamed as National Institute of Educational Planning and Administration in 1980.

Recommendations which Received Little Attention

Following areas have remained ignored by and large. They have not received the due attention they deserved:

1. Development of a 'streak of quality' programme.
2. Creation of school complexes.
3. Development of 'neighbourhood' concept of educational institutions.
4. Establishment of suitable organisations for assessing manpower needs and of employment opportunities at the national and state levels.
5. Provision of part-time education on a large scale.
6. Evolving integrated plans of development.
7. Development of a large programme of scholarships at all states and in all sectors.
8. Creation of Indian Education Service.
9. Creation of District School Boards.
10. Strengthening of the Offices of the District Educational Officers.
11. National Education Act.
12. Creation of a National Board of School Education.

13. Establishment of a Farm University in each State.
14. Recognition of autonomous educational institutions.
15. Freedom to Headmasters.
16. Making Institutional Plans as an integral part of District, State and National Plan of Education.
17. Developing partnership between educational authorities and industry.
18. Discouragement to public schools.
19. Spending 6 per cent of GNP on education.

This is the most discouraging aspect. This indicates that education has not received the desired attention of the Government.

Contribution of the Report of the Education Commission (1964-66)

There is no exaggeration in the statement that there is no report of any educational commission and committee in India which has made such a valuable contribution to the role of education, its contents, development, expansion and planning etc. as the report of the Education Commission (1964-66). The present educational system in India, by and large, draws its inspiration from this report. The report, no doubt, has brought about radical cnanges in education in India. The National Policy of Education (1986) is based on it.

The report provided not only sound philosophical and sociological bases of education but also a reasonably working programme for implementation.

The most notable feature of the educational programme is that it also took note of the financial aspects of various programmes it suggested.

The Commission considered the entire programme of educational reconstruction in the light of the needs, aspirations ideals and values set forth in the Constitution of free India.

NATIONAL STRUCTURE OF EDUCATION – PROPOSED BY KOTHARI COMMISSION

The new educational structure will consist of:

1. *Duration.*

(a) One to three years of pre-school education.
(b) A primary stage of 7 to 8 years divided into a lower primary stage of 4 or 5 years and a higher primary stage of 3 or 2 years.
(c) A lower secondary stage of 3 to 2 years.
(d) A higher secondary stage of two years of general education or one to three years of vocational education.
(e) A higher education stage having a course of three years or more for the first degree and followed by a course for the second or research degree of varying durations.

2. *Admission Age.* Age of admission to class I ordinarily not to be less than 6.

3. *Public Examination.* First public examination to come at the end of first ten years of schooling.

4. *Diversification of Courses*. The system of streaming in school of general education to be made beyond class X.

5. *Types of Secondary Schools*. Two types of secondary schools, high schools providing a ten-year course and higher secondary schools providing a course of 11 or 12 years.

6. *Upgrading of Schools*. Bigger schools and more efficient schools—about one-fourth of the total number to be upgraded and attempts to upgrade every secondary school to the higher secondary stage to be abandoned.

7. *Location of Pre-university Course*. Transfer of the pre-university course from the universities and affiliated colleges to secondary schools by 1975-76 and the duration of the course to be lengthened to two years by 1985-86; U.G.C. being responsible for effecting the transfer of all pre-university or intermediate work from university and affiliated colleges to schools.

8. *Boards of Education*. Reconstituting Boards of Secondary Education to accept the responsibility for the higher secondary stage also.

9. *Vocational Courses*. Vocationalisation at the secondary stage at two points at the end of Class VII (VIII) and at the end of Class X and provision to be made for the introduction of different types of vocational courses at the lower and higher secondary stages, the duration of these courses to vary from one to three years which would prepare young persons for employment.

10. *Ten Years of Schooling of General Education*. The first ten years of schooling should cover a primary stage of seven or eight years and a lower secondary stage of three or two years providing a course of general education without any specialisation.

11. *Two Years Duration of Higher Secondary Stage*. The Higher Secondary stage should be extended to cover a period of two years and to be located exclusively in schools.

Steps to be taken to implement this reform through a phased programme spread over the next 20 years 1965-85.

Then Existing and Proposed Nomenclatures for Various Stages of Education

Nomenclatures Proposed	*Existing Nomenclatures*
School Education	
1. Pre-primary	1. Pre-primary 2. Pre-basic 3. Kindergarten 4. Montessori, etc.
2. Primary (Classes I-VII or I-VIII)	
(a) *Lower Primary*	1. Primary in some States (e.g. Punjab)
Classes I-IV or I-V	2. Lower primary in some States (e.g. Gujarat) 3. Junior basic

	4. Lower Elementary in some States (e.g., Madras)
(b) *Higher Primary* Classes V-VII or VI-VIII	1. Middle in some States (e.g., Punjab) 2. Junior High School (e.g. U.P.) 3. Upper Primary in some States (e.g. Gujarat) 4. Senior Basic 5. Higher Elementary in some States (e.g. Madras)
3. Secondary Classes VIII-XII or IX-XII	High School; Higher Secondary School
(a) *Lower Secondary Education* Classes VIII-X or IX-X	High School
(b) *Higher Secondary Education* Classes XI-XII	This will include Class XI or PUC in some States (e.g. Rajasthan). It will include Junior Colleges in Kerala. It will include Intermediate Classes in Uttar Pradesh. It will also include terms like pre-professional, pre-medical and pre-engineering.
4. Higher Education	
1. *Professional Degrees*	All degrees which lead to a professional qualification (e.g., M.A.; M.Sc., M. Com.; B.E.; M.B.B.S.; B.T.; LL. B.; B.Ag.; etc.
2. *General Degrees*	All degrees other than professional ones.
3. *Undergraduate*	All courses leading to the first degree
4. *Post-graduate*	All courses beyond the first degree (excluding certain first degrees given after the first degree e.g. B.Ed.).
5. General	
First Level of Education	This will include pre-school and primary education.
Secondary Level of Education	This will include high school and higher secondary education.
Third Level of Education	This will include undergraduate and post-graduate education and research.

Evaluation : Why 12 Years of Schooling Before a Three-Year First Degree

The present educational structure popularly known as the 10+2+3 finds its origin in the recommendations of the Kothari Commission Report. It will be observed that since 1975, (the beginning year of the introduction of the new pattern of education), it has been gradually introduced in all parts of the country. The duration of secondary education was increased by one year with the introduction of the New Pattern of Education, popularly called 10+2 in 1975 by the Central Board of Secondary Education in its affiliated schools. Since then it has been adopted almost by all States and Union Territories. Under this pattern, there is 12 years of schooling (8 years of elementary and 4 years of secondary) and three years of the first degree. Previously, secondary education structure consisted of 3 years.

Now, why 15 years! It was felt the standard of education must be raised if India has to take her rightful place among other nations. No advanced country in the world honours a young man with the award of a first degree in less than 15 years of preparation and hard work. In the U.S.A., the high school is up to 12th grade which is followed by a 4-year course in a college or university leading to a bachelor's degree. In the erstwhile U.S.S.R., the complete secondary education ended with grade 10 and then began 5 years of higher education in a university. In England, after 13 years of schooling, three years are needed in a college or university to obtain the first degree. Thus it will take total 16 years in U.S.A., 15 years in U.S.S.R. and 16 years in England to be awarded the first degree. Which is why a graduate from India was not considered equivalent to a graduate in U.K. and therefore a graduate needed to graduate again in U.K. before pursuing higher education for which B.A. is the minimum qualification. The 10+2+3 pattern or extension of one year in secondary education provides the answer.

The new structure of secondary education does not envisage mere addition of one year to the total period of secondary education. It envisages raising the standard of education.

EDUCATION COMMISSION ON CURRICULUM REFORM

Need for a Enrichment and Improvement in the Quality of the Curriculum. The Commission stated: "The explosion of knowledge in recent years and the reformulation of many concepts in the sciences have highlighted the inadequacy of existing school programmes and brought about a mounting pressure for a radical reform of school curriculum. A unified approach should be taken to the framing of the entire school curriculum, a new definition of the content of general education and a new approach to the place of specialisation."

Organisation of the Curriculum. The Commission made the following recommendations:

1. *Common Curriculum for Ten Years.* In general or non-vocational schools, a common curriculum of general education should be provided for the first ten years of school education, and diversification of studies and specialisation

should begin only at the higher secondary stage. Moreover, standards of attainment should be clearly defined at the end of each sub-stage.

2. *Curriculum at the Lower Primary Stage.* At the lower primary stage, the curriculum should be simple with reduced load of formal subjects and emphasis on language and elementary mathematics.

A study of problems relating to beginning reading accompanied by a vigorous programme of improving reading instruction at the lower primary stage should receive great emphasis.

At the lower secondary stage, study of subjects should gain in vigour and depth.

3. *Curriculum at the Higher Primary Stage*: At the higher primary stage, the curriculum will broaden and deepen, teaching methods will become more systematic, and standards of attainment more specific.

4. *Curriculum at Higher Secondary Stage*: At the higher secondary stage of general education, courses to be diversified in such a manner as to enable pupils to study a group of any three subjects in depth with considerable freedom and elasticity in the grouping of subjects. A student, for example, may specialise in any three subjects of the science group or in combination of subjects from the science and the humanities. In order to ensure the balanced development of the adolescent's total personality, the curriculum at this stage should provide half the time to the electives, one-fourth of the time to the language, and one-fourth to physical education, arts and crafts, and moral and spiritual education.

5. *Provision for Ordinary and Advanced Course*: Wherever possible courses should be provided at two levels—ordinary and advanced—beginning with Class IX. For the lower classes beginning with Class V, enrichment programmes should be provided for the talented children. It may take the form of additional subject or greater depth in the same subject. The programme may be done within or outside school hours or on a self-study basis. A beginning may be made with advanced courses in mathematics, science and languages at the lower secondary stage and in all the specialised subjects at the higher secondary stage.

6. *Enrichment Programmes at Different Stages:* At the primary stage, it is difficult to provide separate advanced courses. Enrichment programmes should, therefore, be created for talented children, so that they may get more challenging and more satisfying learning experiences from their studies. Such programmes may start in Class V or VI. It may, for instance, be in the form of additional science, which may involve more extensive reading, practical work and application of knowledge to life situations. It may also mean additional work in language or art, leading to the development of creative self-expression. It is better if the planning of the enrichment programme is done by teachers and pupils together. General guidelines can be given in the curriculum materials, and the teacher will also need some additional help in the form of special types of work-books and facilities for the establishment of subject clubs. Work under this programme may be done outside the schools hours.

7. *Standards of Attainment at Different Stages*: Though the curriculum of the first ten years of general education covering seven years of primary education (four years of lower primary and three years of upper primary and three years of lower secondary education should be organised as a continuous programme of studies, the standard of attainment at the end of each sub-stage in the total course should be clearly indicated. The standards should be defined in terms of the knowledge, skills, abilities and attitudes to be developed with reference to the overall objectives of school education.

Subject Areas at Different Stages of Education

1. *Lower Primary Stage (Classes I-IV)*
   - (a) One language—the mother tongue of the regional language.
   - (b) Mathematics.
   - (c) Study of the Environment (covering Science and Social Studies in Classes III and IV).
   - (d) Creative Activities.
   - (e) Work-Experience and Social Service.
   - (f) Health Education.
2. *Higher Primary Stage (Classes V-VII)*
   - (a) Two languages—(i) the mother-tongue or the regional language, and (ii) Hindi or English.
     (*Note*—a third language (English, Hindi or the regional language) may be studied on an optional basis.
   - (b) Mathematics.
   - (c) Science.
   - (d) Social Studies (or History, Geography and Civics).
   - (e) Art.
   - (f) Work-experience and Social Service.
   - (g) Physical Education.
   - (h) Education in Moral and Spiritual Values.
3. *Lower Secondary Stage (Classes IX-X)*
   - (a) Three Languages.
   - (b) Mathematics.
   - (c) Science.
   - (d) History, Geography and Civics.
   - (e) Art.
   - (f) Work Experience and Social Service.
   - (g) Physical Education.
   - (h) Education in Moral and Spiritual Values.

Higher Secondary Stage (Classes XI-XII)

(1) Any two languages, including any modern Indian language, any modern foreign language and any classical language.

(2) Any three subjects from (a) An Additional Language (b) History (c)

Geography (d) Economics (e) Logic (f) Psychology (g) Sociology (h) Art (i) Physics (j) Chemistry (k) Mathematics (l) Biology (m) Geology (n) Home Science.

(3) Work-Experience and Social Service.
(4) Physical Education.
(5) Art or Craft.
(6) Education in Moral and Spiritual Values.

Difference in Organisation of the Curriculum as Recommended by the Kothari Commission and Secondary Education Commission

1. *Curriculum of the First Ten Years.* In the Kothari Commission's recommendations for the vast majority of pupils there would be a single curricular stream from Class I to Class X, ending with the first external or public examination, and there would be no 'steaming' or specialisation in this general course.

2. *Scheme of Multipurpose Schools.* On the recommendations of the Secondary Education Commission a number of multipurpose higher secondary schools were opened offering different groups of elective subjects to students in the last three classes. Students are divided into streams according to their optional groups, and the opportunities for further education are determined, by and large, in terms of the groups selected.

3. *Specialisation.* One of the major weaknesses in the scheme as suggested by the Secondary Education Commission is that specialisation of studies begins too early. At the age of 13 or 14, the students are classified as belonging to the pre-engineering or the pre-medical section. The streaming of pupils in this way into specialised groups from Class IX upwards is undesirable. The recent world trends in secondary education are in the direction of lengthening the period of general education and postponing diversification and specialisation to the second cycle or senior stage of secondary education.

4. *Emphasis on Science and Mathematics.* The Kothari Commission laid emphasis on these two subjects on account of their special importance in the technological age.

5. *Work Experience.* This has been included to initiate students into the 'world of work'.

EDUCATION COMMISSION AND TEACHERS

Important recommendations regarding teachers are briefly given here.

Stimulating Conditions of Teachers. The Commission observed, "In creative work like teaching or research, the provision of stimulating conditions of work and adequate opportunities for professional advancement are extremely important and can play a very significant role in attracting and retaining the right type of persons in the profession. The conditions of work in educational institutions should be such as to enable teachers to function at their highest level of efficiency."

The Commission, therefore, made several suggestions for enhancing the status of teachers and their salary scales.

	Teachers	*Remuneration*	*Rs.*
1)	Teachers who have completed the secondary course and have received two years of professional training	Minimum for trained teachers	150
		Maximum salary (to be reached in a period of about 20 years)	250
		Selection grade (for about 15 p.c. of the cadre)	250-300
2)	Graduates who have received one year's professional training	Minimum for trained graduates	220
		Maximum salary (to be reached in a period of 20 years)	400
		Selection grade (for about 15 p.c. of the cadre)	300-500
3)	Teachers working in secondary schools and having postgraduate qualifications		300-600
4)	Heads of secondary schools	Depending upon the size and quality of the school and also on their qualifications, the headmasters should have one or other of the scales of pay for affiliated colleges recommended below.	
			Rs.
5)	Teachers in affiliated colleges	Lecturer	300-25-600
		Junior scale	400-30-640-40-800
		Senior Lecturer/ Reader	700-40-1100
		Principal I	700-40-1100
		II	800-50-1500
		III	1000-50-1500
6)	Teachers in university departments	Lecturer	500-40-800-50-950
		Reader	700-50-1250
		Professor	1000-50-1300-60-1600

Note: These scales are exclusive of allowances.

6. *Same Pay in Different Managements*. The scales of pay of school teachers belonging to the same category but working under different managements such as government, local bodies or private organisations should be the same.

The minimum salaries of primary, secondary and university teachers should be in the ratio of 1:2:3.

7. *Liberal Assistance to States*. Liberal Central assistance should be given to State Governments for improving the salaries of school teachers as recommended by us.

8. *Retirement Age.* Normal retirement age for teachers be 60 years and there should be a provision for extension up to 65 years provided the person is physically fit and mentally alert to discharge his duties efficiently.

Note: These scales are exclusive of other benefits.

Evaluation of the Recommendations

The Commission's recommendations on teacher's status, service conditions, pay scales and civic and political rights have been hailed as 'Magna Caarta' for the teachers. It provided quite reasonable pay scales and service conditions for them.

Earlier, teachers teaching same classes in schools of different managements like local bodies, aided schools, public schools and government schools were getting different pay scales and other benefits. The Commission removed this distinction.

Almost all recommendations for teachers were accepted.

The Commission's recommendation regarding permitting teachers to contest election is open to question.

It is painfully observed that with the passage of time and availability of several new types of careers offering far better scales and service conditions, talented male teachers are, generally speaking, not coming forward to the teaching profession. Of course, women teachers from higher strata of society are greatly attracted to it.

EDUCATION COMMISSION AND THREE LANGUAGE FORMULA

Meaning of the Three Language Formula. The three language formula implies the learning of three languages. It specifies the stage of education at which one, two or three languages are to be studied at the school stage.

Origin of the Three Language Formula. The formula finds its origin in the recommendations of the Central Advisory of Education which it made in 1956. The final shape to this formula was given by the Kothari Commission (1964-66).

Operation of the Three Languc.ge Formula at Different Stages

Classes I-IV The study of only one language should be compulsory. It will naturally be the mother-tongue.

Classes V-VIII The study of two languages should be compulsory at this stage. First language should be the mother-tongue. The second language may be either the official language of the Union (Hindi) or the associate official language of the Union(English), so long as it is thus recognised.

Classes IX-X The study of three languages should be obligatory at this stage and one of these three languages should be the official language of the Union or the associate official language whichever was not taken up in classes V-VIII.

Classes XI-XII The study of two languages should be compulsory. The student should be given the option to select any two languages.

General Observations: The approach of the Commission was very pragmatic. It should serve as a practical basis of compromise on various schools of thought on this vexed question.

National Policy on Education and the Three Language Formula.

The National Policy on Education, 1968 and the National Policy on Education, 1986 have upheld the views of the Education Commission. The 1968 observed, "At the secondary stage, the State Governments should adopt and vigorously implement the three-language formula." The National Policy on Education 1986 made these observations on this issue. "The Education Policy of 1968 had examined the question of the development of languages in great detail; its essential provisions can hardly be improved upon and are as relevant today as before. The implementation of this part of the 1968 Policy has, however, been uneven. The Policy will be implemented more energetically and purposefully."

Difficulties in the Implementation of Three Language Formula. Difficulties are given below:

1. The study of three languages puts heavy load on the students.
2. Since the time to be devoted to the study of language/languages is limited, students do not acquire proficiency in any of the three languages.
3. A school is expected to engage a large number of teachers with the result that there is a heavy financial burden on the institution.
4. A compulsory study of three languages is not in conformity with the concept of 'child-centred' education. A student is compelled to study three languages, irrespective of any utility to him.
5. There is little motivation among the students to learn three languages.
6. On the one hand there is resistance to Hindi in the non-Hindi speaking areas and on the other hand, Hindi speaking areas pay little attention to the learning of a language of the South.
7. There are political pulls and pressures in the proper implementation of the Three-Language Formula.

Concluding Remarks. Under the existing linguist, political and social scenario in the country, it would be appropriate not to interfere in the existing scheme of languages, notwithstanding its limitations. 'Let sleeping dogs lie' seems to be the best policy.

MISCELLANEOUS RECOMMENDATIONS

A-Common School System

Why Common School system?

The Commission observed, "In a situation of the type we have in India, it is the responsibility of the educational system to bring the different social classes and groups together and thus promote the emergence of an egalitarian and integrated society."

The Commission stated that if these evils are to be eliminated and the educational system is to become a powerful instrument of national development in general and social and national integration in particular, we must move towards the goal of a common school system of public education.

Characteristics of the Common School System

1. It will be open to all children irrespective of caste, creed, community, religion, economic sanctions or social status;
2. In this system access to good education will depend, not on wealth or class, but on talent.
3. It will maintain adequate standards in all schools and provide at least a reasonable proportion of quality institutions.
4. In this system no tuition fee will be charged; and
5. It would meet the needs of the average parent so that he would not ordinarily feel the need to send his children to expensive school outside the system.

Observations

It is really very sad that the words of wisdom of the Kothari Commission have not been heeded by the policy makers and administrators. There is very little hope that with the present system of education having public schools, semi-public schools, aided schools, state schools, local bodies schools, sainik schools, Navodaya schools, etc. cater to different categories of society admission generally speaking depending upon monetary considerations.

B. Social, Moral and Spiritual Values

The Commission has observed that the expanding knowledge and the growing power which it places at the disposal of modern society must, therefore, be combined with strengthening and deepening of the sense of social responsibility and keener appreciation of moral and spiritual values.

C. Secularism and Religion : Religious Education and Education About Religious

The Commission was very emphatic that in a multi-religious society like ours, it is necessary to define the attitude of the State to religion, religious education and the concept of secularism. The adoption of a secularist policy means that political, economic and social matters, all citizens, irrespective of their religious faith, will enjoy equality of rights, that no religious community will be favoured or discriminated against, and the instruction in religious dogmas will not be provided in State schools. But it is not an irreligious or anti-religious policy; it does not belittle the importance of religion as such. It gives to every citizen the fullest freedom of religious belief and worship. It is anxious to ensure good relations amongst different religious groups and to promote not only religious tolerance but also an active reverence for all religions.

The Commission made a distinction between 'religious education' and 'education about religions'. The former is largely concerned with the teaching of the tenets and practices of a particular religion, generally in the form in which the religious group envisages them, whereas the latter is a study of religious and religious thought from a broad point of view—the eternal quest of the spirit. It would not be practicable for a secular State with many religions to provide education in any one religion. It is, however, necessary for a multi-religious democratic State to promote a tolerant study of all religions so that its citizens can understand each other better and live amicably together. It must be remembered that, owing to the ban placed on religious instruction in schools and the weakening of the home influences which, in the past, often provided such instruction, children are now growing up without any clear ideas of their own religion and no chance of learning about others. In fact, the general ignorance and misunderstanding in these matters are so widespread in the younger generation as to be fraught with great danger for the development of a democracy in which tolerance is rated at a high value. We suggest that a syllabus giving well-chosen information about each of the major religions should be included as a part of the course in citizenship or as part of general education to be introduced in schools and colleges up to the first degree. It should highlight the fundamental similarities in the great religions of the world and the emphasis they place on the cultivation on certain broadly comparable moral and spiritual values.

D. Science and Spiritualism

The greatest contribution of Europe doubtlessly is the scientific revolution. If science and *ahimsa* join together in creative synthesis of belief and action, mankind will attain a new level of purposefulness, prosperity and spiritual insight. Can India do something in adding a new dimension to the scientific achievement of the West? This poses a great challenge and also offers a unique opportunity to the men and women of India, and especially to the young people who are the makers of the future. In this context we cannot do better than to quote Pandit Jawaharlal Nehru:

'Can we combine the progress of science and technology with this progress of the mind and spirit also? We cannot be untrue to science because that represents the basic fact of life today. Still less can we be untrue to those essential principles for which India has stood in the past throughout the ages. Let us then pursue our path to industrial progress with all our strength and vigour and, at the same time, remember that material riches without toleration and compassion and wisdom may well turn to dust and ashes.'

E. Public School and the Education Commission

High Fees. The Commission has spoken of these institutions in scathing terms. The system of schools largely reserved for those who have the capacity to pay high fees, "was transplanted in India by British administrators and we have clung to it so long because it happened to be in tune with the traditional hierarchal structure of our society".

Wide Gulf Between the Classes and Masses. The Commission has regretfully noted that "what is worse, this segregation is increasing and tending to widen the gulf between the classes and the masses."

Undemocratic. This undemocratic feature of the Indian school system has been described by the Commission as one of the major weaknesses of the present educational structure. The children of the masses are compelled to receive sub-standard education and, as the programme of scholarships is not very large, sometimes even the ablest among them are unable to find access to such good schools as exist, while the economically privileged parents are able to "buy good education for their children".

The Commission has stated that whatever the past history of the so-called public schools they have no valid place in the new democratic society we desire to create.

4

National Policy on Education — NPE (1986) and Programme of Action (1986)

NEED FOR FORMATION AND CONTENTS OF THE NATIONAL POLICY ON EDUCATION

Need for the Policy. The Education Commission 1964-66 recommended that the Government of India should issue a statement on the National Policy on Education which should provide guidance to the State Governments and the local authorities in preparing and implementing educational plans. In 1967 the Government of India constituted a committee of Members of Parliament on Education to prepare the draft of a statement on the National Policy of Education. The Committee brought together, for the first time in recent history, leading members of almost all the political parties in the country and prepared a draft which was considered by the Central Advisory Board of Education. A general consensus on the national policy on education emerged in the course of the Board's deliberations. Thereafter the Government of India issued the Resolution on National Policy on Education in 1968.

The National Policy on Education (1968) stipulated that the implementation of the various educational programmes undertaken in accordance with its directions should be reviewed every five years. However, no such review was done in the next 17years. It was, therefore, felt that a review should be made. The then Prime Minister Rajiv Gandhi took the initiative in this regard.

FORMATION OF THE NPE

As a first step a Document entitled *Challenge of Education : A Policy Perspective* was prepared. The contents of the document were debated in the country at various conferences, seminars and study circles etc. It is of great interest to note that the document was translated practically into all the regional languages. 5,80,000 copies of this document in English, 2,40,000 in Hindi and 4,000 in Urdu were distributed by the Ministry, inviting suggestions and comments from all sections of the people. As a part of the nation-wide debate for the formulation of the new policy on education, 12 National Seminars and 17 sponsored seminars were organised by the Ministry of Education and its national organisations. All State Governments and Union Territories also organised seminars, workshops and symposia. A detailed analysis was made of all the communications and recommendations received in the Ministry. Thereafter, the Ministry of Human Resource Development brought out a revised document 'National Policy on Education 1986—A Presentation'. This paper was discussed at the meetings of the State Ministers of Education, the National Development Council and the Central Advisory Board of Education. It was revised in the light of these discussions and the 'Draft National Policy on Education 1986' was finally laid on the table of Parliament in the first week of May,1986.

The National Policy on Education was adopted by the Lok Sabha on May 8, 1986 and the Rajya Sabha on May 13, 1986.

Contents of the NPE. The NPE contains XII Parts and 157 paragraphs on different aspects of education.

POLICY INDICATORS AND MAIN FEATURES OF NPE

I. Essence and Role of Education

This includes:

1. Education for all and for all round development.
2. Education for cultural development.
3. Education for developing ideals of democracy, socialism and secularism as enshrined in the Constitution.
4. Education for the development of mind and spirit.
5. Education for the development of scientific temper.
6. Education for the development of manpower for economy.

II. National System of Education

Education to be made available up to a given level for all, irrespective of any consideration.

(Discussed in detail separately)

III. Education for Quality

1. Education to provide equality of opportunity for all.
2. Removal of illiteracy particularly in the age group 15-35 years.

IV. Reorganisation of Education at Different Levels

1. Child-centred education.
2. Operation Blackboard to be launched for improving the quality of primary education (Discussed separately).
3. A Resolve regarding achieving the Constitutional provisions by 1995 (Discussed separately).
4. Establishment of Pace Setting Schools (Discussed separately).
5. Introduction of vocational education programme (Discussed separately.

V. Technical and Management Education

1. It is essential to look at technical and management education together in view of their close relationship and complementary concerns.
2. As computers have become important and ubiquitous tools, a minimum exposure to computers and a training in their use will form part of professional education.

VI. Making the System Work

1. Education needs to be managed in an atmosphere of utmost intellectual rigour, seriousness of purpose and, at the same time, of freedom essential for innovation and creativity.
2. All teachers should teach and all students study.

VII. Reorienting the Content and Process of Education

1. De-culturalisation and de-humanisation to be avoided at all costs and fine synthesis between change oriented technologies and the country's continuity of cultural traditions.
2. Fostering eternal and universal values.
3. Providing meaningful work experience.
4. Developing consciousness of environment.
5. Examination for qualitative improvement.

VIII. The Teacher

The status of the teacher reflects the socio-cultural ethos of society; it is said that no "people can rise above the level of its teachers."

Teacher education is a continuous process and its pre-service and in-service components are inseparable.

IX. The Management of Education

Overhaul of the system of planning and the management of education will receive high priority.

X. Resources and Review

1. "It will be ensured that from the Eighth Five Year Plan onwards it (investment) will uniformly exceed to 6 per cent of the National Income."
2. "The implementation and parameters of the New Policy must be reviewed every five years."

XI. Future

1. "The future shape of education in India is too complex to envision with precision, yet, given our tradition which has almost always put a high premium on intellectual and spiritual attainment, we are bound

to succeed in achieving our objectives."

2. "The main task is to strengthen the base of the pyramid, which might touch a billion people at the turn of the century. Equally, it is important to ensure that those at the top of the pyramid are among the best in the world."

NATIONAL POLICY ON EDUCATION AND EARLY CHILDHOOD EDUCATION AND CARE (ECCE)

Important Features and Programmes

1. The NPE has used the term ECCE in place of pre-primary or nursery education. NPE lays stress on the holistic nature of child development, *viz.*, nutrition, health and social, mental, physical, moral and emotional development and recommends that ECCE should be suitably integrated with the Integrated Child Development Services (ICDS) Programme, wherever possible.
2. The span under consideration in ECCE is from conception to about 6 years.
3. ICDS includes six services: supplementary nutrition, immunisation, health check up referral services, health education and non-formal pre-school education.
4. Day-care centres should be provided as a support service for universalisation of primary education to enable girls engaged in taking care of siblings to attend school and as a support service for working women belonging to poorer sections.
5. Programmes of ECCE should be child-oriented.
6. Programmes of ECCE should be focussed around play and the individuality of the child.
7. Formal methods and introduction of the 3 R's should be discouraged at this stage.
8. The local community should be fully involved in ECCE programmes.
9. A full integration of child care and pre-primary education should be brought about, both as a feeder and strengthening for primary education and human resource development.

EVALUATION OF THE NPE

The most important significant aspect of the NPE is that for the first time in the history of India, an education policy was formulated at the initiative of a Prime Minister.

The second aspect is that a nation-wide debate was held on different aspects of education before the NPE came into being.

The third aspect is that it was discussed in the Parliament.

Lastly, a Programme of Action was chalked out for its implementation.

Merits of the NPE

Among the most important merits, following may be mentioned:

1. *National System of Education.* The NPE proposed a national system of education to provide access to education of a comparable quality to all students, to have a common educational structure with national curricular framework containing a common core.

2. *Improvement in Primary Education.* The NPE very rightly laid stress on the qualitative improvement of elementary education.

3. *Pace Setting Schools.* Setting up of Navodaya Vidyalayas is a great landmark in the history of education in India.

4. *Vocational Targets.* The policy fixed somewhat realistic targets of covering 10 per cent of higher secondary students by 1990 and 25 per cent by 1995 in vocational courses.

5. *Delinking Degrees from Jobs.* Beginning to be made in delinking degrees from jobs in selected areas.

6. *Performance and Accountability.* Stress was laid on performance and accountability at all levels.

7. *Decentralisation of the Management of Education.* The policy very aptly called for evolving a strategy of decentralisation and the creation of a spirit of autonomy for educational institutions.

8. *Indian Education Service.* It envisaged that the Constitution of the Indian Education Service would bring about a national perspective in education.

9. *National Testing Service.* This is likely to be helpful in determining suitability of candidates for specified jobs and to pave the way for the emergence of norms of comparable competence across the nation.

10. *Raising Resources.* The policy has suggested appropriate methods of financing education. These are: (i) Beneficiary communities to maintain school buildings and supplies of some Consumables; (ii) Raising fees at the higher levels of education; (iii) Levying a cess or charge on users of research and development agencies; and (iv) Affecting savings by the efficient use of facilities.

Missing Links and Limitations of the New Policy

1. *Financial Aspects not Worked Out.* It is very unfortunate that financial implications have not been worked out. Targets in different areas have not been fixed. Any workable document must be backed by financial resources otherwise it will remain a 'paper' document.

2. *No Reference to Basic system of Education.* There is no reference to the Basic System of Education at the School Stage.

3. *Working Hours in Schools.* For making the optimum use of human resources, increased working hours in educational institutions should have been recommended.

4. *Too Much Expectation from Community Help.* There is very little hope of obtaining Community funds for educational purposes as there has developed a strong tendency on the part of the rich members of the community to

contribute to political parties due to obvious reasons.

5. *Neighbourhood School Concept Ignored.* The neighbourhood school concept advocated by the Kothari Commission for eliminating the segregation that now takes place between the schools for the poor and the under-privileged classes and those for the rich and the privileged, has been completely ignored.

6. *Silent on the Existence of Public Schools.* The NPE has evaded the issue of the 'Commercialisation' of education by most of the public schools in the country.

7. *No Check on the Working of Minority Schools.* The Policy does not propose any checks to prevent the management of the public schools from exploiting the staff working there.

8. *Multiplication of Institutions.* Setting up State Advisory Boards of Education, District Institutes of Education and Training and District Boards of Education is not likely to serve any useful purpose.

IMPLEMENTATION OF THE POLICY: PROGRAMME OF ACTION (1986)

After the declaration of the National Policy on Education, 1986, the Ministry of Human Resource Development, (formerly known as Ministry of Education), Government of India, announced the Programme of Action for its implementation. This was the first time in the history of educational development in independent India that such a follow up programme was prepared. Twenty-three Task Forces were prepared and each was assigned a specific topic covered by the National Policy on Education, 1986 (NPE). Eminent educationists, experts, senior bureaucrats and representatives of the Central and State Governments were associated with these Task Forces. Each Task Force examined the situation in respect of the subject assigned to it and elaborated upon the implications of the specific statements contained in the NPE. Necessary action was also projected and the broad lines indicated by each Task Force.

The reports of the Task Forces were discussed in a series of meetings convened by the Minister of Human Resource Development. A conference of Education Secretaries of the State Governments and Union Territories also considered these reports in July 1986. Further the document on Programme of Action was discussed in the meeting of the Central Advisory Board of Education held at New Delhi on the 1st and 2nd of August, 1986. The Final Programme of Action was presented to Parliament on August 8, 1986. The Lok Sabha and the Rajya Sabha discussed and approved the Programme of Action on 22 and 23 August 1986 respectively.

The Programme of Action covers a vast gamut of the crucial educational parameters. It surveys the educational scene in the country, points out the implications of the statements contained in the NPE and suggests strategies of implementation. It contains twenty-four well-intentioned excellent essays on various aspects of education.

MAIN SCHEMES LAUNCHED AS A RESULT OF THE PROGRAMME OF ACTION (1986) IN PURSUANCE OF THE NPE (1986)

1. National System of Education.
2. Reconstruction of Curriculum
3. Operation Blackboard (Discussed in the next chapter)
4. Navodaya Schools.
5. Vocationalisation of Education (Discussed in the next chapter)

National System of Education

The most distinct feature of the NPE (1986) is the formulation of the national system of education. For the first time since independence, the concept of the national system was developed. Its various parameters were detailed and action started.

Main Features of the National System of Education

The National Policy on Education, 1986 has envisaged the following main features of the National System of Education:

1. *Philosophical and Sociological Foundations Based on Constitutional Principles*. The National System of Education derives its inspiration from the ideals and values of democracy, secularism and socialism.

2. *Universal Access to Education.* The National System of Education implies that up to a given level, all students, irrespective of caste, creed, location or sex, have access to education of a comparable quality. To achieve this, the Government will initiate appropriately funded programmes. Effective measures will be taken in the direction of the Common School System recommended in the 1968 Policy.

3. *Common Educational Structure.* The National System of Education envisages a common educational structure. The 10+2+3 structure has now been accepted in all parts of the country. Regarding the further break-up of the first 10 years efforts will be made to move towards an elementary system comprising 5 years of primary education and 3 years of upper primary, followed by 2 years of High School.

4. *National Curricular Framework with a Common Core.* The National System of Education will be based on a national curricular framework which contains a common core along with other components that are flexible. The common core will include the history of India's freedom movement, the constitutional obligations and other content essential to nurture national identity. These elements cut across subject areas and will be designed to promote values such as India's common cultural heritage, egalitarianism, democracy and secularism, equality of the sexes, protection of the environment, removal of social barriers, observance of the small family norm and inculcation of the scientific temper. All educational programmes will be carried on in strict conformity with secular values.

5. *Education for International Understanding.* India has always worked for peace and understanding between nations, treating the whole world as one family. True to this hoary tradition, education has to strengthen this world view and motivate the younger generations for international cooperation and peaceful coexistence. This aspect cannot be neglected.

6. *Equality of Opportunity of Education.* To promote equality, it will be necessary to provide for equal opportunity to all not only in access, but also in the conditions for success. Besides, awareness of the inherent equality of all will be created through the core curriculum. The purpose is to remove prejudices and complexes transmitted through the social environment and the accident of birth.

7. *Determination of Minimum Levels of Learning.* Minimum levels of learning will be laid down for each stage of education. Steps will also be taken to foster among students an understanding of the diverse cultural and social systems of the people living in different parts of the country.

8. *Promotion of State Languages.* Besides the promotion of the link language, programmes will also be launched to increase substantially the translation of books from one language to another and to publish multi-lingual dictionaries and glossaries. The young will be encouraged to undertake the rediscovery of India, each in his own image and perception.

9. *Universal Character of Higher Education.* In higher education in general, and technical education in particular, steps will be taken to facilitate inter-regional mobility by providing equal access to every Indian of requisite merit, regardless of his origins. The universal character of universities and other institutions of higher education is to be underscored.

10. *Network Arrangement of Pooling of Resources.* In the areas of research and development, and education in science and technology, special measures will be taken to establish network arrangement between different institutions in the country to pool their resources and participate in project of national importance.

11. *Priorities of Educational Reforms.* The nation as a whole will assume the responsibility of providing resource support for implementing programmes of educational transformation, reducing disparities, universalisation of elementary education, adult literacy, scientific and technological research, etc.

12. *Extensive facilities for Open and Distance Learning.* Life-long education is a cherished goal of the educational process. This presupposes universal literacy. Opportunities will be provided to youth, housewives, agricultural and industrial workers and professionals to continue the education of their choice at the pace suited to them. The future thrust will be in the direction of open and distance learning.

13. *Strengthening of National Institutions.* It is proposed to strengthen national institutions like the University Grants Commission, NCERT, NIEPA,

All India Council of Technical Education, Indian Council of Educational Research, the Indian Medical Council, etc.

14. *Meaningful Partnership*. The Centre and States will make their partnership in the field of education meaningful.

15. *Expenditure on Education*. Efforts to be made to spend 6% of GNP on education.

16. *Education for All*. Attempts to made to provide elementary education and adult education to all.

NATIONAL POLICY ON EDUCATION AND RECONSTRUCTION OF CURRICULUM

Importance of Curriculum. Curriculum is the one of the most important elements of education through which it can bring about the 'fine synthesis between change-oriented technologies and the country's continuity of cultural traditions', as observed by the NPE. Curriculum contains subject-matter of various disciplines and activities. It fulfills the tasks set. The NPE provided the directions and the Programme of Action (1986) formulated for their implementation worked out the details of the curriculum.

Special Features of the Curriculum

1. *Common Core Curriculum*. The National System of Education will be based on a national curricular framework which contains a common core along with other components that are flexible. The common core will include the history of India's freedom movement, the constitutional obligations and other content essential to nurture national identity. These elements will cut across subject areas and will be designed to promote values such as India's common cultural heritage, egalitarianism, democracy and secularism, equality of the sexes, protection of the environment, removal of social barriers, observance of the small family norm and inculcation of the scientific temper. All educational programmes will be carried on in strict conformity with secular values.

2. *Minimum Levels of Learning*. Minimum levels of learning will be laid down for each stage of education. Steps will also be taken to foster among students an understanding of the diverse cultural and social systems of the people living in different parts of the country.

3. *The Cultural Perspective*. The existing schism between the formal system of education and the country's rich and varied cultural traditions need to be bridged. The preoccupation with modern technologies cannot be allowed to sever new generations from the roots in India's history and culture. De-culturisation, dehumanisation and alienation must be avoided at all costs. Education can and must bring about the fine synthesis between change-oriented technologies and the country's continuity of cultural traditions.

The curricula and processes of education will be enriched by cultural content in as many manifestations as possible. Children will be enabled to develop sensitivity to beauty, harmony and refinement.

4. *Value Education.* The growing concern over the erosion of essential values and an increasing cynicism in society has brought to focus the need for readjustments in the curriculum in order to make education a forceful tool for the cultivation of social and moral values.

In our culturally plural society education should foster universal and eternal values, oriented towards the unity and integration of our people. Such education should help eliminate obscurantism, religious fanaticism, violence, superstition and fatalism.

5. *Languages.* The Education Policy of 1968 had examined the question of the development of languages in great details; its essential provisions can hardly be improved upon and are as relevant today as before. The implementation of this part of the 1968 Policy has, however, been uneven. The Policy will be implemented more energetically and purposefully.

6. *Media and Educational Technology.* Modern communication technologies have the potential to bypass several stages and sequences in the process of development encountered in early decades. Both the constraints of time and distance at once become manageable. In order to avoid structural dualism, modern educational technology must reach out to the most distant areas and the most deprived sections of beneficiaries simultaneously with the areas of comparative affluence and ready availability.

The media has profound influence on the mind of children as well as adults; some of it has encouraged consumerism, violence etc., and thus had a deleterious effect. Radio and TV programmes which clearly militate against proper educational objectives will be prevented. Steps will be taken to discourage such trend in the films and other media also. An active movement will be started to promote the production of children's films of high quality and usefulness.

7. *Work Experience.* Work experience, viewed as purposive and meaningful manual work, organised as an integral part of the learning process and resulting in either goods or services useful to the community, is considered as an essential component at all stages of education, to be provided through well-structured and graded programmes. It would comprise activities in accordance with the interests, abilities and needs of students, the level of skills and knowledge to be upgraded with the stages of education. The experience would be helpful on entry into the workforce. Pre-vocational programmes provided at the lower secondary stage will also facilitate the choice of the vocational courses at the higher secondary stage.

8. *Education and Environment.* There is a paramount need to create a consciousness of the environment. It must permeate all ages and all sections of society, beginning with the child. Environmental consciousness should inform teaching in schools and colleges. This aspect will be integrated in the

entire educational process.

9. *Teaching of Mathematics.* Mathematics should be visualised as the vehicle to train a child to think, reason, analyse and to articulate logically. Apart from being a specific subject, it should be treated as a concomitant to any subject involving analysis and reasoning.

With the recent introduction of computers in schools, educational computing and the emergence of learning through the understanding of cause-effect relationships and the interplay of variables, the teaching of mathematics will be suitably redesigned to bring it in line with modern technological devices.

10. *Science Education.* Science education will be strengthened so as to develop in the child well defined abilities and values such as the spirit of inquiry, creativity, objectivity, the courage to question, and an aesthetic sensibility.

Science education programmes will be designed to enable the learner to acquire problem solving and decision making skills and to discover the relationship of science with health, agriculture, industry and other aspects of daily life. Every effort will be made to extend science education to the vast numbers who have remained outside the facility of formal education.

11. *Sports and Physical Education.* Sports and physical education are an integral part of the learning process, and will be included in the evaluation of performance. A nation-wide infrastructure for physical education, sports and games will be built into the educational edifice.

The infrastructure will consist of playfields, equipment, coaches and teachers of physical education as part of the School Improvement Programme. Available open spaces in urban areas will be reserved for playgrounds, if necessary by legislation. Efforts will be made to establish sports institutions and hostel where specialised attention will be given to sports activities and sports-related studies along with normal education. Appropriate encouragement will be given to those talented in sports and games. Due stress will be laid on indigenous traditional games. As a system which promotes an integrated development of body and mind, Yoga will receive special attention. Efforts will be made to introduce Yoga in all schools; to this end, it will be introduced in teacher training courses.

12. *Education for International Understanding.* India has always worked for peace and understanding between nations, and treating the whole world as one family. True to this hoary tradition, education has to strengthen this world view and motivate the younger generations for international cooperation and peaceful co-existence. This aspect cannot be neglected.

13. *Curriculum at Different Stages of School Education*

(1) *Curriculum at pre-elementary stage.* Recognising the holistic nature of child development, *viz.*, nutrition, health and social, mental, physical, moral and emotional development, Early Childhood Care and Education (ECCE) will receive high priority and be suitably integrated wherever possible. Day-

care centres will be provided as a support service for universalisation of primary education, to enable girls engaged in taking care of siblings to attend school and as a support service for working women belonging to poorer sections.

Programme of ECCE will be child-oriented, focused around play, and the individuality of the child. Formal methods and the introduction of the 3R's will be discouraged at this stage. The local community will be fully involved in these programmes.

A full integration of child care and pre-primary education will be brought about, both as a feeder and a strengthening factor for primary education and for human resource development in general. In continuation of this stage, the School Health Programme will be strengthened.

(2) *Curriculum at the Elementary Stage: Child-centred Approach.* A warm welcoming and encouraging approach, in which all concerned share a solicitude for the needs of the child, is the best motivation for the child to attend school and learn. A child-centred and activity-based process of learning should be adopted at the primary stage. First generation learners should be allowed to set their own pace and be given supplementary remedial instruction.

(3) *Curriculum at the Secondary Stage.* Secondary education begins to expose students to differentiated roles of science, the humanities and social sciences. This is also an appropriate stage to provide children with a sense of history and national perspective and give them opportunities to understand their constitutional duties and rights as citizens. Conscious internalisation of a healthy work ethos and of the values of a humane and composite culture will be brought about through appropriately formulated curricula. Vocationalisation through specialised institutions or through the refashioning of secondary education can, at this stage, provide valuable manpower for economic growth.

National Curriculum for Elementary and Secondary Education (1988)

For carrying out the directives in the policy, the National Council of Educational Research Training, New Delhi, prepared a National Curriculum for Elementary and Secondary Education. It included the emerging curricular concerns and imperatives based on socio-cultural, political and economic considerations.

Revised Curriculum 2000

The NCERT revised the curriculum in 2000. Three pillars of the revised policy are: 1. 'Relevance', 2. 'Equity' and 3. 'Excellence'. It is based on the following objectives which by and large are the same as contained in NPE 1986 and as modified in 1992.

1. Developing a cohesive society.
2. Strengthening national unity.

3. Preserving cultural heritage and improving the indigenous knowledge.
4. Highlighting India's contribution to mankind.
5. Responding to the challenge of globalisation.
6. Meeting the challenges of information and communication technologies.
7. Linking education with life skills.
8. Developing values.
9. Relating education to the 'World of work'.
10. Reducing the curriculum load.
11. Making child as a instructor of knowledge.
12. Developing interface between cognition and emotion.
13. Promoting cultural specific pedagogies.
14. Developing aesthetic sensibilities.
15. Making comprehensive and continuous evaluation.

NAVODAYA/JAWAHAR VIDYALAYAS (PACE-SETTING SCHOOLS)

Origin of the Navodaya Schools. The National Policy on Education, 1986, pointed out the need for setting up pace-setting schools which came to be known as Navodaya Vidyalayas or Jawahar Navodaya Vidyalayas. At present more than 400 such Vidyalayas are functioning in different parts of the country. Eventually the Central Government plans to open one such school in every district.

Need for the Pace-Setting Schools. The NPE observed , "It is universally accepted that children with special talent or aptitude should be provided opportunity to proceed at a faster pace through quality education, irrespective of their capacity to pay for it."

Main Features of Navodaya Schools

1. They cater to the talented students.
2. They are residential.
3. They provide free education.
4. They cater primarily to rural areas. 75 per cent seats are reserved for rural areas.
5. They have reserved seats for SC and ST as per their actual population in the district subject to a minimum of nationally prescribed figure of 15 per cent and 7.5 per cent for SC and ST respectively.
6. They are expected to foster national integration by providing opportunities of living and learning together.
7. A certain proportion of students comes from other States.
8. Special emphasis is laid on diagnostic and remedial teaching.
9. They are expected to provide full scope for innovation and experimentation.
10. They are expected to become catalysts of nation-wide programme of school improvement.

11. Selection for admission is based on different types of scholastic aptitude tests which aim at eliminating the element of subjectivity.
12. It is envisaged that in these schools three-language formula will be implemented in its true spirit.

Organisation of Navodaya Vidyalayas. A Navodaya Vidyalaya Samiti, an autonomous organisation in the Ministry of Human Resource Development has been set up to manage these schools. These schools are affiliated to the Central Board of Secondary Education, Delhi. The Central Government bears 100 per cent expenditure for running these institutions and it is the responsibility of the State Governments to provide a plot of land, about 30 acres in area, free of cost.

The Navodaya Vidyalayas (NVs) have started functioning in almost all the States with some glaring exceptions—Tamil Nadu and West Bengal, for instance, have not yet agreed to the scheme for certain reasons which include opposition to Hindi as a medium of instruction.

Snags in the Scheme of Navodaya Vidyalayas

1. It appears that these schools had been started in great haste, without the necessary infrastructure or operational facilities which reveals a lack of proper planning. However, these defects have been removed gradually.
2. By and large, Navodaya Vidyalayas are facing the problem of inadequate accommodation.
3. There are instances in which these schools have been set up in obscure location.
4. Another major problem has been the non-availability of experienced staff. Merited teachers are not willing to work in remote villages. Also according to the initial policy laid down by the Navodaya Vidyalaya Samiti, teachers can only join on deputation which means teaches will have very little affinity with these schools.
5. The library facilities provided are far inferior to the stipulated requirement.
6. Suitable playgrounds are not available, which is indeed sad.

Criticism of the Scheme

The critics point out the following demerits:

1. Admission tests do not take into consideration rural background.
2. On account of special coaching facilities, children of middle class income group are able to get admission in large numbers at the cost of lower income group.
3. By opening these schools, the government has discarded the Common School System. Another category of public schools has emerged.
4. These schools put a heavy burden on the State. This money should be spent in providing elementary universal education.

Conclusion. Despite these snags and shortcomings, they are serving the purpose to a considerable extent for which they were created. Nevertheless, there is a lot of scope in improving the admission tests and bringing about qualitative improvement in the standard of teaching.

5

Modified National Policy on Education (1992)

FORMULATION OF THE NATIONAL POLICY ON EDUCATION (1992)

The NPE was adopted by Parliament in May, 1986. It was followed up by the Programme of Action which was adopted by Parliament in August, 1986. The NPE could be implemented only for about three years. The Janata Governments headed by Shri V.P. Singh (December 2, 1989 to November 7, 1990) and Shri Chandra Shekhar (November 10, 1990 to March 6, 1991) were somewhat lukewarm to the NPE formulated by the Congress Government headed by Shri Rajiv Gandhi. A Review Committee with Acharya Ramamurti as Chairman was appointed in May 1990. The Committee submitted its report on NPE on December 26, 1990. The report was placed in the meeting of the Central Advisory Board of Education held on March 8-9, 1991. A Committee with Shri N. Janardhana Reddy, Chief Minister and of Education Minister, Andhra Pradesh as its Chairman was appointed on July 31, 1991 to review the NPE and the recommendations of the Ramamurti Review Committee. On the recommendations of the Janardhana Committee, certain modifications were made in the NPE, 1986. These changes were announced in the Parliament in the month of May, 1992.

MAJOR ORIGINAL PROVISIONS AND REVISED POLICY CHANGES

National System on Education (1986)

NPE 1986 Para 3.3

The National System on Education envisages a common educational structure. The 10+2+3 structure has now been accepted in all parts of the country. Regarding the further break-up of the first 10 years efforts will be made to move towards an elementary system comprising 5 years of primary education and 3 years of upper primary, followed by 2 years of High School.

Elementary Education

NPE, 1986, Para 5.5

The new thrust in elementary education will emphasise two aspects: (i) universal enrolment and universal retention of children up to 14 years of age, and (ii) a substantial improvement in the quality of education.

A Resolve

NPE, 1986, Para 5.12

The New Educational Policy will give the highest priority to solving the problem of children dropping out of school and will adopt an array of meticulously formulated strategies based on micro-planning, and applied at the grassroots level all over the country, to ensure children's retention at school. This effort will be fully coordinated with the network of non-formal education. It shall be ensured that all children who attain the age of about 11 years by 1990 will have had five years of schooling, or its equivalent through the non-formal stream. Likewise, by 1995 all children will be provided free and compulsory education up to 14 years of age.

Vocationalisation

NPE, 1986, Para 5.23

It is proposed that vocational courses cover 10 per cent of higher secondary students by 1990 and 25 per cent by 1995. Steps will be taken to see that a substantial majority of the products of vocational courses are employed or become self-employed. Review of the courses offered would be regularly undertaken. Government will also review its recruitment policy to encourage diversification at the secondary level.

Revised NPE, 1992, Para 3.3

The National System of Education envisages a common educational structure. The 10+2+3 structure has now been accepted in all parts of the country. Regarding the further break-up of the first 10 years efforts will be made to move towards an elementary system comprising 5 years of primary education and 3 years of upper primary, followed by 2 years of High School. Efforts will also be made to have the +2 stage accepted as a part of school education throughout the country.

Revised NPE, 1992, Para 5.5

The new thrust in elementary education will emphasise three aspects: (i) universal access and enrolment, (ii) universal retention of children up to 14 years of age; and (iii) a substantial improvement in the quality of education to enable all children to achieve essential levels of learning.

Revised NPE, 1992, Para 5.12

The New Educational Policy will give the highest priority to solving the problem of children dropping out of school and will adopt an array of meticulously formulated strategies based on micro planning, and applied at the grassroots level all over the country, to ensure children's retention at school. This effort will be fully coordinated with the network of non-formal education. It shall be ensured that free and compulsory education of satisfactory quality is provided to all children up to 14 years of age before we enter the twenty-first century. A national mission will be launched for the achievement of this goal.

Revised NPE, 1992, Para 5.23

It is proposed that vocational courses cover 10 per cent of higher secondary students by 1995 and 25 per cent by 2000. Steps will be taken to see that a substantial majority of the products of vocational courses are employed or become self-employed. Review of the courses offered would be regularly undertaken. Government will also review its recruitment policy to encourage diversification at the secondary level.

Resources and Review

NPE Para 11.4

11.4 In view of these imperatives, education will be treated as a crucial area of investment for national development and survival. The National Policy on Education, 1968, had laid down that the investment on education be gradually increased to reach a level of expenditure of 6 per cent of the national income as early as possible. Since the actual level of investment has remained far short of that target, it is important that greater determination be shown now to find the funds for the programmes laid down in this policy. While the actual requirements will be computed from time to time on the basis of monitoring and review, the outlay on education will be stepped up to the extent essential for policy implementation in the Seventh Plan. It will be ensured that from the Eighth Five Year Plan onwards it will uniformly exceed 6 per cent of the National Income.

NPE Para 11.4

11.4 In view of these imperatives, education will be treated as a crucial area of investment for national development and survival. The National Policy on Education, 1968, had laid down that the investment on education be gradually increased to reach a level of 6 percent of the national income as early as possible. Since the actual level of investment has remained far short of that target, it is important that greater determination is shown now to find the funds for the programmes laid down in this policy. While the actual requirements will be computed from time to time on the basis of monitoring and review, the outlay on education will be stepped up to ensure that during the Eighth Five Year Plan and onwards it will uniformly exceed 6 per cent of the National Income.

Chief Features of Programme of Action, 1992 (POA-1992)

1. *Meaningful Partnership in the Implementation of Programmes.* The NPE, 1986 has the distinction of giving an operational meaning to concurrency. Given that Education is a concurrent subject, the POA, 1992 can be implemented only if the Union and the States/Union Territories (UTs) work together in meaningful partnership. The POA, 1992 has to be perceived as a charter for action of the nation as a whole requiring a co-operative effort of the Union, States/UTs, the education community, and the community at large. Given the rich diversity of our continental nation it would be in the fitness of things if each State and UT formulates a State POA which is in line with the situational imperative as well as with the POA, 1992. This process has to be carried to its logical conclusion with each district and educational institution formulating a POA of its own. In this context it is necessary to stress that what is presented here is not an inflexible structure but only a projection of the direction with varying degrees of detail. A certain amount of flexibility is assumed which will help the implementing agencies in tailoring the POA, 1992 to suit their contexts and emerging scenarios.

2. *Flexible Approach.* In the ultimate, resources and management would define implementation. In developing this document the resource availability indicated for the 8th Five Year Plan (1992-97) was kept at the back of the mind; but at the same time the long term perspective has not been lost sight of. Many actions envisaged by the POA, 1992 span not only the 8th Five Year Plan but also the 9th and even beyond. Phasing has, therefore, to be left somewhat flexible so that the pace of implementation can match the mobilisation of resources.

3. *Cost Effectiveness and Accountability:* The national resolve of raising the outlay on education to 6% of the national income should be translated into practice at the earliest possible. As envisaged by the NPE, 1986 and through the modalities it outlined, the nation as a whole, should assume responsibility of providing the resource support for education. The logical corollary of this proposition is that an ethos of cost-effectiveness and accountability should permeate every part of the education system. To say the least, unplanned proliferation of sub-standard institutions should stop here and now; programmes should cease to be driven by budgets and instead should stress processes and outcomes; efficiency should be rated not by the ability to consume budget and demand more but by performance and delivery. All this calls for extra-ordinary attention to the management of education which is often neglected. It is obvious that the many tasks which the NPE, 1986 and POA, 1992 envisage cannot be performed in a state when even routine tasks like supply of textbooks, conduct of examinations and operation of academic calendar leave much to be desired. Reform of management in its entirety should be the first and foremost task of the education community.

4. *Involvement of the People.* While the Union and State Governments

will fully shoulder these responsibilities it is people's involvement in the educational reconstruction which will make the real difference. The total literacy campaigns have demonstrated that, given the will, and the right strategy and appropriate structures, people's involvement can be elicited on a large scale. The management challenge in education lies in creating appropriate arrangements for a similar involvement to take on long-standing problems like the Universalisation of Elementary Education (UEE). There is no better way to ensure accountability than an awakened and "demanding" community.

5. *Establishing Linkages Between Education and Other Related Services*. Another important challenge is establishing linkages between education and other related services like child care, nutrition and health. As it is, the responsibility for educational administration is fragmented in most States, with more than one Education Secretary and several Directors of Education. There is need for greater coordination amongst these multiple agencies and functionaries on the one hand and between Education and other areas of HRD on the other. Appropriate mechanisms should be developed.

6. *Empowerment of Women Through Education*. Education for Women's Equality is a vital component of the overall strategy of securing equity and social justice in education. There is the need for institutional mechanisms to ensure that gender sensitivity is reflected in the implementation of all educational programmes across the board. It is being increasingly recognised that the problem of UEE is, in essence, the problem of the girl child. It is imperative that participation of girls is enhanced at all stages of education, particularly in streams like science, vocational, technical and commerce education where girls are grossly under-represented. The education system as a whole should be re-oriented to promote women's equality and education.

7. *Special Strategy for the Education of the Disadvantaged Sections*

Another facet of the overall strategy of securing equity and social justice in education is the concern for the educational needs of SCs/STs, minorities, and the physically and mentally handicapped. Here again it is necessary for educational system to be sensitive to the educational needs of these groups; it should be geared up to promote equalisation of educational opportunities.

Main Area's Covered by Programme of Action, 1992.

1. Education for Women's Equality
2. Education of Scheduled Castes, Scheduled Tribes and Other Backward Sections
3. Minorities' Education
4. Education of the Handicapped
5. Adult and Continuing Education
6. Early Childhood Care and Education
7. Elementary Education
8. Secondary Education
9. Navodaya Vidyalayas

10. Vocational Education
11. Higher Education
12. Open Education
13. Delinking Degrees from Jobs and Manpower Planning
14. Rural Universities and Institutes
15. Technical and Management Education
16. Research and Development
17. The Cultural Perspective
18. Development of Languages
19. Media and Educational Technology
20. Sports, Physical Education and Youth
21. Evaluation Process and Examination Reforms
22. Teachers and Their Training
23. Management of Education

Major Initiatives/Programmes as a Follow-Up of POA (1992)

Elementary Education (UEE)

1. District Primary Education Programme (DPEP) started in 1994.
2. National Programme of Nutritional Support to Primary Education (Mid-day Meals) – started in 1995.
3. Lok Jumbish – started in 1992.
4. *Sarva Shiksha Abhiyan* – started in 2000 (Discussed separately)

Higher Education

Constitution of National Assessment and Accredition Council (NAAC) (Discussed separately)

6

Universalisation of Elementary Education (UEE)

MEANING OF UNIVERSALISATION OF ELEMENTARY EDUCATION

Universalisation of elementary education in India implies that all children in the age-group 6 to 14 (Class I to VIII), belonging to the rich and the poor, the male and female, the rural and the urban and in places which are accessible with difficulty must be provided with elementary education.

Universalisation of elementary education also means free education. In some of the advanced countries free education means no fees, free books and stationery, free mid-day meals and free school transport. But in developing countries like India, it has not been possible to provide all these facilities free of cost. Of course, education at this stage is free of tuition fee in state run/local bodies aided schools. Other facilities on a selective basis are also provided.

Universalisation of primary of elementary education involves the following three stages or steps:

(a) Universalisation of Provision.
(b) Universalisation of Enrolment.
(c) Universalisation of Retention.

(a) *Universalisation of Provision.* It means that school facilities should be provided to all the children between the age group 6 to 14 years in the country within the walking distance of a child. We have fairly succeeded as far as this provision is concerned.

(b) *Universalisation of Enrolment.* All children between the age group 6 to 14 years must be enrolled. For this, compulsory legislation must be passed. Under legislation, parents can be fined for not sending their children to schools. However this provision has not been fulfilled in our country.

(c) *Universalisation of Retention.* By this we mean that once a child joins an elementary/primary school, he should remain there till he completes all 8 classes. If the child leaves the school in between, the idea of universalisation stands defeated. Unfortunately, in our country 55% of all the first admission leave the primary school before completing it. It gives birth to problem of wastage. Mere enlistment of children is not enough. They have to be retained for eight years from Classes I to VIII.

SIGNIFICANCE OF UEE

It is universally accepted that the provision of UEE is the true index of the general, economic, political and social development of a country. Primary education contributes to national development. Various studies have clearly demonstrated that countries which have made proper provision for UEE are far ahead of those with inadequate provision. On account of its importance, the Constitution of India enjoins upon the State to make provision for it. UEE assumes special significance for a developing country like India where elementary education is the end of nearly 45 per cent of the people.

UEE education is needed on account of the following considerations:

1. Preservation and promotion of culture.
2. Enrichment of life of an individual.
3. Promotion of values like give and take, mutual appreciation and tolerance.
4. Constructive participation in political and social life.
5. Development of vocational efficiency.
6. Development of basic and upgraded skills.
7. Improvement in the quality of followership and leadership.
8. Deriving benefit from new knowledge.
9. Development of basic essentials for a healthy life.
10. Development of worthy leisure time pursuits.
11. Development of values of emotional integration and national unity.
12. Development of awareness regarding work done during Five Year Plans.
13. Liquidation of elements of fatalism and superstitions.
14. Inculcation of scientific temperament.

NON-FULFILMENT OF CONSTITUTIONAL COMMITMENT TO UNIVERSAL ELEMENTARY EDUCATION

The universalisation of elementary education has been one of the most important goals of educational development in India since independence. It found expression in Article 45 of the Indian Constitution as a Directive Principle of State Policy under the caption *Provision for Free and Compulsory Education for Children*: "The State shall endeavour to provide, within a period of ten years from the commencement of the Constitution, for free and compulsory education for all children until they complete the age of fourteen years." In other words this task should have been completed by 1960. However this resolve could not be accomplished on account of several problems such as the rehabilitation of displaced persons after partition and lack of resources. As a result the target date had to be revised first to 1970, then to 1976 and later on to 1990. The target date, according to the National Policy on Education, 1986 was 1995. The Resolve contained in the policy reads as : "The new Education Policy will give the highest priority to solving the problem of children dropping out of school and will adopt an array of meticulously formulated strategies based on micro-planning, and applied at the grass-roots level all over the country, to ensure children's retention at school. The effort will be fully coordinated with the network of non-formal education. It shall be ensured that all children who attain the age of about 11 years by 1990 will have had five years of schooling, or its equivalent through the non-formal stream. Likewise, by 1995 all children will be provided free and compulsory education up to 14 years of age." The modified NPE 1992, has further revised the date. It states, "It shall be ensured that free and compulsory education of satisfactory quality is provided to all children up to 14 years of age before we enter the twenty first century. A National Mission will be launched for the achievement of this goal." Alas ! This goal is also elusive.

Now the present goal according to '*Sarva Shiksha Abhiyan*' (Education for All) (Discussed separately).

PROGRESS IN UEE SINCE INDEPENDENCE

The total enrolment at the primary and upper primary school levels in India has witnessed a steady increase (Table 6.1). Total enrolment at the primary stage (grades I-V) increased 6 times from 19.2 million in 1950-51 to about 128.3 million in 2003-2004. Total enrolment at the Upper Primary levels (grades VI-VIII) increased by 14 times, from 3.1 million in 1950-51 to 48.7 million in 2000-2001. The growth rate of girls' enrolment at the elementary level was higher as compared to that of the boys. Participation of girls at all levels of school education has improved appreciably over the years.

Table 6.1: Sex-wise Enrolment at Primary Stage (1950-51 to 2003-2004)

Year	*Classes I to V*			*Classes VI to VIII*		
	Boys	*Girls*	*Total*	*Boys*	*Girls*	*Total*
1950-51	13.8	5.4	19.2	2.6	0.5	3.1
1960-61	23.6	11.4	35.0	5.1	1.6	6.7
1970-71	35.7	21.3	57.0	9.4	3.9	13.3
1980-81	45.3	28.5	73.8	13.9	6.8	20.7
1990-91	57.0	40.4	97.4	21.5	12.5	34.0
2000-2001	64.0	49.8	113.8	25.3	17.5	47.8
2003-2004	68.3	59.0	128.3	27.3	21.4	48.7

Note: Gross Enrolment Ratio (GER) is defined as the percentage of the enrolment in classes I-V and VI-VIII and/or I-VIII to the estimated child population in the age groups 6 to 11 years and 11 to 14 and or 6 to 14 years respectively. Enrolment in these stages include under-age and over-age children. Hence the percentage may be more than 100% in some cases.

The Gross Enrolment Ratio (GER) at Primary and Upper Primary levels improved perceptibly from 1950-51 to 2003-2004. The GER rose at the primary level from 42.6 per cent in 1950-51 to 98.3 per cent in 2003-2004.

Table 6.2: Trends in Gross Enrolment Ratios in India

(In per cent)

Year	Primary (I-V)		Upper Primary (VI-VII)		Elementary (I-VIII)	
	Boys	Girls	Boys	Girls	Boys	Girls
1950-51	60.6	24.8	20.6	4.6	46.4	17.7
1960-61	82.6	41.4	33.2	11.3	65.2	30.9
1970-71	95.5	605	46.5	20.8	75.5	44.4
1980-81	95.8	64.1	54.3	28.6	82.2	52.1
1990-91	114.4	85.5	76.6	47.0	100.0	70.8
1991-92	112.3	86.9	75.1	49.6	101.2	73.2
2003-04	100.7	95.7	98.3	68.8	57.6	62.4

Table 6.3: No. of Recognised and Middle Schools

Year	Primary	Middle
1950-51	2,09,671	13,596
1960-61	3,30,399	49,663
1970-71	4,08,378	90,621
1980-81	4,94,503	1,18,555
1990-91	5,60,935	1,51,456
2000-2001	6,38,738	2,06,269
2003-2004	7,12,239	2,62,286

Note: Use of the terms 'Primary' and 'Elementary' has not been uniform. Sometimes they are used interchangeably. Sometimes 'primary' (lower Primary) class I to V and upper Primary (classes VI to VIII) or Middle are used. Middle Schools sometimes include classes I to VIII and mostly classes VI to VIII.

Table 6.4: Expansion of Educational Facilities since 1950-51

	Stage/Classes	1950-51	2003-2004	Increase Approximate
I.	Enrolment in Primary			
	Class I to V: Age Group 11-14 years			about
	Boys	13.8 million	68.3 million	5 times
	Girls	5.4 million	59.0 million	10 times
	Total	19.2 million	128.3 million	6 times
II	Enrolment in Middle (Upper Primary): Age Group 11-14 years			
	Boys	2.6 million	27.6 million	10 times
	Girls	0.5 million	21.4 million	43 times
	Total	3.1 million	48.7 million	16 times
III	No. of Primary Schools	2,10,000	7,10,471	3 times
IV.	No. of Middle Schools (Upper Primary)	13,596	2,06,249	15 times
V.	Literacy Rate (2001)			
	Male	27.15%	75.85%	48.70%
	Female	8.56%	54.16%	45.60%
	Total	18.33%	65.38%	47.05%

Enrolment for girls rose from 24.8 per cent to 95.7 per cent during this period. The boys/girls differential also declined substantially. The GER at the Upper Primary level improved from 12.7 per cent in 1950-51 to 62.4 per cent in 2003-2004 with what that for girls increasing from 4.6 per cent to 57.6 percent for this period. Though the participation of girls at levels of school education has increased substantially, the proportion of girls enrolled both at the Primary and Upper Primary levels continues to be lower than the gross enrolment of boys. Vast disparities exist amongst the States/UTs in terms of enrolment with educationally backward states having a lower GER than the all India average.

CAUSES AND PROBLEMS FOR NON-FULFILMENT OF CONSTITUTIONAL PROVISIONS REGARDING UEE

Following are the important cause and problems of slow progress:

1. Problems of priority to Elementary Education.
2. Problems of Finance.
3. Problem of Reconstruction of the Education System.
4. Problem Resulting from Poverty of Parents.
5. Problem of Unattractive Schools.
6. Problem of Wastage and Stagnation.
7. Problem of Girls Education.
8. Problem of States with Low Enrolment.
9. Problem of Education of Backward Sections and Classes.
10. Problem of Small Habitations.
11. Problem of the Education of the Handicapped.
12. Problem of Enforcing Compulsory Primary Education Acts.
13. Rigidity of School Programmes.
14. Problem of Teachers.
15. Adult Illiteracy
16. Lack of part-time educational facilities.

MEASURES FOR THE ACHIEVEMENT OF THE GOAL OF UEE

1. *Priority to Elementary education.* Elementary education should be developed on priority basis and percentage of budget under this sector should be suitably raised. There has been a decline in expenditure in this sector. From 55 percent of the total educational budget spent on elementary education during the First Plan, it came down to 36 percent in the Sixth Plan, 34 per cent in the Seventh Plan and 47 percent in the Eighth Plan.

2. *Rational Use of Finance.* Cost on elementary education may be rationalised by:

(a) Introducing double shift wherever possible.
(b) Harnessing community resources in men, material and monetary terms.
(c) Evolving a system of voluntary service in the form of teaching by young persons who have completed secondary school or college.

3. *Restructuring Education.* The single point entry system must be replaced by multiple entry system under which it will be open for older children of 9, 11 or 14 to join primary schools in separate classes organised for their needs. Facilities for part time education even at primary stage should be introduced. It should also be made possible for older children to join the prescribed courses at any time and also complete them in much shorter period.

4. *Provision of Facilities to Poor Students.* Facilities such as free supply of books and stationery, free uniforms and school means can be helpful in retaining children in schools. But more than that is the need for providing part-time educational facilities to the children from the poor families.

5. *Attractive School Environment.* Education should be suited to the environment and lives of children so that they do not regard it as a waste of time. Audio-visual aids should be made available in schools. Methods of teaching should arouse the curiosity and interest of children.

6. *Checking Wastage and Stagnation.* Nearly 60 per cent of the students enrolled in class I reach class V and only 45 percent reach class VIII. To reduce wastage and stagnation a number of steps need to be taken. The holding power of schools should be increased through the provision of better teachers and equipment. (For details see 4.8)

7. *Promoting Girls' Education.* Although girls education has made much headway since independence, yet there is still a wide gap between the education of boys and girls. Adequate attention should be given to education of girls at all stages. Special schemes should be prepared for this purpose and the funds required for them should be provided on a priority basis.

8. *Special Attention to States with Low Enrolment.* Special attention to universal enrolment has to be paid in these States. Provision for part-time education should be made and more schools should be set up at suitable places.

9. *Education of Backward Classes.* The Backward classes include the Scheduled Castes, the Scheduled Tribes, Denotified Communities and few nomadic and semi-nomadic groups.

The Scheduled Castes and Scheduled Tribes constitute respectively 15 per cent and 7 per cent of the total population of the country. Special efforts should be made to enrol girls, children of Scheduled Castes and Scheduled Tribes and children of other weaker sections like landless agricultural labourers.

10. *Providing Education in Small Habitations.* The number of small habitations with a population of less than 200 is nearly four lakhs and a half. The population of these habitations is nearly 15 per cent of total rural population. Suitable measures need to be devised to tackle this problem.

11. *Education of the Handicapped.* According to the Programme of Action 1986, the population of handicapped children of the school going age is about 43 lakhs. This also requires special attention.

12. *Enforcing Compulsory Primary Education Act.* Although the

Compulsory Primary Education Act have been passed, yet this has not been properly enforced. Parents who wilfully do not send their children to school should be fined as provided in the Act.

13. *Providing Some element of Autonomy to Schools*

Each school, primary or middle, may be made fully responsible and accountable for formulating and implementing strategies for UEE in villages/ habitations/*mohallas* in the area under its coverage. For this purpose, vest the school with the necessary authority and autonomy to decide upon their mix of strategies and measures (e.g. adult education, para-schools, Operation Blackboard). Provide each school through the avenue of the Educational Complex adequate funds and intellectual resources to implement its programme of universalisation.

14. *Recruitment of 'Para teachers'*: The School Head Master/Head Mistress may be authorised to recruit 'para-teachers' (*Shiksha Karmis*) for reaching out either to unserved habitations or to those children who cannot attend the school during the day hours.

15. *Population Education.* The problem of population explosion has upset all our planning including education. Family planning must be adopted as a way of life. Population education should be promoted in educational institutions.

16. *Adult Literacy.* Nearly 50 per cent of the people in India are illiterate and as such they do not fully realise the importance of education for their children. They are indifferent to education. The prevalence of illiteracy is one of the factors that has stood in the way of universalisation of primary education. A massive programme for removing adult illiteracy should be taken up.

17. *Strengthening and Popularisation of Non-Formal Education Revised as Education Guarantee Scheme and Alternative and Innovative Education.* The scheme of Non-Formal Education (NFE) was introduced in 1979-80 to those children in the age group of 6-14 years who had remained outside the formal system of schooling. The prime focus of this programme was 10 educationally backward States. But it also covered urban slums, hilly, tribal and desert areas. The programme was implemented both by the States/UTs as well as NGOs in the ratio of 60:40 for running co-educational centres, 90:10 for girls' centres and 100 per cent assistance to voluntary agencies. A total number of 2,33,946 centres were run through State/UT governments and another 58,618 through 816 voluntary agencies.

In order to make the scheme a viable alternative to formal education, it has been revised as Education Guarantee Scheme and Alternative and Innovative Education (EGS and AIE). The revised scheme will cover all the unserved habitations throughout the country where there are no learning facilities. It has not achieved the desired results. It needs to be made more attractive.

NEW INITIATIVES IN UNIVERSALISATION OF ELEMENTARY EDUCATION

Since the formulation of the National Policy on education —NPE, (1986) and the Programme of Action—POA (1986), several new schemes for the qualitative as well as quantitative improvement of primary education and reaching the goal of UEE, have been initiated by the Government of India, Ministry of Human Resource Development (MHRD), Department of Education. Some of the old schemes have also been revised and strengthened. In this regard, a brief review of the following scheme is provided in this chapter.

1. District Primary Education Programme (DPEP)
2. Elementary Education as a Fundamental Right.
3. Lok Jumbish (LJ).
4. Minimum Levels of Learning (MLLs).
5. National Elementary Education Mission(NEEM).
6. National Programme of Media Publicity and Advocacy of UEE.
7. Non-Formal Education (NFE).
8. National Programme of Nutritional Support to Primary Education (NP-NSPE) or Mid-Day Meals.
9. Operation Blackboard (OBB).
10. *Shiksha Karmi* Project (SKP).
11. Teacher Education: Restructuring and Reorganisation.
12. *Sarva Shiksha Abhiyan* (Education for All)

District Primary Education Programme (DPEP)

DPEP launched in 1993 is a national initiative to achieve Universalisation of Elementary Education (UEE) through district level intervention. The overall goal of the programme is the reconstruction of primary education system to operationalise the strategy of UEE as envisaged in NPC 1986 (as updated in 1992) and its Programme of Action—POA (1992) through decentralised planning and management, disaggregated target setting, community mobilisation and population specific planning. The fundamental principle of DPEP is to evolve strategy at state and district level. It goes beyond the conventional packages such as opening of new schools and appointing new teachers, and addresses the issues of content, process, quality and equity in education.

Objectives

The objectives of DPEP are:

(i) to reduce difference in enrolment, drop-out and learning achievement among gender and social groups to less than 5 per cent.

(ii) to reduce overall primary drop-out rates for all students to less than 10 per cent.

(iii) to raise average achieved level.

Coverage. By 2001-2003, 271 districts spread over 19 states had been covered.

Funding of DPEP. DPEP is a Centrally Sponsored Scheme and is funded by World Bank and several international organisations.

National Programme of Nutritional Support to Primary Education (NP-NSPE) or Mid-Day Meals

Objective

A nation-wide programme of NP-NSPE launched on August 15, 1995 is intended to give a boost to universalisation of primary education by increasing enrolment, retention and attendance and simultaneously to make an impact on nutritional levels of students in primary classes.

The ultimate aim under the programme is the provision of wholesome cooked/processed food having a calorific value equivalent to 100 gms. of wheat/rice per student per school day.

Implementing Agency. The implementing agencies of the programme, namely, local bodies/authorities, as, Panchayats and Nagarpalikas.

Central Support. The Central support under this programme is on the following lines:

(i) Provision of foodgrains free of cost to the implementing agencies.

(ii) Reimbursement of transportation cost to district authorities for moving of foodgrains from Food Corporation of India godowns to schools/villages at the rate of Rs. 25/0 per quintal as applicable under RPDS.

(iii) Besides, labour charges for conversion of foodgrains into cooked food as well as expenditure on construction of kitchen sheds, will be eligible for coverage under the Poverty Alleviation Schemes being administered by the Ministry of Rural Development.

Coverage. The coverage of children during 1995-96, 1996-97, 1997-98 and 1998-99 was 3.34 crore, 5.57 crore, 9.10 crore and 9.75 crore respectively.

Shiksha Karmi Project (SKP)

Shiksha Karmi Project started in Rajasthan in 1987 remained in operation up to June 1998. It was a scheme jointly sponsored by Swedish International Development Agency (SIDA), Government of India and the State of Rajasthan.

Aims of the Project.

1. Universalisation of education.
2. Checking drop-out.
3. Qualitative improvement of primary education.

Target Area. Socio-economically backward villages in Rajasthan.

Target Group. Specially girls.

Teachers. Replacement of regular teachers by local teachers who were less qualified but specially trained. A '*Shiksha Karmi*' (SK) was a local person with minimum educational qualifications of class VIII for men and class V for women. To overcome the basic lack of qualification, special training was given to these teachers.

Role of the Community. Active involvement of the Non-Government Organisations (NGOs) and the Village Education Committees (VECs).

Prehar Pathshalas (PPs): (School of Convenient Timings) providing educational programmes for out of school children who cannot attend regular day schools. About 22,000 girls who constituted 71% of learners in PPs have been benefited.

Coverage. About 2 lakh children (1.18 lakh boys and 0.82 lakh girls) in 32 districts, 146 blocks attending 2,697 day schools and 4,335 Prehar *Pathshalas*. Number of *Shiksha Karmis*: 6,285.

Evaluation. A unique successful experiment. Positive results with minimum costs.

Teacher Education Restructuring and Reorganisation

Objectives. As envisaged in the NPE and Programme of Action (POA), 1996, a Central Scheme of Restructuring and Reorganisation of Teachers Education was taken up in 1987 for the following purposes:

(i) Creating a viable institutional infrastructure of teacher education.

(ii) Building up an academic and technical base for orientation, training and continuous upgrading of knowledge, competence and pedagogical skills of elementary school teachers in the country.

Components of the Scheme. (i) Setting up of District Institute of Education and Training (DIETs) in each district to provide academic and resource support to elementary education teachers, and non-formal and adult education instructors.

(ii) Establishment of Colleges of Teacher Education (CTEs) and Institutions of Advanced Study in Education (IASEs) to organise pre-service and in-service training for secondary teachers.

About 350 DIETs have been set up. It has been envisaged to cover all districts in the country *i.e.*, DIET in each district during the Tenth Plan.

DIETs have been playing an important role in the new educational initiatives like DPEP.

Operation Blackboard (OBB)

Objective. The scheme of Operation Blackboard started in 1987, is a Centrally Sponsored Scheme for bringing about improvement in primary education by providing additional facilities to the schools already established.

Use of the word 'Operation' indicates that there is an urgency in this programme. Its goals are clear and well-defined and the government is determined to achieve these goals with the cooperation of the people within a pre-determined time frame.

Components of the Scheme. There are three components of Operation Blackboard:

1. Provision of at least two reasonably large rooms that are usable in all weathers, with a deep veranda along with separate toilet facilities for boys and girls.

2. Provision of at least two teachers, as far as possible, one of them a woman, in every primary school.
3. Provision of essential teaching and learning materials.

Responsibility. For the operation of the Scheme, responsibility is shared by the Central Government, State Government and the local community.

Role of the community in OBB scheme is as under:

(a) Necessary land for the construction of school building including land for games and sports has to be provided by the local community.
(b) The local community, preferably Village Education Committees, have to give a formal undertaking that they will accept responsibility for repair and maintenance of the building.
(c) The local community has also to accept responsibility for an appropriate fencing around the school compound.

Hundred per cent Central assistance is provided for appointment of an additional teacher in the single teacher schools.

Problems. Financial sanctions for the programme reach towards the fag end of the year resulting in purchase of material which sometimes is sub-standard. Sometimes locally made material is not included in the list of approved articles.

Suggestions. 1. Demands for the required material must come from the grass roots level.

2. Necessary timely sanctions for the equipment needed for storage of material should also be made.

3. It must be ensured that the teachers selected join the institutions immediately after their selection. At the same time, sanctioned posts of teachers may not exist on paper only.

Lok Jumbish (People's Mobilisation). An innovative project called "Lok Jumbish"—People's movement for Education of All—with assistance from Swedish International Development Authority (SIDA) has been undertaken in Rajasthan. The basic objective of the project is to achieve education for all by the year 2000 through people's mobilisation and their participation. Government of India approved the first phase of the project for a period of two years, 1992-94 to cover 25 blocks spread over several districts with an estimated cost of Rs.18 crores to be shared by SIDA, Government of India and Government of Rajasthan in the ratio 3:2:1. The Phase-I concluded on 30th June, 1994. The Second Phase of the project was taken up for implementation during 1994-98. The project covered 75 blocks.

The LJ, has undertaken environment building activities in 5,683 villages. 383 new schools have been opened while 227 primary schools have been upgraded.

An innovative and successful NFE programme launched by LJ has spread to more than 3,000 centres. The programme has close linkage with the community. The NFE centres are called "Sahaj Shiksha Centres".

Universal Elementary Education as a Fundamental Right. The Central Cabinet in 1997 approved the proposal to make education as a fundamental right. It involves amending the Constitution of India. There was no such provision in the Constitution. With this amendment it would be possible to achieve the target of providing UEE. The Ninety Third Amendment of the Constitution passed by the Parliament received President's assent in December 2002. With this the Government will be required to take vigorous steps including compulsory enforcement of Compulsory Education Acts. The parents would be required to ensure that their children of primary school age attend school. However it is not clear how vast funds required for this would be forthcoming.

Sarva Shiksha Abhiyan at the Elementary Stage

The *Sarva Shiksha Abhiyan* was launched towards the end of the Ninth Plan to achieve the goal of UEE through a time-bound integrated approach, in partnership with states. The medium-term goals for the scheme are given in the Box (page 253). The programme, which aims to provide elementary education to all children in the 6-14 age group by 2010, is an effort to improve the performance of the school system and provide community-owned quality elementary education in the mission mode. It also envisages bridging of gender and social disparities at the elementary level. The *Sarva Shiksha Abhiyan* has a special focus on the educational needs of girls, SCs and STs and other children in difficult circumstances.

Objectives of Sarva Shiksha Abhiyan

— All children to be in schools, Education Guarantee Scheme centres, alternative schools, back-to-school camps by 2003;
— All children to complete five years of primary schooling by 2007;
— All children to complete eight years of schooling by 2010;
— Focus on elementary education of satisfactory quality with emphasis on education for life;
— Bridging all gender and social disparities at the primary stage by 2007 and at the upper primary level by 2010; and
— Universal retention by 2010.

DROP-OUTS AT THE ELEMENTARY STAGE OF EDUCATION—A MAJOR ISSUE IN UEE

Whereas the rising enrolment in elementary schools is a source of satisfaction, there is concern about the percentage of students actually attending school and those dropping out of the education system altogether. Nearly 79 percent of the 6-14 age group were attending school that is, of the population of 200 million in this age group in the year 2000, the number of children attending school was about 158 million. The student retention rate at the primary school stage was about 58 per cent (1990-95). Drop-out rates at the primary and upper primary level have decreased over the years. From 64.9 per cent at the primary level in 1960-61, the drop out rate decreased to 40.25 per cent in 1999-2000 and from 78.3 in upper primary level in 1960-61, it decreased to 54.33 per cent in 1999-2000. Though drop-out rates at the elementary education stage have declined over the years, they are still relatively high especially in the case of girl students for whom the rates are 42 per cent and 58 per cent at the primary and upper primary stages respectively.

Strategies Planned by the Government Towards UEE and Checking Drop-Outs, Stagnation and Wastage

Following are the salient features of the strategies:

1. Laying emphasis on retention rather than on merely enrolment.
2. Strengthening the alternatives of schooling, particularly, the Non-Formal Education System for working children, girls and children from other disadvantaged or marginalized sections of the society.
3. Shifting focus from educationally backward states to educationally backward districts.
4. Preparing and implementing district specific and population-specific plans.
5. Providing more facilities to girls.
6. Introducing Minimum Levels of Learning for the enhancement of learner's achievement.
7. Improving teacher competence, training and motivation.
8. Decentralising planning and management through Panchayati Raj Institutions, Village Education Committees.
9. Coordinating all early childhood care and education and school health and nutrition programmes, etc.
10. Following non-detention policy at the elementary stage of education.
11. Abolishing corporal punishment.
12. Adopting child-centred approach.
13. Establishing Ashram Schools in the sparsely populated and tribal areas.
14. Providing free mid-day meals, uniforms, textbooks and other instructional material.

(*See* Various New Initiatives like DPEP, etc.)

STRATEGIES FOR UNIVERSALISATION OF ELEMENTARY EDUCATION : TENTH FIVE YEAR PLAN (2002-2007)

The strategies and interventions during the Tenth Plan will mainly be guided by three major considerations: (a) magnitude of the task; (b) present challenges; and (c) the existing administrative and policy framework and the one that will be in place during the Plan period.

Goals and Targets : Magnitude of the Task. The year-wise estimated additional enrolment during the Plan period are given in Table 6.5.

Present Challenges. Achieving the goal of UEE poses three main challenges: (i) access to basic education for the unreached segments and social groups; (ii) qualitative improvement in content and processes so as to raise

Table 6.5: Year-wise Estimated Additional Enrolment

(in million)

Year	*Additional Enrolment*					
	Primary (Grade-I-V)			*Upper Primary (Grades VI-VIII)*		
	Boys	*Girls*	*Total*	*Boys*	*Girls*	*Total*
2002-03	0.67	2.01	2.68	1.14	1.44	2.58
2003-04	0.67	2.10	2.77	1.19	1.54	2.73
2004-05	0.67	2.18	2.85	1.25	1.67	2.92
2005-06	0.69	2.27	2.96	1.31	1.81	3.12
2006-07	0.69	2.37	3.06	1.37	1.35	3.32
Total	3.39	10.93	14.32	6.26	8.41	14.67

learning achievements; and (iii) tackling high drop-out and low retention rates in primary and upper primary schools.

Universal Access

— All children in the 6-14 age group should have access to primary schools, upper primary schools or their alternatives within a walking distance of one km. and three km. respectively.
— All children in the 3-6 age group must have universal access to early childhood care and education centres.
— Need-based expansion of upper primary education facilities, particularly for the disadvantaged sections. There should be one upper primary school for every two primary schools.
— All schools should have buildings, toilets, drinking water, electricity, playgrounds, blackboards and other basic facilities. There must be provision of one classroom for every teacher at the elementary stage.

Universal Enrolment

— Enrolment of all children in schools or alternative arrangements by 2003.
— All children to complete five years of primary schooling by 2007.

Universal Retention

— Universal retention in the primary stage by 2007.
— Drop-out rate to be reduced to less than 10 per cent for grades VI-VIII by 2007.

Universal Achievement

— Improve the quality of education in all respects (content and process) to ensure reasonable learning outcomes at the elementary level, especially in literacy, numerics and in life skills.

Strategies for Quality Improvement

A qualitative improvement in the content and processes of basic education, in order to make them more responsive to the learning needs of individuals and the development needs of different socio-economic sectors, continues to be a major challenge. The challenge for providing quality education at the elementary level involves: (i) improvements in the preparation, motivation and deployment of teachers, (ii) the quality of textbooks and of infrastructural facilities, (iii) making education relevant to society's needs, (iv) strengthening the management and institutional capacity of educational institutions especially at the state, district and local levels.

Summing Up

Universalisation of Elementary Education

Universalisation of Elementary Education (UEE) has been accepted as a national goal. The Tenth Five Year Plan envisages UEE to mean universal access, universal retention and universal achievement. As a result of the efforts made by the Central and State Governments, 94 per cent of country's rural population have primary schools within one km. At the upper primary stage, 84 per cent of the rural population have schools within a distance of three km.

The Central and State governments have over a period of time evolved strategies to check drop-out rates and improve levels of achievement in the schools, the key elements of which include: (i) creating parental awareness and community mobilisation; (ii) involvement of communities and Panchayati Raj Institutions (PRIs) PRIs (73rd and 74th Constitutional Amendments); (iii) economic incentives; (iv) improvement in the infrastructure facilities in schools; (v) District Primary Education Programme initiative; (vi) National Programme of Nutritional Support to Primary Education (Mid-Day Meals Scheme); (vii) Education Guarantee Scheme and Alternative and Innovative Education; (viii) Teacher Education Schemes; (ix) *Sarva Shiksha Abhiyan* initiative; and (x) elementary Education as Fundamental Right.

The Government formulated a revised Constitution Amendment Bill (93rd amendment) and it was presented in Parliament. The Lok Sabha passed the bill on 28 November, 2001. It was considered by the Rajya Sabha on 14 May, 2002. It got President's Assent on December 12, 2002.

The scheme of *Sarva Shiksha Abhiyan* (SSA) was approved in November, 2000. The goals of SSA are: (a) that all 6-14 age children (i) are in school/ Education Guarantee Scheme (EGS)/bridge course by 2003; (ii) complete five year primary education by 2007; (iii) complete eight years of schooling by 2010; (b) Focus on elementary education of satisfactory quality with emphasis on education for life; (c) bridge all gender and social category gaps at primary stage by 2007 and at elementary education level by 2010; and (d) Universal retention by 2010.

The SSA will cover the entire country with a special focus on educational needs of girls, Scheduled Castes and Scheduled Tribes and other children in difficult circumstances.

RIGHT TO EDUCATION: ARTICLE 21A: AMENDMENT IN ARTICLE 45

Provision for Free and Compulsory Education for Children

The State shall endeavour to provide, within a period of the years from the commencement of this constitution, for free and compulsory education for all children until they complete the age of fourteen years. This has been deled and following amendments have been made in the constitution by Eight-Sixth Amendment Act, 2002.

1. Article 45

Provision for Early Childhood Care and Education to Children below the Age of Six Years—The State shall endeavour for provide early childhood care and education for all children until they complete the age of six years.

2. Article 21A

Right to Education—The State shall provide free and compulsory education to all children of the age of six to fourteen years in such manner as the state may, by law determine.

3. Clause 'K' has been Added in 51 A Fundamental Duties

It shall be the duty of every citizen of India (K) "who is parent or guardian to provide opportunities for education to his child or, as the case may be, ward between the age of six amd fourteen years."

7

Women's Education

HIGH STATUS AND WIDESPREAD EDUCATION OF WOMEN IN ANCIENT INDIA

The 'Vedas' accord a very honourable and respectable status to women. Accordingly they were not only eligible for education but also received higher education and status. They could occupy administrative and other important jobs mostly performed by men. It was only during the middle ages that their education and status began to decline. Here we are giving a few quotes from the Vedas and other ancient literature which bring out the factual position of the status and education of women in earlier times in this country.

Just as boys acquire sound knowledge and education by the practice of 'Brahmacharya' and then marry girls of their own kind and choice, who are young, well educated, loving and of like temperament, so should a girl practice 'Brahmacharya', study the Vedas and other sciences and thereby perfect her knowledge, refine her character, give her hand to a man of her own choice, who is young, learned and loving. (A.V. XI. 16.3.18).

In the battlefield, in the absence of the king, the queen should take command of the forces and should inspire them. (R.V.X. 159.2).

O Learned Lady! All life is dependent upon you because you impart education to all. (R.V.2, 49.17).

From the point of view of reverence due, a teacher is ten-fold superior to mere lecturer, a father—a hundred fold to teacher, and a mother—a thousand fold to father. '*Vashisht Dharmsutra*' (13.480).

Where women are respected, there the Gods delight, and where they are not, there works and efforts come to naught, there is no hope of rise for that family or country where they live in sadness. ('*Manusmriti*').

What can the fire not burn.
What cannot merge into the ocean
What can the weaker section not achieve
And what can escape death ('*Ramcharitmanas*', '*Ayodhyakand*')

IMPORTANCE OF WOMEN'S EDUCATION

Women plays a prominent role in the cultural, economic, political, religious and social life of a country. The ancient people of India fully realised this fact and accorded a reasonable status to women and encouraged their education. According to Vedas, women should have opportunity to attain knowledge of the Vedas from all four courses (Rig Veda 14.9.64). More than 400 verses in the Vedas are ascribed to 24 women seers. In the Vedas, women have been called 'Updeshtri' of knowledge and this indicates, women working as teachers (Rig Veda 1.3.11).

Swami Vivekananda has emphasised, "If you do not raise the women who are living embodiment of the divine mother, don't think that you have any other way to rise."

Gandhiji stated the importance of women education in these words, "I am strongly of the opinion that women should have the same facilities as men and even special facilities where necessary."

Jawaharlal Nehru very rightly observed, "Education of a boy is the education of one person, but education of a girl is the education of entire family."

In view of the importance of women education in national development, the University Education Commission 1948-49 remarked, "There can't be an educated people without education of women. If general education had to be limited to men or to women, then opportunity should be given to women, from them it would more surely be passed to the next generation."

Similarly, the Kothari Commission 1964-66, stated, "For full development of human resources, the improvement of human beings and for moulding the character of children during the most impressionable years of infancy, the education of women is of great importance than that of men."

PROGRESS OF WOMEN EDUCATION

Tables 7.1 to 7.7 reflect the progress of girls and women education at different levels since 1950-51.

Table 7.1: Progress of Women Education : Literacy Rates (1951 to 2001)

Census Year	*Persons (Total)*	*Males*	*Females*	*Male-Female Gap in Literacy Rates*
1951	18.33	27.16	8.86	18.30
1961	28.30	40.40	15.75	25.05
1971	34.45	45.96	21.98	23.98
1981	43.37	56.38	29.76	26.62
1991	52.21	64.13	39.29	24.84
2001	65.38	75.85	54.16	21.69

(*Source*: Census 2001).

Observations. In spite of increase in literates, there were nearly 19 crore illiterate females (7 years and above).

Table 7.2: Number of Literates and Illiterates Among Populated Aged 7 Years and Above and Their Change in India (1991 and 2001)

Literates/Illiterates	*Persons/Total*	*Males*	*Females*
Literates			
1991	358,402.626	228,983,134	129,419,492
2001	562,010,745	336,969,695	225,041,048
Increase in 2001 over 1991	203,608,117	107,986,561	95,621,556
Illiterates			
1991	328,167,288	128,099,211	200,068.077
2001	296,208,952	106,654,066	189,554,886
Decrease in 2001 over 1991	31,958,336	21,445,145	10,513,191

Observations. In spite of increase in literates there were nearly 19 crore illiterate females (7 Years and above)

Table 7.3: Percentage of Girls Enrolment to Total Enrolment by Stages since 1950-51

Year	*Primary I-V*	*Middle VI-VIII*	*Sec./Hr.Sec./ 10+2/Inter*	*Hr. Education (Degree & above level)*
1950-51	28.1	16.1	13.3	10.0
1960-61	32.6	23.9	20.5	16.0
1970-71	37.4	29.3	25.0	20.0
1980-81	38.6	32.9	29.6	26.7
1990-91	41.5	36.7	32.9	—
2000-2001	44.0	40.5	39.0	38.6

Table 7.4: Gross Enrolment Ratio of Girls at the Primary Stage Since 1950-51

Year	*Classes I to V*		*Classes VI to VIII*	
	Girls	*Total*	*Girls*	*Total*
1950-51	24.8	42.6	4.6	12.7
1960-61	41.4	62.4	11.3	22.5
1970-71	60.5	78.6	20.8	33.4
1980-81	64.1	80.5	28.6	41.9
1990-91	85.5	100.1	47.0	62.1
2000-2001	85.9	95.7	49.07	58.6
2003-2004	95.6	98.2	57.6	62.0

Table 7.5: Sex-wise Enrolment by Stages/Classes Since 1951 (in Million)

Year	*Primary*			*Middle/Upper Primary*			*High/Hr. Secondary*		
	Boys	*Girls*	*Total*	*Boys*	*Girls*	*Total*	*Boys*	*Girls*	*Total*
1950-51	13.8	5.4	19.2	2.6	0.5	3.1	1.3	0.2	1.5
1960-61	23.6	11.4	35.0	5.1	1.6	6.7	2.7	0.7	3.4
1970-71	35.7	21.3	57.0	9.4	3.9	13.3	5.7	1.9	7.6
1980-81	45.3	28.5	73.8	13.9	6.8	20.7	7.6	3.4	11.0
1990-91	57.0	40.4	97.4	21.5	12.5	34.0	12.8	6.3	19.1
2000-2001	64.0	49.8	113.8	25.3	17.5	42.8	16.9	10.7	27.6
2003-2004	68.4	59.9	128.3	27.3	21.4	48.7	20.6	14.3	34.9

Table 7.6: Drop-out Rates Sex-wise at Primary and Middle Stages (1960-61 to 2003-2004)

	1960-61	*1970-71*	*1980-81*	*1990-91*	*1992-93*	*1997-98*	*2003-04*
Class I-V							
Boys	61.7	64.5	56.2	40.1	43.83	38.23	33.7
Girls	70.9	70.9	62.5	46.0	46.67	41.34	28.6
Total	64.9	67.0	58.7	42.6	45.01	39.58	31.5
Class I-VIII							
Boys	75.0	74.6	68.0	59.1	58.23	50.72	51.8
Girls	85.0	83.4	79.4	65.1	65.21	58.61	53.9
Total	78.3	77.9	72.7	60.9	61.10	54.14	52.3

The total enrolment at primary stage (classes I to V) during the period 1950-51 to 1998-99 increased by 6 times while for the girls the increase is nine times. At the upper primary stage of education, the increase during this period is more than 14 times while that of girls the increase is more than 34 times, while is quite appreciable. At the secondary and senior secondary stage the total increase is more than 18 times and that of girls the increase is about 53 times.

The participation of girls at all stages of education has been increasing steadily over the time as may be seen from the above tables. However, the percentages are still much below fifty per cent at all stages of education.

TEACHERS

The percentage of female teachers to total in 2003-2004 was about 35% in primary schools, 36% in Upper Primary Schools and 35% in High and Sr. Secondary Schools.

Table 7.7: No. of Women Universities, Women Vice-Chancellors (2004)

Year	*No. of Women Universities*	*No. of Women Vice-Chancellors*	*% of Women as Professors/Heads of Deptt.*
2000	5	17	2%

1. S.N.D.T. Women's University
2. Mother Teresa Women's University
3. Shri Padmavati Mahila Vishwavidyalaya
4. Avinashilingam Institute for Home Science and Higher Education for Women
5. Banasthali Vidyapeeth

Teacher-pupil ratio in 2003-2004 at the primary stage was 1:43 and at the upper primary it was 1:38.

Table 7.8: No. of Women Colleges Since 1986-87 to 2003-2004

Year	*No. of Women's Colleges*	*Year*	*No. of Women's Colleges*
1986-87	780	1999-2000	1503
1996-97	1195	2000-2001	1578
1997-98	1260	2001-2002	1600
1998-99	1359	2003-2004	1798

Table 7.9: Percentage of Women Students in Higher Education in Select States 1998-99 and 2003-2004

Sl. No.	*States*	*% of Women Students in Higher Education*	
		1998-99	2003-2004
1.	Kerala	53.6	60.6
2.	Goa	51.4	58.8
3.	Punjab	51.5	51.4
4.	Jammu & Kashmir	40.6	46.6
5.	Tamil Nadu	40.1	45.5
6.	Manipur	43.4	44.8
7.	Gujarat	40.1	44.2
	Overall Percentage	38.4	40.2

Source: Annual Report 2003-2004, UGC.

Table 7.10: Women Enrolment by Faculty: 2003-2004

Sl. No.	*Faculty*	*Women Enrolment*	*Percentage of Total Women Enrolment*
1.	Arts	20,41,706	51.01
2.	Science	8,09,368	20.22
3.	Commerce/Management	6,57,682	16.43
4.	Education	76,154	1.90
5.	Engineering/Technology	1,65,316	4.13
6.	Medicine	1,45,302	3.63
7.	Agriculture	9,981	0.25
8.	Veterinary Science	3,138	0.08
9.	Law	62,523	1.56
10.	Others	31,637	0.79
	Total	40,02,807	100.00

Source: Selected Educational Statistics – 2000-2001.

Table 7.11: Women Students Per Hundred Men Students

Year	*Total Women Enrolment*	*Enrolment Per Hundred Men*
1950-51	40,000	14
2003-2004	40,02,807	67

SLOW BUT ENCOURAGING PROGRESS OF GIRLS AND WOMEN EDUCATION

The above table clearly illustrates that girls and women have now increasingly pursuing higher and professional courses. The emerging courses that girls are now entering into are M.Com., BSc., BSc. (Hons.), BE, BSc, BArch., MBBS etc. This is an encouraging trend. It shows that parents, especially from urban areas and from relatively better socio-economic backgrounds, are sending their daughters to higher education/professional courses. Participation of women in non-traditional courses has gradually eroded the myth of gender bias and sex stereotyping in courses and professions. This phenomena also depicts why there is a gradual rise in the status of women. However, this change is by and large confined to urban areas and among the educated classes.

From the figures given above, it is quite clear that there has been phenomenal progress on women's education since independence but still there is a wide gap between female education and male education.

Usually following causes of slow progress are mentioned:

(i) Lack of proper social attitudes in the rural and backward areas for the education of girls.
(ii) Lack of educational facilities in rural areas.
(iii) Economic backwardness of the rural community.
(iv) Conservative nature and co-educational aspects.
(v) Lack of suitable curriculum.
(vi) Lack of proper incentives to parents and children.
(vii) Lack of women teachers.
(viii) Lack of proper supervision and guidance due to inadequate women personnel in the Inspectorate.
(ix) Uneducated adult women and lack of social education.
(x) Social ills.
(xi) Inadequate systematic publicity.
(xii) Indifference of Panchayats.

MEASURES FOR THE PROMOTION OF WOMEN'S EDUCATION

Following measures are suggested:

I. *Creating Proper Social attitude in the Rural and Backward Areas for the Education of Girls*: Following measures may be taken:

(1) To study the problems relating to women's education and to get detailed scientific data, a thorough research should be taken up by the Institutes of Education and allied institutions in different States and coordinated at the national level.
(2) Separate schools for girls at the middle and high school stages should be established where needed.
(3) School Mothers in co-education primary schools should be appointed.
(4) Creches and nursery classes wherever possible should be opened.
(5) Public opinion in favour of girls' education should be created.

II. *Providing Adequate Educational Facilities in Backward and Rural Areas*: The target should be to have at least one primary school within a radius of one kilometre from every home which is within the walking distance of a child. Following steps are needed:

(1) Hostel for girls at the middle and high school stages.
(2) Maintenance stipends to girls residing in hostels for meeting their board and lodging expenses, at least in part.

(3) Subsidised transport facilities, wherever necessary and possible.
(4) All priority to be given to the construction of suitable buildings for girl's schools.
(5) Free education for girls.

III. *Removing Economic Backwardness of the Rural and Backward Areas*: The girls are very useful at home for carrying out domestic duties and so mothers are reluctant to send them to school. A large number of children in the rural areas are under-nourished. They hardly have a square meal a day. Unless the parents are given some kind of economic relief, it will be impossible to achieve the targets.

Following measures should prove very useful:

(1) Free uniforms and free books to the needy and deserving children should be provided.
(2) Attendance scholarships which serve as a compensation to the parents should be given. This will also ensure reduction of wastage and stagnation.
(3) Mid-day meals should be made available free of charge.

IV. *Conservative Nature of Parents and Co-education*: Parents in rural areas and backward communities tend not to send the girls to co-educational schools. Their apprehensions have to be removed with a thought-out plan of educating them in this regard (see next part).

V. *Provision of Suitable Curriculum*: Curriculum, by and large, has not met the requirements of women.

Following suggestions made by Smt. Hansa Mehta Committee (1962) deserve careful consideration:

(1) No differentiation should be made in the curricula for boys and girls at the primary and middle stages of education.
(2) Steps should be taken to improve the instruction of home economics.
(3) Steps should be taken to improve the teaching of music and fine arts and liberal financial assistance should also be made available to girls' schools for the introduction of these courses.
(4) Universities should review periodically the provision they have made for the courses designed to meet the special needs of girls and take necessary action to remove the deficiencies discovered.

VI. *Proper Incentives to Parents and Girls*. The following measures have been suggested:

(1) The number of attendance scholarships should be doubled in the Ninth Plan.
(2) The allowance of the School Mothers should be enhanced so that qualified women may be attracted to take up the work.
(3) The number of maintenance stipends should be doubled in the Ninth Plan and the rate of such stipends should be adequately increased in view of the rising prices all over the country.
(4) The number of sanitary blocks in co-educational primary schools be adequately increased during the Ninth Plan.
(5) Larger allocation of funds should be made in the budget for construction

of hostels for girls during the Ninth Plan.

VII. *Provision for Providing Adequate Number of Women Teachers*: Following steps are suggested:

(1) A large number of training institutions have to be provided for women, especially in the backward states. These institutions should generally be located in rural areas and they should generally recruit their trainees from that area.

(2) Condensed course centres should be started in these backward areas to open up avenues to adult unqualified women for employment as teachers. Wherever possible such centres should be attached to the training institutions.

(3) A large number of quarters for women teachers should be provided, particularly in rural areas. Our target should be to provide at least 50 per cent of the women teachers with quarters in primary schools.

(4) All women teachers employed in rural areas should be given adequate rural allowance.

(5) Special stipends should be given to girls in high and higher secondary schools with aptitude for teaching.

(6) Whenever possible husbands and wives should be posted in the same place even if they work in different departments of the Government.

(7) Free training should be imparted with stipends to all candidates of training institutions.

(8) In-service education training should be given to untrained women teachers who have put in at least two years of service. The period of training of education should be treated as on duty.

VIII. *Proper Supervision and Guidance*: For providing proper guidance and supervision, following steps should be taken:

(a) Increase in the number of women inspecting officers, particularly in the backward states, at different levels including State level and Directorate level.

(b) Provision of adequate transport for all district women inspecting officers.

(c) Adequate office staff and equipments.

(d) Residential facilities to all women officers at all levels.

(e) Adequate funds at the disposal of the State Council for closer contact with rural areas.

IX. *Facilities for Education of Adult Women*: Girls education and education of adult women suffers on account of lack of social education. This problem can be tackled in the following ways:

(1) By opening adult literacy classes in large number.

(2) By teaching simple skills like sewing, knitting, handicrafts etc., and knowledge of basic principles of health and food habits.

(3) New attitudes towards community living, family planning, superstitions, caste, etc.

This programme can be tackled effectively with the help of the Education Department in cooperation with other departments concerned like the

Community Development, Health and Social Welfare.

X. *Eradicating Social Ills*: The *Purdah* System (in some States such as in Orissa, Uttar Pradesh, Bihar and Rajasthan) and certain other harmful social customs in these States and in others stand in the way of the development of girls' education. In some places caste barriers also contribute to this. Social reformers and other voluntary organisations may be motivated to take up this work.

XI. *Wide Systematic Publicity*: For educating the parents to take interest in the education of girls, press and electronic media may be used extensively.

XII. *Awards to Panchayats*: Panchayats should be given some motivation to take up work in this area.

Concluding Remarks: The role of women outside the home has become an important feature of the social and economic life of the country and in the years to come this will become still more significant. From this point of view greater attention will have to be paid to the problems of training and development of women. The education of girls, therefore, should be emphasised not only on grounds of social justice, but also because it accelerates economic and social transformation.

COMMITTEES AND COMMISSIONS ON WOMEN EDUCATION

Following Committees and Commissions have discussed the various issues relating to women's education:

1. The University Education Commission (1948-49).
2. Smt. Durgabai Deshmukh Committee (1959).
3. Smt. Hansa Mehta Committee (1962).
4. M. Bhaktvatsalam Committee to look into the causes of Public Support particularly in Rural Areas for girls Education and to enlist Public Cooperation.
5. Education Commission (1964-66).
6. Resolution on the National Policy on Education (1968).
7. Report of the Committee on the status of Women in India (1974).
8. Challenge of Education 1985.
9. National Policy on Education 1986.
10. Programme of Action 1986.

NPE (1986 AND 1992) AND PROGRAMME OF ACTION (1992)

Education for Women's Equality

Education will be used as an agent of basic change in the status of woman. In order to neutralise the accumulated distortions of the past, there will be a well conceived edge in favour of women. The National Education system will play a positive, interventionist role in the empowerment of women. It will foster the development of new values through redesigned, curricula, textbooks, the training and orientation of teachers, decision-makers and administrators, and the active involvement of educational institutions. This will be an act of faith and social engineering. Women's studies will be promoted as a part of various courses and educational institutions encouraged to take up active programmes to further women's development.

The removal of women's illiteracy and obstacles inhibiting their access to, and retention in, elementary education will receive overriding priority, through provision of special support services, setting of time targets, and effective monitoring. Major emphasis will be laid on women's participation in vocational, technical and professional education at different levels. The policy of non-discrimination will be pursued vigorously to eliminate sex stereotyping in vocational and professional courses and to promote women's participation in non-traditional occupations, as well as in existing and emergent technologies.

8

Distance Learning

MEANING OF DISTANCE EDUCATION AND ITS NOMENCLATURE

Distance education as the name indicates is a form of education in which there is usually a long distance between the learner and the teacher. (The word 'long' is a relative term and it has no limits). It is in a sense a remote control system of education wherein the learner and the teacher may not be face to face. They are separate by physical distance. Some of the important definitions of distant education are given below:

(1) In the words of Dohmen (1967) "Distance education is a systematically organised form of self-study in which student counselling, the presentation of learning material and the securing and supervising of students success is carried out by a team of teachers, each of whom has responsibilities. It is made possible at a distance by means of media which can cover long distances. The opposite of 'distance education' is 'direct education', or 'face-to-face education' : a type of education that takes place with direct contact between lecturers and students."

(2) Peter (1973) defines distance education as "Distance teaching/education (Fernunterricht) is a method of imparting knowledge, skills and attitudes which is rationalised by the application of division of labour and organisational principles as well as by the extensive use of technical media, especially for the purpose of reproducing high quality teaching material which makes it possible to instruct great numbers of students at the same time wherever they live. It is an industrialised form of teaching and learning. It is a method of indirect instruction implying geographical and emotional separation of the teacher and the taught. Whereas in mainstream of education, the relationship between teacher and students in the classroom is based upon social norms, in distance education it is based upon technological norms."

(3) In the words of Holmberg (1979) "The term Distance Education covers the various forms of study at all levels which are not under the continuous, immediate supervision of tutors present with their students in lecture rooms or on the same premises, but which, nevertheless, benefit from the planning, guidance and tuition of a tutorial organisation". It is 'guided didactic conversation' with 'two-way communication'."

(4) Moore's (1991) definition is "The transaction that we call distance

education occurs between individuals who are teachers and learners, in an environment that has the separation of one from another, and a consequent set of special teaching and learning behaviours. It is the physical separation that leads to a psychological and communication gap, a space of potential misunderstanding between inputs of instructor and those of the learner, and this is the transactional distance."

(5) Mackenzie N., Postgate R. and Scupham (1975) use the term '*Open Learning*'. According to them Open Learning Systems are designed to offer opportunities for part-time study, for learning at a distance and for innovations in the curriculum. They are intended to allow access to wider sections of adult population, to enable students to compensate for lost opportunities in the past or to acquire new skills and qualifications for the future. Open Learning systems aim to redress social and educational inequality and to offer opportunities not provided by conventional colleges or universities."

(6) Wedemeyer (1971) discusses the concept '*Independent Study*' which "consists of various forms of teaching-learning arrangements in which teachers and learners carry out their essential tasks and responsibilities apart from one another, communicating in a variety of ways for the purpose of freeing internal learners from inappropriate class pacing or patterns, of providing external learners with opportunities to continue learning in their own environment, and of developing in all learners the capacity to carry on self-directed learning."

A perusal of the above definitions indicates that the educators and researchers have defined the term distance education in different ways, each stressing certain aspects of the system.

Distance education is known by different names. On account of a variety of terms used for distant education, Prof. F.R. Jevons (1983) called it a "bewildering nomenclature". Important terms associated with this type of education are as under:

(1) Continuing Education; (2) Correspondence Education; (3) Correspondence Learning; (4) Correspondence Course; (5) Correspondence School; (6) Correspondence Teaching; (7) Distance Education; (8) Distance Learning; (9) Distance Teaching; (10) External Degree Programme; (11) External Studies; (12) Extra-mural System; (13) Home Study; (14) Home Tuition; (15) Independent Learning; (16) Independent Study; (17) Life Long Education; (18) Non-Formal Education; (19) Off-Campus Study; (20) Open Education; (21) Open Learning; (22) Open School; (23) Open; (24) Open University; (25) Out of School Education; (26) Postal Courses; (27) Teach Yourself Programme; (28) Tele University; (29) University of the Art; (30) University without Walls.

All the above mentioned terms are associated with non-traditional and non-conventional teaching-learning programme. These terms derive their names from the medium of communication. By and large, they are based on same economic, educational, philosophical and psychological basis.

CHIEF CHARACTERISTICS OF DISTANCE EDUCATION

1. There is physical distance between the teacher and the learner.
2. There is little face-to-face relationship.
3. There is no fixed classroom or lecture room.
4. There is less of oral instruction.
5. There is no immediate supervision by the tutor present with his students.
6. Learning is on an individual basis and not on group basis.
7. There is multi-media use i.e., use of postal services, radio, TV, etc.
8. Industrial form of production is used.
9. Learning is on part-time basis.
10. Learner is more motivated.
11. It also provides for a two-way communication when contact courses are organised.

CORRESPONDENCE EDUCATION, OPEN EDUCATION, FORMAL EDUCATION AND DISTANCE EDUCATION

Correspondence Education and Distance Education. The basic difference between the correspondence education and distance education is the use of mode of communication. In correspondence education, postal system is the mode whereas in distance education postal system and multimedia are used.

Distance Education and Open Education. In distance education there may be minimum educational qualifications prescribed for joining a course but in open education there may not be any such qualifications required for pursuing a course. Open education is not limited to geographical boundaries.

	Distance Education		*Formal Education*
1.	It is indirect education, as it is not centred on face-to-face communication.	1.	It is direct education, as it is centred on face-to-face communication.
2.	It is part-time education.	2.	It is usually full-time education.
3.	It concentrates on the needs of the learner.	3.	It puts the institution first.
4.	It is flexible in the sense that a course can usually be completed in number of years.	4.	A course is to be completed within a given period.
5.	It takes into account the convenience of the learner.	5.	It is teacher centred.
6.	It looks for unorthodox modes and means of educating all those who are willing to be educated.	6.	It depends upon conventional means of education.
7.	Its place of instruction is not fixed.	7.	Its place is fixed usually four walls of the school or college.
8.	There is separation of the learner from his peer group.	8.	Learners are in close contact.
9.	It lacks a certain kind of vitality which only the presence of a teacher can generate.	9.	It provides vitality with the presence of the teacher.

10.	It uses media like computer, radio and television.	10.	Print word is the most prominent element.
11.	It is flexible with regard to qualifications for entry.	11.	It is rigid.
12.	It may or may not be for a degree or diploma.	12.	It is for a degree or diploma.
13.	It is a system of mass education	13.	Education is imparted in a group.
14.	It is available even in the areas where there is no school or college.	14.	It is not possible without educational institution.
15.	It is available even to those with poor health or disadvantageous psychological conditions that inhibit them from undergoing institutionalised education.	15.	It is not available to such groups as they cannot attend educational institutions.

MAIN OBJECTIVES OF DISTANCE EDUCATION

1. To provide a suitable alternative path to wider opportunities in education and especially higher education.

2. To provide an efficient and less expensive system of education.

3. To provide opportunities to students who had to discontinue their formal education on account of various circumstance—pecuniary etc.

4. To cater to the educational needs to people residing in geographically remote areas.

5. To provide for educational opportunities to students who had to discontinue studies because of lack of aptitude and motivation but who may later on become motivated.

6. To provide opportunities for citizens who are willing to improve their standard of knowledge and learning through continuing education while in business.

7. To provide opportunities to students who cannot find a seat or do not wish to join a regular college or university department although they possess the necessary qualifications to pursue higher education.

8. To provide opportunities to persons engaged in different professions to get higher degrees or certificates which may enable them to get higher jobs or promotions or better emoluments.

9. To cater to the needs of citizens who look upon education as a life-long pursuit and may like to refresh their knowledge and skill or to acquire knowledge and skills in new areas.

10. To provide opportunities for promoting aesthetic, citizenship and cultural values.

11. To provide courses according to the specific needs of individuals.

12. To provide opportunities for in-service training to teachers.

13. To provide opportunities for pre-service training to teachers.

14. To enable the students to learn while they earn.

15. To enable the students to earn while they learn.

16. To provide opportunities for getting education, vocational and personal guidance.

17. To help socio-economically backward students to receive education.

18. To make the educational institution go to the students, rather than the students coming to the university.

19. To provide opportunities to the educated citizens to study further while remaining at the places of their work.

20. To train in-service personnel in different fields to make them more efficient in their work.

21. To provide instruction in technical and vocational courses.

22. To impart basic knowledge to the farmers regarding modern ways of farming.

23. To enhance the technical knowledge of the farmers to such a level that they would take full advantage of printed literature dealing with agricultural sciences.

24. To enable farmers to pass on the acquired knowledge to others.

25. To assist elderly people, people in armed forces, dependents of embassies abroad, and others in improving their qualifications.

26. To solve the problem of increasing pressure on formal education.

27. To minimise the gap in the academic standard of the regular and private students through planned and regular postal education.

28. To ease the problem of financial constraints on the part of the government to start new educational institutions.

MERITS AND LIMITATIONS OF DISTANCE EDUCATION

Merits and Salient Features of Distance Education

1. It fulfills the needs of various categories of persons who are unable to make use of the formal system of education.

2. It is a very flexible educational system which is not limited by time and place restrictions.

3. Under this system a learner can progress at his own speed.

4. Distance education makes higher education accessible to all sections of society.

5. The courses cater to all segments of society.

6. There is no need to spend on buildings and other equipment.

7. In-service personnel, housewives, disabled persons, under-privileged people, people residing in remote areas, school drop-outs, etc., can all avail of the courses offered.

8. The inherent flexibility of distance education system is conducive to a greater variety of subjects of study.

9. It leads to self-learning.

10. It can reach remote areas through postal service or radio or TV.

11. It is an economical method of teaching-learning as compared to the regular formal system.

12. Teaching-learning can be made more efficient and powerful through the media like radio and TV.

13. It can supplement the studies of regular students.

14. It can be used at various levels.

15. Learners can take advantage of the lectures of the most efficient teachers which is not always possible in all conventional educational institutions.

16. Contact courses provide opportunities for face-to-face learning also.

17. Limited full-time academic staff is needed. Part-time teachers can deliver the goods.

18. Students are not concentrated in the campuses and there is little chance of student unrest.

19. Number of students in an open university system may be unlimited.

20. The Indira Gandhi National Open University has its jurisdiction over whole of the country.

21. The likely higher quality of the self-instructional package produced by multidisciplinary team of experts for use in distance education seems likely to enhance the learning experience of distance students.

22. It suits all age groups.

23. It is very flexible. It even arranges courses as demanded by specific groups.

24. It provides equality of opportunity irrespective of income and status of individuals.

Limitations of Distance Education

1. The system of distance education has very limited scope for making people aware of cultural change and social development.

2. The courses become stereotyped in due course.

3. The scope for practical experience is very negligible.

4. Usually the provision for study-centres and book banks is very meagre.

5. The experts do not have the adequate means to ensure whether the students are entirely satisfied with the material given.

6. Normally suggestions are not invited from the students about the utility of the material.

7. The students are given extensive written material through post but the same is not suitably supplemented by discussion on radio or TV.

8. Periodic review of the courses is not frequent.

9. The students hardly get opportunities for different types of co-curricular activities during contact programmes except listening to lectures.

10. Opportunities of learning through social contact among students are very limited.

11. Generally speaking, same importance or weightage is not given to distance education degrees as is given to the degrees and diplomas obtained through formal education. By and large, it is considered an inferior type of education.

BRIEF HISTORY OF DISTANCE EDUCATION IN INDIA

University of Delhi was the first University to start correspondence course in higher education in 1962.

Andhra Pradesh was the first Open University to be opened in the country in 1982.

The National Policy on Education – 1986 (revised in 1992) says:

"The open learning system has been initiated in order to augment opportunities for higher education, as an instrument of democratising education and to make it a lifelong process. The flexibility and innovativeness of the open learning system are particularly suited to the diverse requirements of the citizens of our country, including those who had joined the vocational stream.

The Indira Gandhi National Open University, established in 1985 in fulfilment of these objectives, will be strengthened. It would also provide support to establishment of Open Universities in the State."

OPEN SYSTEM OF EDUCATION

Indira Gandhi National Open University (IGNOU)

The University came into being on December 1985 by an Act of Parliament.

Mission and Objectives of IGNOU. These included the following:

— Introduction and promotion of open university and distance education system in the educational pattern of the country.

— Widening access to higher education for large segments of the population, particularly the disadvantaged groups.

— Ensuring relevance to programmes of education by relating them to the needs of economic development, employment and empowerment of the people of India.

The Strategic Goals of the Open System of Education

The strategic goals the IGNOU sets for itself are:

(i) To expand higher education facilities and widen access to education that will empower increasing diversity of people.

(ii) To ensure relevance for educational programmes by diversifying the course provisions and developing high-quality, multi-media open learning curriculum, designed to meet the academic, technical and vocational needs of diverse student groups.

(iii) To reach out to large number of learner groups, especially those who have no opportunities to pursue good quality higher education programme, and enable them to acquire knowledge, skills and competence to become productive participants in development.

(iv) To foster and lead development in knowledge related technologies relevant to large scale distance education.

(v) To establish and operationalise a major open education network comprising IGNOU, the State Open Universities and other distance education institutions to extend the outreach of distance education programmes to all parts of the country.

(vi) To establish and develop large networks, especially in the spheres of communication (broadcasting teleconferencing) and of computers, etc., of physical and intellectual resources for technological support in the delivery of high-quality educational programmes.

(vii) To organise research and development activities through projects, fellowships and other programmes in distance education, its methodologies and practices.

(viii) To undertake an active role in the process of globalisation of education by increasing world-wide access to Indian open education programmes by promoting enrolment in Indian institutions and the use of their learning packages by institutions and students outside the country.

(ix) To establish and develop a significant national resource base for the growth and development of the open learning system in the country in such areas as electronic media production and diffusion, human resource development etc.

(x) To develop instruments and methods by which the quality of programmes, products and services provided by the open university system is assured and mobility of students among open universities and between the open and the traditional systems is promoted through credit transfer, provision of multiple entry and exit points, modularity of programmes, and so on.

(xi) To develop a cutting edge for Indian education in the global context and establish a healthy competitiveness for Indian degrees.

(Source : *Open and Distance Education—2002 : IGNOU*)

Special Features of IGNOU

University stands significantly apart from others because of:

— national jurisdiction;
— flexible admission rules;
— individualised study : flexibility, in terms of place, pace and duration of study;
— use of latest educational and communication technologies;
— student support services;
— cost-effective programmes;
— modular programmes;
— resource sharing, collaboration and networking between other Open Universities.

DISTANCE SYSTEM OF EDUCATION AT WORK

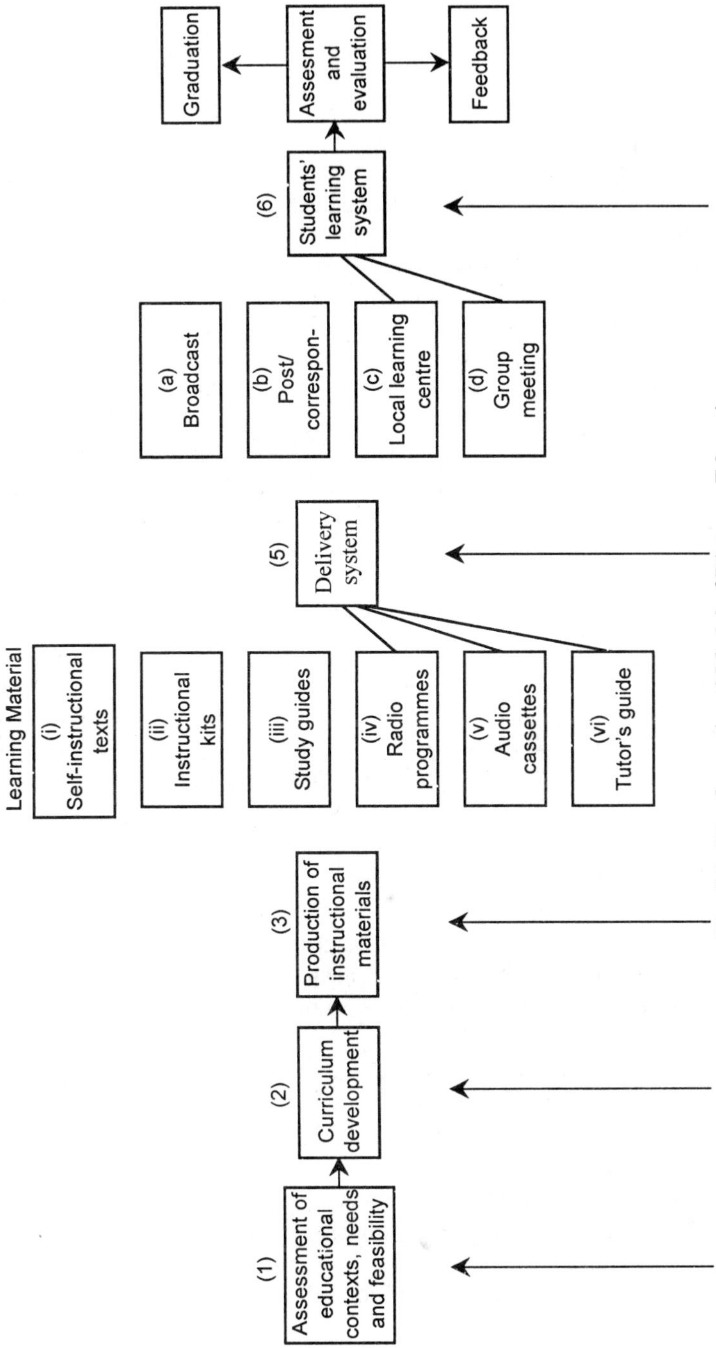

Fig. 8.1: The Operational Model of Distance Education

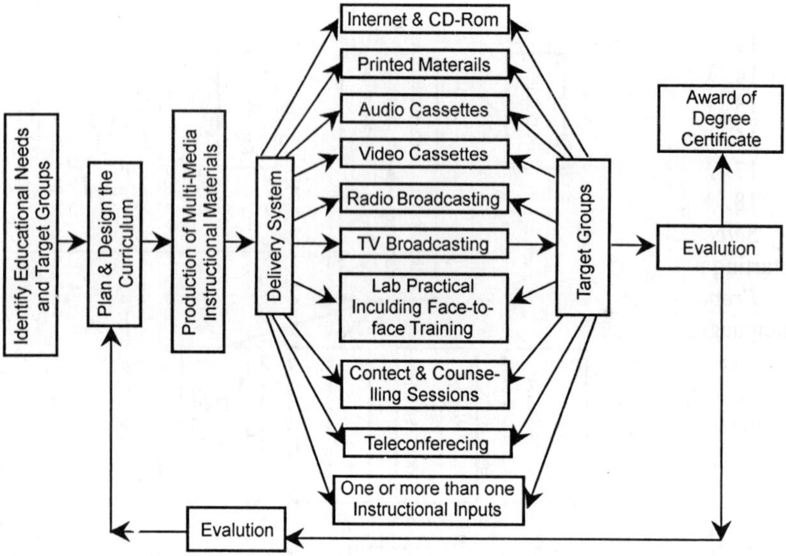

The degree and diplomas of this University are recognised and have the same status as those of any other Central or State University in the Country

(IGNOU, Public Information Unit)

Fig. 8.2: Instructional System in IGNOU

The Indira Gandhi National Open University (IGNOU) established in 1985, has 1.2 million students on its rolls and offers 72 programmes. The University has created a countrywide network of student support structures, with 46 regional centres and 765 study centres. It has also created a media network and teleconferencing system to electronically link all distance-teaching institutions in the country.

PROBLEMS OF DISTANCE EDUCATION AND MEASURES FOR STRENGTHENING IT

1. Selection of Need Based Courses.
2. Preparation of Material Reviews.
3. Selection of Course Writers Editors
4. Printing of Material
5. Provision of Infrastructural Facilities
6. Coordination with Postal Authorities
7. Guidelines for Correspondence Students
8. Timely Dispatch of Material
9. Evaluation of Response Sheets
10. Arranging Contact Programmes
11. Setting up Study Centres
12. Provision of Travel Facilities to Students

13. Provision of Board and Lodging
14. Use of Electronic Media
15. Cost Factor
16. Training of Staff
17. Study Habits of Students
18. Notion of Distance Education as Second Hand Education

Selection of Need-Based Courses: Courses should be need-based. Before starting a course, its potential users should be kept in view.

Preparation of Material: Material should be prepared in the regional language to be used in the course. Translation of material from English does not serve the purpose as sometimes it becomes superficial.

Selection: Sufficient care should be exercised in the selection of course writers, editors and reviewers. Experts and scholars are not necessarily most suited for this purpose. Persons with experience should be selected. Guidelines for each category of staff should be prepared.

Printing of Material: Printing of thousands of copies is a very challenging task. Related to this process are items like selection of printing press, type face, size of the booklet, procurement of white paper, art work, etc.

Infrastructural Facilities: The Open University will have to make use of the infrastructural and other facilities of the existing colleges. It will, therefore, be very necessary to maintain proper liaison with them. Programmes will have to be organised in such a way as to get the optimum results. The timings of the contact courses, will have to be adjusted suitably.

Timely Preparation and Dispatch of Material: It must be ensured that the material is prepared in time and dispatched properly.

Coordination with Postal Authorities: Dispatch of course materials requires proper planning and coordination with the postal authorities.

Guidelines for Correspondence Students: A correspondence student first be helped by supplying him with a brochure which should enable him to understand the method of studying the lessons before the first lesson is set to him.

Regular Evaluation of Assignments: A good deal or success of the distance education depends on the regular receipt of studiously prepared lessons and honesty done assignments by the students. But just as in the case of colleges, the house tests have lost their relevance or seriousness so in the same manner, the assignments in correspondence institutions are not taken in a very serious manner by the students. The universities must insist that at least 50% of the total number of assignments given to the students are responded by them. The quality of education imparted through correspondence courses would greatly depend on the steady and continuous two-way flow.

Arranging Contact Programmes: Contact programmes should be properly planned and executed.

Setting Up Study Centres: Study Centres should be set up at places convenient to students and having requisite infrastructure.

Provision of Travel Facilities to Students: Concerned transport authorities should be contacted to ensure the availability of reasonable facilities to students.

Provision of Board and Lodging Arrangement: All efforts should be made to make proper arrangements at reasonable cost.

Use of Electronic Media and Proper Communication: One of the most important features of the Distance University is the effective utilisation of the latest educational technology and audio-video media and their integration in an effective manner with the print material. This pre-supposes a well-equipped audio-video studio for the purpose of producing the audio-video tapes and also getting them ready for broadcasting the lessons.

Cost Factor: The expense of distance education is another constraint to its full development. One of its most important goals is to provide new opportunities to those who for socio-economic reasons could not remain in the formal system. As it is, in most cases, not designed for learners who can pay, distance education will remain largely dependent on government support and subsidies; it must, therefore, be viewed as a long-term investment in a country's future. In terms of its cost effectiveness and the large numbers of people it can reach, however, distance education does not appear to be an extravagance.

Training of Personnel: On a more practical level, the lack of trained personnel to develop distance education materials is a stumbling block. Most of the people working in distance education have come from the formal system and are attuned to the methods of traditional education. Their new roles demand a new set of skills and attitudes. Personnel must be reoriented and retrained for their changed task. Qualified producers, script-writers, technical support staff and presenters are all required. On the receiving end, the classroom teachers who will use distance learning methods must be trained to take full advantage of them.

Study Habit of Students: Since time for individual study is quite limited at the disposal of a correspondence student, only selected Indian books should be recommended.

Notion of Second Rate Education: As an alternative to face-to-face teaching, distance education has yet to gain full acceptance. Many students and educators still consider it to be second-rate and the second-choice education for those who for some reason did not make it in the formal system. A way round this constraint is found where equal status is awarded to the degrees given in the conventional and the distance teaching systems. As the two systems are fully integrated, learners can transfer from conventional to distance education and vice-versa. This situation points out the strong need to take a more confident approach to distance education.

Present Position of Distance Education System

Besides IGNOU, there are nine Open Universities and 64 Institutions of Correspondence Courses and Directorates of Distance Education in Conventional Universities in India.

Total enrolment through this non-formal system of learning is nearly 13 per cent of the total enrolment of nearly 7.8 million students enrolled in Universities and Colleges.

National Open School, now called National Institute of Open Schooling

At the school level, the Central Board of Secondary Education set up the National Open School in July 1979 which subsequently became an autonomous organisation under the Ministry of Human Resource Development, Department of Education, Government of India. It offers a number of programmes.

SUMMING UP

Demand for higher education places is constantly rising. The average rate of growth in enrolment in the traditional higher education system is currently about 5-6% per annum. The participation ratio in higher education is about 6.5% of the relevant age group. On the other hand there is an ever increasing number of mature learners, including working people, who are looking for opportunities for higher education. All indications are that the demand for initial education (age group 17) and continuing education (mature persons) at advanced levels will increase further.

The development in communication technology have opened up unprecedented opportunities for large scale dissemination of knowledge and information. The multimedia learning packages are fast replacing the traditional practice of classroom instruction. The adoption of these technologies in India will provide the education system with the means to reach out to large numbers and transform the teaching-learning process significantly. There is, therefore, an urgent need to strengthen distance education system in India.

SOME WELL KNOWN OPEN UNIVERSITIES OF THE WORLD

1. United Kingdom Open University, Walton Hall, Milton Kenyes, MK7 6 AA, United Kingdom (1969).
2. Universidad Nacional de Educacion a Distancia, Madrid, Spain (1972).
3. Allama Iqbal Open University, Islamabad, Pakistan (1974)
4. Everyman's University, Israel (1974).
5. Fern Universitat, Fleyer Strasse 204, D 5800 Hagen, West-Germany (1974).
6. Athabasca University, Box 10,000, Athabasca, Alberta, Canada, TOG 2 RO (1975).
7. Universidad Estatal a Distancia, Costa Rica (1977).
8. Universidad Nacional Abierta, Venezuela (1977).

9. Central Radio and Television University, Beijing, China (1978).
10. Sukhothai Thammathirat Open University, 9/9 M009 Tambo Bangpood, Nonthaburi-11120 Bangkok, Thailand (1978).
11. The Open University of Sri Lanka, P.O. Box 21, Nawala, Nugegoda, Sri Lanka (1981).
12. Korea Air and Correspondence University, 169, Dongsuog-dong, Chongro-ku, Seoul-110, Korea (1982).
13. University of Air, Wakaba, 2-Chome, Chiba, 260 Japan (1983).
14. Universitas Terbuka, Kotak POs 6666, Jakarta-10001, Indonesia (1984).
15. Indira Gandhi National Open University, Maidan Garhi, New Delhi-110 068 (1985).

9

National and Emotional Integration

MEANING OF NATIONAL AND EMOTIONAL INTEGRATION

Usually national and emotional integration is treated as a single term and not taken as two terms *i.e.*, national integration and emotional integration. Sometimes only the term national integration is used.

Emotional integration may imply several things, *i.e.*, individual emotional integration or emotional integration of personality of an individual, family emotional integration *i.e.*, integration with the family, caste emotional integration, linguistic emotional integration, regional emotional integration and national emotional integration.

The terms in educational psychology, the term emotional integration is used with reference to the integration of the personality of an individual.

National and Emotional Integration denotes only one meaning *i.e.*, emotional integration with the nation. Thus national and emotional integration implies a feeling of oneness which may transcend all groups or cultural differences and synthesise the different religions, castes, linguistic communities emotionally into a compact whole. It implies a feeling among citizens of India that India is 'One' and we belong to it culturally and emotionally. "What is in the interest of India, it is in our interest. Country comes first and other loyalties are subservient to it. We must share and respect common objectives, purposes or ideas and give them a higher place over sectional, linguistic, racial and other loyalties.

The Kothari Commission defines it as, "National integration includes a confidence in nation's future development of feeling of values and duties."

WHY NATIONAL AND EMOTIONAL INTEGRATION : NEED FOR NATIONAL AND EMOTIONAL INTEGRATION.

India is a land of so many faiths, creeds, castes, languages etc. It is very essential that people of different faiths and creeds, etc. think in terms of nationalism and place the welfare of the country above such narrow considerations. In the words of the Emotional Integration Committee, "One of the hardest problems before us today is the building up of a national mind by curbing the religious, linguistic and communal conflicts which tend to disunite us." Jawaharlal Nehru observed that national integration would weld Indian people into one and make India into "one strong national unit maintaining at the same time all our wonderful diversity."

Following are the main reasons for bringing about national and emotional integration of India:

1. Developing broadmindedness among the people.
2. Economic development of India.
3. Raising the standard of living and life of the people.
4. Developing patriotism and national spirit among the people.
5. Safeguarding the unity and integrity of India.
6. Making democracy successful.
7. Safeguarding national defence.
8. Developing spirit of mutual toleration and understanding.
9. Bringing harmony among people of diverse outlooks.

CONSEQUENCES OF LACK OF NATIONAL AND EMOTIONAL INTEGRATION

1. Rise of communal tendencies in communal riots.
2. Spread of the cult of casteism.
3. Narrow regional outlook.
4. Growth of separatist tendencies.
5. Rise of terrorism.
6. Danger to national unity.
7. Hurdles in law and order.

FAVOURABLE FACTORS FOR NATIONAL AND EMOTIONAL INTEGRATION

1. Constitutional provisions regarding equality of opportunity.
2. Declaring India as a secular state and freedom of worship etc.
3. Provision of special facilities for the disadvantaged sections.
4. Constitution of All India Services.
5. Division of powers between the Union and State Governments.
6. National symbols.
7. Special financial help to backward regions.
8. Cultural unity and teachings of great saints.
9. Network of masses of communications.

BARRIERS TO NATIONAL AND EMOTIONAL INTEGRATION

Major barriers to national and emotional integration in India are as under:

— Casteism
— Classism
— Communalism
— Ignorance
— Illiteracy
— Linguism – Narrow mindedness

— Provincialism – Political ambitions
— Regionalism
— Religious fundamentalism
— Sectarianism
— Selfishness of leaders
— Uneven regional development

ROLE OF EDUCATION IN DEVELOPING NATIONAL INTEGRATION

In the words of Dr. Radhakrishnan, "National integration cannot be built by brick and mortar, it cannot be built by chisel or hammer. It has to grow silently in the minds and hearts of men. The only process is the process of education."

The Emotional Integration Committee (1961) highlighted the role of education as "Education can play a vital role in strengthening emotional integration. It is felt that education should not only aim at imparting knowledge but should develop all aspects of a student's personality. It should broaden the outlook, foster a feeling of oneness and nationalism and a spirit of sacrifice and tolerance so that narrow group interests are submerged in the larger interests of the country.

APPOINTMENT OF THE EMOTIONAL INTEGRATION COMMITTEE (1961) AND ITS RECOMMENDATIONS

At the conference of the Education Ministers held in November, 1960, the distressing frequency with which disruptive tendencies were making themselves in the country was discussed. It was felt that such tendencies, if unchecked, might threaten the unity of the country. In the circumstances, the importance of the role of education in counteracting such divisive trends and in fostering unity was stressed. The Conference recommended that a Committee be set up to study the problem and to suggest positive educational measures for promoting integration. This was followed by the appointment of the Committee in May 1961 by the Ministry of Education.

Dr. Sampurnanand was the Chairman of the Committee. Among the other nine members, Shrimati Indira Gandhi, who after a few years became the Prime Minister, was also a member of the Committee.

Terms of Reference

(a) To study the role of education in considering and promoting the process of emotional integration in national life and to examine the operation of tendencies which come in the way of their development; and
(b) In the light of such study, to advise on the positive educational programmes for youth in general and students in schools and colleges in particular, to strengthen in them the processes of emotional integration.

Major Recommendations of the Emotional Integration Committee

1. *Reorientation of the Curriculum*: The school and college curriculum should be re-oriented to suit the needs of a secular state.

At the primary stage the importance of stories, poems, folklore and teaching of social studies, national anthem and other national songs should be emphasised.

Daily morning prayer should be held.

At the secondary stage the curriculum should include, among other things, the study of language and literature, social studies, moral and religious instruction and co-curricular activities.

At the university level the study of different social sciences, languages and literature, culture and art and also the exchange of teachers and students should play an important role.

2. *Co-curricular Activities*: The place of co-curricular activities in the curriculum is considered to be very important. These activities include common observance and celebration of festivals and events of national importance, sports, educational excursions, tours, and picnics, military training like the NCC, ACC, scouts and guides, student camps, debates, symposia, dramatics, and youth festivals. The use of audio-visual aids like films, pictures, radio and TV should also be made.

It is felt that participation in co-curricular activities helps in the growth of a well-balanced and well-adjusted personality. It creates a group feeling of oneness and brotherhood, broadens the outlook and develops a catholicity of spirit and tolerance which are necessary for good citizenship.

3. *Special Stress on the Teaching of Social Studies*: The teaching of social studies at all levels *i.e.*, the primary, secondary and university stages would impart knowledge of the geographical, historical and cultural background of the country and of the world as a whole. Books on social studies should include reference to the lives and works of the great men of India and of the world and also stories from ancient books like the *Ramayana* and the *Mahabharata*.

4. *Textbooks*: In order that the textbooks play their legitimate role in strengthening of emotional integration, it is necessary that they be re-oriented and improved. In the preparation of history textbooks special care needs to be taken to see that facts are not misrepresented, distorted or exaggerated to create prejudice.

5. *Language and Script*:

(i) The use of the Roman script may be permitted in certain areas for an interim period to enable persons to improve their acquaintance with Hindi.

(ii) Throughout India the international numerals must be used.

(iii) To reduce the burden of three scripts, Hindi may be learnt in the non-Hindi areas in the regional script.

(iv) To popularise the study of Hindi in non-Hindi speaking areas, a beginning may be made with the publication of Hindi books in the Roman script and the compilation of simple dictionaries in Hindi — other languages, also in the Roman script.

(v) Hindi books may be published in the regional scripts and the compilation of Regional Language — Hindi dictionaries should be encouraged.

(vi) At the high school stage Hindi must be taught in the Devnagri script, keeping in view the constitutional provisions.

(vii) The two link languages—Hindi and English should be effectively taught at university level so that conditions of emotional and intellectual isolation are not created.

(viii) It is necessary to ensure that in implementing any language policy the rights of minorities are adequately projected.

6. *Uniform for School Children*: It is desirable to have a uniform for school children; one common uniform for the whole of India is not necessary; schools may have their own preference in regard to colour and pattern.

7. *Singing of National Anthem*: Children should be taught to sing the National Anthem in unison and behave in a disciplined way when it is sung. They should also be the taught meaning of the verses.

8. *Reverence for National Flag*: Students should be told the history of the National Flag and taught at the earliest stage to show reverence for the National Flag.

9. *Celebration of National Days*: National Days—January 26, August 15 and October 2—should be celebrated in schools with the full participation of the teachers, the students and the community.

10. *Special Talks on the Unity and Oneness of the Country*: Special meetings of the school assembly should be held from time to time and the speakers speak to the children on topics dealing with the unity and oneness of the country.

11. *Taking Pledge*: Students may be asked to repeat a pledge twice a year dedicating themselves to the service of their country. A draft of such a pledge in English is given below:

India is my country, all Indians are brothers and sisters.

I love my country, and I am proud of its rich and varied heritage,

I shall always strive to be worthy of it.

I shall give my parents, teachers and all elders respect and treat everyone with courtesy. I shall be kind to animals.

To my country and my people, I pledge my devotion. In their well-being and prosperity alone lies my happiness.

12. *Open-Air Dramas*: Open-air dramas emphasising the ideals of national unity may be staged four times a year by every school.

At least one play should be based upon a theme derived from the classic or from the history of ancient India. In predominant Hindu areas there should be some plays dealing with non-Hindu lives and *vice-versa*.

13. *Student Exchange and Tours*: Such tours should be conducted from one State to another. The inter-state visits if properly organised should do much to acquaint both teachers and children with different parts of the country.

A network of youth hostels should be set up by all the States in selected places.

14. *School Improvement*: Students should be associated with the cleanliness of the school premises. This would not only increase their pride in it and loyalty to the school but would also help in improving the school for future students.

15. *Admissions*: Admissions to schools, colleges and other educational institutions should not be given on the basis of caste but on the basis of means and merits.

16. *Recognition of Institutions*: Recognition should not be given to institutions where divisive tendencies are encouraged.

17. *Freeship and Scholarships*: These should be awarded only on the basis of means and merit.

18. *No domiciliary Restrictions*: Domiciliary restrictions in regard to migration of students between one State and Other should be removed.

19. *Suitable Handbooks for Teachers*: Suitable handbooks for teachers in the social studies and languages should be published.

20. *All-India Award*: An annual all-India award for the best general essay on different States in India should be instituted.

21. *Educational and Travel Documentaries*: Educational and travel documentaries with particular emphasis on various aspects of Indian scenery, flora and fauna, on various developmental and reconstruction programmes should be produced for use in schools and these should form a regular feature of the schools.

22. *School Projects*: Schools may conduct several projects which improve their general knowledge of the country. For instance 'Know Your Country' project can be undertaken during which children may share in the collection of information about a State in the Indian Union other than their own.

23. *Exchange of Professors*: Distinguished professors should also be deputed periodically to different universities so that a large range of students can benefit from their experience.

24. *All-India Youth Council*: An all-India youth council should be set up to coordinate all the youth programmes taken up by the Central and State Governments and also to help various agencies to extend their efforts.

25. *Teachers*: The Union Ministry of Education should implement a scheme providing for a national minimum scale of salaries for teachers in the primary, middle and secondary schools.

26. *Recommendations of the Education Commission.* Following recommendations of the Education Commission (1964-66) may be added:

(i) *Provision of Quality Education.* A reasonable quality of good education should be made available to all irrespective of any consideration.

(ii) *Common School System.* A common school system should be established.

(iii) *No Public Schools.* Public schools should not be permitted as they breed inequality.

(iv) *Three Language Formula.* Three language formula should be followed.

(v) *Regional Language on Medium of Instruction.* The use of regional languages as media of education from the lowest to the highest stage was a matter of 'profound importance for national integration'.

27. *National Policy on Education (1986 and Modified in 1992) on National Integration : Common Core Curriculum)*: The NPE provides for a common core curriculum including the History of Indian Freedom Movement, the constitutional obligations and other content essential to national identity. These contents are expected to cut across subject areas and designed to promote values such as India's common cultural heritage, egalitarianism, democracy and secularism, equality of the sexes, protection of the environment, removal of social barriers, etc.

28. *Uniform Educational Structure*: A uniform educational structure should be established, all over the country.

30. *Equality of Opportunity*: Equal educational opportunities should be provided to all.

32. *Educational Opportunities in all Parts*: All parts of the country should be provided with suitable educational institutions.

33. *Social and National Service*: Social and national service should be made an integral part of education as its absence is also responsible for increasing the gulf between the educated and the uneducated classes.

PROGRAMMES UNDERTAKEN FOR PROMOTING NATIONAL INTEGRATION

1. Setting up of the National Integration Council.

2. Setting up of National Integration *Samities* in universities and colleges for the purpose of promoting mutual understanding and appreciation among persons coming from different parts of India. At present there is a total number of 105 *Samities* functioning in the country.

3. Formation of committees composed of members drawn from various fields of national life to act as spearheads for a mass movement in the cause of national integration.

4. Survey of textbooks and elimination of biased and prejudiced material leading to hatred among different communities.

5. Establishing planning forums for disseminating information.

6. Organisation of writers' camps.
7. National Integration Inter-State Student-Teacher Camps.
8. Celebration of centenaries.
9. *Community Singing*: A National Integration Project as a national movement has been launched by the Ministry of Human Resource Development for the promotion of community singing. NCERT has been organising community singing camps for music and musically inclined teachers drawn from different States and Union Territories of the country. Several Camps of State and National levels on community singing have been organised and several thousand music and musically inclined teachers drawn from States have been trained in community singing. Under the scheme every trained teacher is given an illustrated book entitled, "Let's Sing Together". A recorded cassette containing 15 songs in different Indian languages and a tape recorder is also given to each teacher.

Concluding Observation

In the end, it must be stressed that the major responsibility for the promotion of values of national integration among the people of India rests with the political and religious leaders. Here also, political leaders have the most prominent role to play. It is they who, by and large, are responsible for sowing the seeds of disintegration. However, this is not to minimise the role of education in this respect.

10

Medium of Instruction

IMPORTANCE OF THE MEDIUM OF INSTRUCTION

The importance of the medium of instruction in the educative process has been highlighted by the Education Commission (1964-66) in these words, "The medium selected should enable students to acquire knowledge with facility to express themselves with clarity and to think with precision and vigour." It further observed, "As a matter of sound education policy, the medium of education in school and higher education should generally be the same."

MOTHER-TONGUE AS THE MEDIUM OF INSTRUCTION

Rabindranath Tagore (1861-1941) expressed the value of learning through mother-tongue as, "It was because we were taught in our mother-tongue that our mind quickened. Learning should as far as possible follow the process of eating. When the taste begins from the first bite the stomach is awakened to its function before it is loaded so that its digestive juices get full play. Nothing of this sort happens when the Bengali boy is taught in English."

Gandhiji (1869-1948) advocated the use of mother-tongue on account of the following reasons:

1. Our language is the reflection of ourselves and foreign language is the reflection of foreigners.
2. The babe takes its first lesson from its mother.
3. We cling to our mother-tongue as to our mother's breast as it alone can give us the life-giving milk. No other milk is its appropriate substitute.
4. Instruction through mother-tongue lays the solid foundation of our many-sided development.
5. Instruction through mother-tongue allows us to think freely.
6. Instruction through mother-tongue develops originality.
7. Instruction through mother-tongue enables us to be creative.

DEMERITS, LIMITATIONS AND SHORTCOMINGS OF FOREIGN MEDIUM OF INSTRUCTION

Gandhiji was convinced that, "the foreign medium has made our children practically foreigners in our own land. It is the greatest tragedy of the existing system." He further states with great anguish, "I am certain that the children of the nation that receive education in a tongue other than their own commit suicide".

Writing about the merit of the mother-tongue as the medium of instruction and demerits of the foreign language he writes, "I know now that what I took from years to learn of Arithmetic, Geometry, Algebra, Chemistry and Astronomy, I should have learnt easily in one year, if I had not to learn them through English but Gujarati."

Following shortcomings are quite evident from the use of foreign medium of instruction:

1. The students lose their originality.
2. The students become like birds without wings in the views of Gandhiji.
3. Foreign medium puts a severe strain on students' nervous energy.
4. Foreign medium makes students imitators.
5. Foreign medium saps the energy of the students.
6. Foreign medium estranges the students from their parents.
7. Foreign medium makes education unnecessarily expensive.
8. Foreign medium robs the nation of its soul.
9. Foreign medium stunts the natural growth of the students.
10. Foreign medium kills the originality of the students.
11. Foreign medium causes a brain fag.
12. Foreign medium makes students crammers.
13. Foreign medium makes students foreigners in their own lands.
14. Foreign medium creates barriers between the educated few and the masses.

Gandhiji wrote that "I am certain that the children of the nation that receive instruction in a tongue other than their own commit suicide." Gandhiji, in view of the harmful effects of the foreign medium emphatically stated, "The medium of instruction must be altered at once and at any cost, the provincial languages being given their original place. I would prefer temporary chaos in higher education to criminal waste that is daily accumulating."

OPPOSITION TO HINDI AS MEDIUM OF INSTRUCTION. CAN THERE BE A UNIFORM MEDIUM OF EDUCATION IN INDIA?

The Education Commission (1964-66) gave a careful consideration to the issue of medium of instruction at the University stage and observed "It is sometimes argued that there should be a single medium of education at the University stage—English for the time being, to be ultimately substituted by Hindi—on the ground that it would promote mobility of teachers and students from one part of the country to another, provide for easy communication between academic and professional men and administrator, further intellectual cooperation amongst the universities and help in other ways in developing a corporate intellectual life in the country. We are inclined to think, on a balance of considerations, that this solution is not feasible. In practice, it will probably mean the indefinite continuance of English as the only medium of education—a development we cannot support in the larger interest of the country. The adoption of Hindi as a common medium of education in higher stages in all parts of India is not possible for some years to come, and in non-Hindi areas, it will still have some of the advantages associated with the use of foreign medium and is likely to be resisted. It would, therefore, be unwise to strive to reverse the present trend for the adoption of the regional languages as media of education at the university stage and insist on the use of a common medium in higher education throughout the country."

In view of the importance of the problem, the Commission suggested

1. UGC and the universities carefully work out a feasible programme suitable for each university or group of universities regarding medium of instruction.
2. The change-over to regional languages should take place as early as possible and, in any case, within about ten years, since the problem will only become more complex and difficult with the passage of time.
3. A large programme of producing the needed literature in the Indian languages will have to be made for the training and retraining of teachers.
4. Suitable safeguards should be devised, in the transitional stage, to prevent any lowering of standards during the process of change-over because of inadequate preparation.

But while we proceed with caution, we would do well to remember that careful action does not mean vacillation or tardy action, or no action at all. Caution is meaningful only if it forms part of a policy of determined, deliberate and vigorous action.

English as the Medium in All-India Institutions. There will, however, be one important exception to this general rule, namely, All-India Institutions which admit, in considerable numbers, students from the different parts of the country. These now use English as the medium of education, which should continue undisturbed for the time being.

Development of Modern Indian Languages. The Commission felt, "It is hardly necessary to emphasise that the development of the Indian languages is essential for the development of the Indian people and as a way of bringing together the elite and the masses. It can make scientific and technical knowledge more easily accessible to people in their own languages and thus help not only in the progress of industrialisation but also in the wider dissemination of science and a scientific outlook."

DOCUMENTS ON THE MEDIUM OF INSTRUCTION

William Bentinck's Policy Resolution (1835). The Policy Resolution in its para 4 clearly stated that all the funds would be spent in imparting the native population a knowledge of English literature and science through the medium of the English language.

It may be observed that Lord Macaulay, whose recommendations were accepted by the Governor General William Bentinck, while stressing the supreme importance of English and European Sciences and Arts, had not used the term medium of instruction although for all purposes his contention implied that English would be the medium of instruction.

Thus with William Bentinck's policy, English became the medium of instruction.

Wood's Despatch (1854). The Despatch recommended that along with English, Indian languages should also be accepted as the medium of instruction. It observed, "while the English language continues to be made use of as by far the most perfect medium for the education of those persons who have acquired a sufficient knowledge of it to receive general instruction through it, the vernacular languages must be employed to teach the far larger classes who are ignorant of it, or imperfectly acquainted with it."

Indian Education Commission or Hunter Commission (1882). The Commission indirectly advocated English as the medium of instruction at the secondary stage of education and gave very little place to the mother-tongue.

Sadler Commission (1917). The Commission recommended the use of mother-tongue as medium of instruction in Intermediate Colleges.

Sargent Report (1944). The medium of instruction at the primary stage should be the mother-tongue of the pupils.

University Education Commission (1948-49). Its recommendations on medium of instruction are:

(a) The Federal Language be developed through the assimilation of words from various sources and the retention of words which have already entered into Indian languages from different sources.

(b) International technical and scientific terminology be adopted, the borrowed words be properly assimilated.

(c) For the medium of instruction for higher education, English be replaced as early as practicable by an Indian language which cannot be Sanskrit on account of vital difficulties.

Secondary Education Commission (1952-53). The mother-tongue or the regional language should generally be the medium of instruction throughout the secondary stage, subject to the provision that for linguistic minorities special facilities be made available.

Education Commission (1964-66). The Commission stated, "The medium selected should enable students to acquire knowledge with facility to express themselves with clarity and to think with precision and vigour. From this point of view, the claims of the mother-tongue are pre-eminent.

Learning through a foreign medium compels the students to concentrate on cramming instead of mastering the subject-matter. Moreover, as a matter of sound education policy, the medium of education in school and higher education should generally be the same. Prior to 1937, the position was at least consistent. English was the medium in the upper stages of the school and in college education. As we have rightly adopted the regional languages as the media of education at the school stage, it follows logically that we should adopt them increasingly at the higher stage also."

National Policy on Education (1968). The Policy observed, "The regional languages are already in use as media of education at the primary and secondary stages. Urgent steps should now be taken to adopt them as media of education at the university stage."

"The Education Policy of 1968 had examined the question of the development of languages in great detail; its essential provisions can hardly be improved upon and are as relevant today as before. The implementation of the part of its 1968 Policy has, however, been uneven. The Policy will be implemented more energetically and purposefully."

PRESENT POSITION OF MEDIUM OF INSTRUCTION : POPULARITY OF ENGLISH AS THE MEDIUM OF INSTRUCTION

Notwithstanding the views of eminent educationists, social reformers and thinkers favouring mother-tongue/regional language as the medium of instruction at all stages of education, English as the medium of instruction has been gaining popularity after independence. Now it has become the status symbol to send a child even at the nursery/preparatory stage to an English medium school.

English is the medium of instruction in almost prestigious schools in the country.

Mother-tongue/regional language is the medium of instruction in general in almost all elementary educational institutions run by the Local Bodies.

The State run schools follow English as well as the regional language/ mother-tongue as medium of instruction at the Secondary/Senior school stage.

Besides English, all the 18 languages mentioned in Eighth Schedule of the Constitution are being used as the medium of instruction in different States/ Regions at various levels and in varying degrees. There is no single medium of instruction. However, as already stated, the recent tendency is to use English as the medium of instruction even at the nursery/pre-primary stage. This is in spite of the views of experts favouring mother-tongue as the medium of instruction. As observed in "*Education To-day*" (July-Sept., 2003) in UNESCO Newsletter.

"Educators are increasingly convinced of the value of multilingual education and studies show that children learn better in their mother-tongue."

The 18 languages recognised in the Constitution of India are:

(1) Assamese, (2) Bengali, (3) Gujarati, (4) Hindi, (5) Kannada, (6) Kashmiri, (7) Konkani, (8) Malayalam, (9) Manipuri, (10) Marathi, (11) Nepali, (12) Oriya, (13) Punjabi, (14) Sanskrit, (15) Sindhi, (16) Tamil, (17) Telugu, (18) Urdu.

MULTILINGUAL EDUCATION AND UNESCO

According to UNESCO "Bilingual and multilingual education means using two or more languages as mediums of instruction". UNESCO adopted the term "Multilingual education" at its General Conference in 1999.

11

Education of Weaker Sections

MEANING OF WEAKER SECTIONS

According to the National Policy on Education, the socially disadvantaged children are those children who belong to the following categories:

1. Scheduled Castes Children.
2. Scheduled Tribes Children.
3. Other Backward Classes (OBC's) Children.
4. Tribal Areas Children.

Constitutional Provisions Regarding Deprived Socially Disadvantaged Sections of Society

Article 15: Prohibition of Discrimination on grounds of religion, race, caste, sex or place of births sub-section (4) states, "Nothing in this Article or in clause (2) of Article 29 shall prevent the State from making any special provision for the advancement of any socially and educationally backward classes or for the Scheduled Castes and the Scheduled Tribes."

Article 46: It reads, "the State shall provide with special care the educational and economic interests of the weaker sections of the people, and in particular, of the Scheduled Castes and Scheduled Tribes and shall protect them from social injustice and all forms of exploitation."

Article 338: It makes provision for the appointment of a Special Officer for SCs and STs.

Article 390: It envisages the appointment of a Commission to investigate the conditions of the Backward classes.

WHY PROMOTION OF EDUCATION OF THE WEAKER SECTIONS' CHILDREN?

The Education Commission 1964-66, in Chapter VI entitled 'Equalisation of Educational Opportunity and Social Change' very aptly observed, "One of the important social objectives of education is to equalise opportunity, enabling the backward or under-privileged classes and individuals to use education as a lever for the improvement of their conditions. Every society that values social justice and is anxious to improve the lot of the common man and cultivate all available talent must ensure progressive equality of opportunity to all sections of the population. This is the only guarantee for the building up of an egalitarian and humane society in which the exploitation of the weak is minimised." The Commission further stated, "The education of the backward classes in general and the tribal people in particular is a major programme of equalisation and of social and national integration. No expenditure is too great for this purpose." Alas! We have not paid heed to these words of wisdom. Non-implementation of this vital recommendation has led to disintegrative tendencies, hatred and strife.

Policies on education—the National Policy on Education, 1968, 1986 and modified Policy Formulation 1992—all stress upon speedy action for the promotion of education of the deprived sections.

EDUCATION OF THE SCHEDULED CASTES

Population of Scheduled Castes. In 2001, the population of Scheduled Castes was 179.7 million, which accounted for 17.5 per cent of the total population (projected on the basis of the trend of their decadal growth rates).

Almost half of the total population of SC is concentrated in the states of Bihar, Haryana, Madhya Pradesh, Punjab, Rajasthan and U.P.—popularly known as Hindi belt in the North.

In the South, SCs are concentrated mainly in Andhra Pradesh and Tamil Nadu.

In the East, they are in Bengal and in the West in Maharashtra.

Origin of the Term Scheduled Caste

The Simon Commission (1928), which was boycotted in India and became responsible for the death of Lala Lajpat Rai on account of '*Lathi Charge*' coined the term Scheduled Caste.

Thereafter, it was used in Government of India Act, 1935. After independence, it found expression in the various provisions of the Constitution.

The Education of Scheduled Castes

The central focus in the SCs' educational development is their equalisation with the non-SC population at all stages and levels of education, in all areas and in all the four dimensions-rural male, rural female, urban male and urban female.

The Measures Contemplated for Education of SCs Include:

(i) Incentives to indigent families to send their children to school regularly till they reach the age of 14;

(ii) Pre-matric Scholarship scheme for children of families engaged in occupations such as scavenging, flaying and tinning to be made applicable from Class I onwards. All children of such families, regardless of incomes, will be covered by this scheme and time-bound programmes targeted on them will be undertaken;

(iii) Constant micro-planning and verification to ensure that the enrolment, retention and successful completion of courses by SC students do not fail at any stage, and provision of remedial courses to improve their prospects for further education and in employment;

(iv) The recruitment of teachers from Scheduled Castes;

(v) Provision of facilities for SC students in hostels at district headquarters, according to a phased programme;

(vi) Location of school buildings, *Balwadis* and Adult Education Centres in such a way as to facilitate full participation of the Scheduled Castes; backward sections of society, particularly in the rural areas. Hill and desert districts, remote and inaccessible areas and islands will be provided adequate institutional infrastructure.

PRESENT STATUS OF THE EDUCATION OF SCs

Table 11.1: Literacy Rates of SCs and Total Literate Population (1971-2001)

Category	*1971*	*1981*	*1991*	*2001*
Total Population*	29.45	36.23	52.21	65.38
Scheduled Castes	14.67	21.38	37.41	Not available
Gap between SCs and Total Population	14.78	14.85	14.80	Not available

Note : * Includes SC population.

Educational Status

Education, being the most important instrument for empowering weaker sections of the society, every effort is being made to improve the educational status of SCs on priority basis. Between 1971 and 1991, the literacy rate of SCs increased by 2.6 times, while that of total population increased by 1.8 times (Table 11.1).

Table 11.2: Female Literacy Rates of SCs and Total Literate Population (1971-2001)

Category	*1971*	*1981*	*1991*	*2001*
Total Population*	18.69	29.85	39.29	54.16
Scheduled Castes	6.44	10.93	23.76	NA
Gap between Female literacy of SCs and Total Population	12.25	18.92	15.53	NA

Note : * Includes SC population.

Table 11.3: Gross Enrolment Ratios of SCs and Total Population Enrolment (1990-91 to 1999-2000)

	Year / *Classes*	*1990-91*		*1999-2000*	
		I to V	*I to VIII*	*I to V*	*I to VIII*
Total Population*	Total	100.1	62.1	94.9	58.8
	Boys	114.0	76.6	104.1	67.2
	Girls	85.5	47.8	85.2	49.7
Scheduled Castes	Total	102.2	47.7	92.4	62.5
	Boys	122.7	61.4	103.6	73.6
	Girls	80.6	33.3	80.5	50.3
GAP	Total	(+)2.1	(-)14.4	(-)2.5	(+)3.7
	Boys	(+)8.7	(-)15.2	(-)0.5	(+)6.4
	Girls	(-)4.9	(-)14.5	(-)4.7	(+)0.6

Note : * Includes SC population.

EDUCATION OF THE SCHEDULED TRIBES

Origin of the Term Scheduled Tribes (ST). As distinct from the so-called mainstream population, the British used this term with respect to groups living in forests and hills, etc. It was also used with the prefix like indigenous people, etc. The term Scheduled Tribes denoted that people belonging to these groups did not have much contact with the main culture.

Traditionally Considered Characteristics of the Tribal People

1. The tribal people live in the rather inaccessible parts of the country.
2. The tribal people live away from the civilised world.
3. They belong to these races—Australoid or Mongoloids or Negrito.
4. They speak tribal dialect.
5. They believe in ghosts and spirits and worship them.
6. They profess primitive religion known as 'Animism'.
7. Their chief occupations are gathering forest products, hunting, etc.
8. They are, by and large, meat eaters.

Total Tribal Population

The population of tribal people in 2001 was estimated to have reached 88.8 million on the basis of the projected figures. This represented 8.6 per cent of country's total population.

Population Profile of the Tribal People

1. The largest concentration of ST population is found in the north-eastern states: Mizoram (94.8 per cent); Nagaland (87.7 per cent); Meghalaya (85.5 per cent); and Arunachal Pradesh; (63.7 per cent).
2. Union Territories: Lakshadweep (93.2 per cent); Dadra and Nagar Haveli (79 per cent); Andaman and Nicobar Islands (5.5 per cent).

3. Madhya Pradesh (23.3 per cent); Orissa (22.2 per cent); Rajasthan (12.4 per cent); Maharashtra (9.3 per cent); Bihar (7.7 per cent); and Madhya Pradesh (6.3 per cent).
4. Almost nil in Haryana, Punjab, Chandigarh, Delhi and Pondicherry.

Promotion of Education among the STs in Accordance with the Provisions of the NPE and Programme of Action (1986 and 1992)

The following measures are being taken urgently to bring the Scheduled Tribes at par with others:

(i) Priority is accorded to opening primary schools in tribal areas. The construction of school buildings will be undertaken in these areas on a priority basis under the normal funds for education, as well as under the Jawahar Rozgar Yojna, Tribal Welfare Schemes, etc.

(ii) The socio-cultural milieu of the ST has its distinctive characteristics including, in may cases, their own spoken languages. This underlines the need to develop the curricula and devise institutional materials in tribal languages at the initial stages, with arrangements for switching over to the regional languages.

(iii) Educated and promising Scheduled Tribe youths are encouraged and trained to take up teaching in tribal areas.

(iv) Residential schools, including Ashram Schools have been established on a large scale.

(v) Incentive schemes have been formulated for the Scheduled Tribes, keeping in view their special needs and life styles. Scholarships for higher education will emphasise technical, professional and para-professional courses. Special remedial courses and other programmes to remove psycho-social impediments are provided to improve their performance in various courses.

(vi) Anganwadis, Non-formal and Adult Education Centres are being opened on a priority basis in areas predominantly inhabited by the Scheduled Tribes.

(vii) The curriculum at all states of education has been gradually designed to create an awareness of the rich cultural identity of the tribal people as also of their enormous creative talent.

OTHER BACKWARD CLASSES (OBCs) AND THEIR EDUCATION

Constitutional Provisions

1. *Article 15(4) of the Constitution*: It enjoins upon the state the creation of special provisions for the advancement of any socially and educationally backward classes of citizens or for the Scheduled Castes and Scheduled Tribes.

2. *Article 16(4)*: It enables the State for making provisions for the reservation of appointments or posts in favour of any backward class of citizens which in

the opinion of the state is not adequately represented in the services under the state.

3. *Article 38*: It makes it obligatory for the State to "strive to promote the welfare of the people by securing and protecting as effectively as it may a social order, in which Justice; Social, Economic and Political shall inform all the institutions of the National Life".

4. *Article 46*: It contains a very significant directive regarding promotion of educational and economic interests of other weaker sections and protecting them from social injustice and all forms of exploitation.

5. *Part XVI of the Constitution*: It contains "special provisions relating to certain classes" and under this part, Article 340 envisages the appointment of a Commission to investigate the conditions of Backward Classes.

With a view to consider measures for the improvement of the conditions of the Other Backward Classes, the Government of India appointed the Mandal Commission in 1978. As far as promotion of education among these sections is concerned, following special measures are being taken:

1. Special schemes for the OBCs after their educational training.
2. Reservation of seats for OBC students in all scientific, technical and professional institutions run by the Centre as well as the State Governments.

POPULARISING EDUCATION AMONG THE WEAKER SECTIONS

It is observed that well-planned, sustained and vigorous efforts as stated below would go a long way in promoting education among the weaker sections.

1. *Introduction of tribal dialects and medium of instruction*: In tribal areas, having a large population where people do not understand the regional language, tribal dialects may be introduced as the medium of instruction wherever possible in the initial stages and then they should be integrated with the general educational system and may be taught regional languages. But in the tribal areas where the children understand the regional language, it can be used as medium of instruction. Such practice will reduce the rate of wastage and stagnation and also create interest among the children.

2. *Suitable curriculum for the schools*: There is a need for evolving a suitable curriculum for the schools functioning in tribal areas. This curriculum may be science-oriented but culture-based. The curriculum should be so framed that this should include the various aspects of tribal life and culture.

3. *Training of teachers*: Such teachers working in the tribal areas who do not possess enough knowledge about the tribal life and culture may be given training in these aspects. The teachers posted in tribal areas should also acquire knowledge of tribal dialects.

4. *Provision of suitable school accommodation*: All the schools functioning in tribal areas should be provided with suitable accommodation.

5. *Provision of hostels and extension of Ashram schools*: Whenever

possible, the schools functioning in tribal areas may be provided with hostels which will solve many problems. Extension of Ashram schools, use of youth dormitories may also solve some of the problems.

6. *Encouragement of participation of tribal parents*: Participation of tribal parents in the educational programmes may also be encouraged. The awareness and interest regarding the utility of education for the children should be created among the parents.

7. *Flexibility in schools hours*: In the tribal areas, the school hours and the duration will have to be adjusted according to the needs of the community. Children in these areas are by nature, playful and not work-oriented. They cannot sit for long hours in the classrooms. In some cases, therefore, schools might have to be opened in the morning and evening hours with a break in between.

8. *Medium of instruction*: To sustain the interest of the little children, it is necessary that at least up to class-III the mother-tongue of the children should be used as the medium of instruction. It will help to reduce the drop-out and stagnation of children in the lower class. There is also a need to develop special reading materials for these children.

9. *Economic incentives to parents*: Since the tribal people are economically backward and the children have to take part in different activities of the economic pursuits, the parents do not care for the education of their children because this sustains economic loss. Thus some economic incentive may be given to students, but not to parents to prosecute their studies.

10. *Special training for talented tribal students*: A scheme to help the talented tribal students may be started. They may be given different types of training and they may be asked to work in tribal areas.

11. *Provision of audio-visual aids*: Provision of audio-visual aids for the development of education of tribal children is essential and may be made available as soon as possible.

12. *Improvement of teacher-community relationships*: Steps to improve the Ashram School education may be taken. The teacher-community relationship may be improved. The cleanliness of the buildings, discipline in the Ashram Schools may be improved and adequate freedom to students for participating in various games may be given. Some courses to train these teachers may be organised.

13. *Relaxation in prescribed norms*: Where needed, prescribed norms for the opening of educational institutions catering to the needs of the backward sections, may be relaxed.

14. *Opening of non-formal centres*: One of the solutions for the problems of education of tribals and nomads would be to open non-formal education centres. These centres would cater to the needs of both parents, dropped out and unenrolled children, mothers, and other adult women folk of the community. The educational programmes will have to be integrated with the

development and social welfare activities of the community. It would include both health, sanitation, agriculture, work-experience and community developmental programmes. It is through this package programme of the non-formal education centres that tribal and normal children could be brought and retrained in large numbers in the folds of education.

15. *Intensive programme of adult education/social education*: In backward areas and among backward sections, intensive adult education and social education programmes may be undertaken for educating the parents.

16. *Relaxation or prescribed pupil-teacher ratio*: Wherever necessary, the prescribed teacher-pupil ratio may be relaxed while sanctioning staff in schools located in backward areas.

17. *Guidance facilities*: A special drive may be launched for acquainting the people with all types of facilities available for weaker sections.

18. *Incentives for students*: Students of weaker sections should be provided with various incentives like tuition free education, free books, free stationery, free uniform and free mid-day meals.

19. *Scholarships*: A special scheme for providing liberal scholarships to students belonging to backward sections should be operated.

20. *Study camps*: During summer, winter and other holidays study camps for students may be organised. Services of teachers from well-established schools may be utilised for the improvement of standards.

21. *New initiatives for universalisation of elementary education*: Preference may be accorded while launching new initiatives to the backward areas/ backward sections of the society. In fact, it would be highly desirable where possible to limit these initiatives to such areas.

Preference should be given for admission to children belonging to backward sections in the following types of programmes: (1) District Primary Education (DPEP), (2) Lok Jumbish (LJ), (3) Non-formal Education Centres (NFECs), (4) National Programme of Nutritional Support to Primary Education (NPNSPE), (5) Operation Black Board (OBB), (6) Shiksha Karmi Project (SKP), (7) Sarva Shiksha Abhiyan — SSA (Education for All), (8) Navodaya Schools, (9) Sainik Schools.

22. *Facilities for teachers*: (1) It may be made obligatory for teachers to stay in the vicinity of the school as far as possible. As an incentive, payment of backward area accommodation allowance to teachers who live within the vicinity of the school, may be considered.

(2) Suitable facilities may be given to the children of school teachers studying in high schools.

(3) Residential type of schools (Ashram Schools) may be established for children of teachers working in very backward areas and the full cost of their education may be borne by the Government.

(4) Reservation of some seats in the Public Schools, Sainik Schools, Navodaya Schools, professional institutions for the teachers working in such

remotes areas may be made.

23. *Conducive environment in educational institutions*: The students should be made to feel that teachers appreciate their problems and difficulties. The teachers, therefore, should demonstrate an encouraging attitude and be patient and sympathetic with them. They should show no discriminatory feelings. They should in no case use sarcastic language as to their caste or family backwardness.

24. *Educational provision in terms of curriculum, teaching methodology and evaluation of the children of weaker sections*

Preparatory classes and compensatory instruction: Many children belonging to the Scheduled Castes ad Scheduled Tribes come from a comparatively poor environment. They may not be neat or smart. Their usage of standard language may be poor. Their vocabulary is underdeveloped as compared to their peers. They may not have formed the initial mathematical concepts. On the other hand they may be more enthusiastic to learn. Because of the lack of a congenial home environment, these children may not be in a position to complete their home assignments. Their parents are usually employed as landless labour or in other manual or agrarian activities. Therefore, such children are not able to conceptualise their future as educated persons.

There is the need to conduct some preparatory classes for children coming from the Scheduled Castes and Scheduled Tribes. The primary objective of conducting such classes is to raise the school entry ability level of such children. This is also helpful in having a somewhat homogeneous grouping in the class. The classes may be conducted two to three weeks in advance of the general admissions. Classes may be conducted on healthy habits, personal and environmental cleanliness, eating habits etc. The children may also be helped in improving the pronunciation of the words and picking up standard language. For this, they may be motivated to participate in discussions, recitation and story-telling etc. Initial concepts of mathematics may also be introduced.

25. *Remedial instruction.* Students coming from Scheduled Castes and Scheduled Tribes are also likely to be deficient in the scholastic areas. The school may provide some remedial education programmes. Adoption of instructional strategies, such as peer group learning, monitorial assistance, diagnostic testing and tutoring would help to improve the educational levels of these learners.

Provision of outdoor games and activities, co-curricular and work experience activities will also help in the retention of such children in the schools and create an interest in them for continuing schooling.

26. *Monitoring of programmes.* A standing Committee of the Central Advisory Board of Education (CABE) under the chairmanship of Minister of Human Resource Development may be constituted to monitor and review implementation of all educational programme for the deprived sections.

27. *Special role of the teacher in the education of children of backward*

sections:

Following are the important points which a teacher should take into account while teaching the students.

1. The teacher should take interest in meeting the needs of every type of child.
2. The teacher should ensure that his own behaviour and behaviour of students is free from bias.
3. The teacher must ensure that the interaction amongst the students is normal.
4. The teacher should understand the learning process in the context of characteristics of learners.
5. The teacher should appreciate that the special educational needs of the students reflect the special requirement of a learner calling for specific adjustment in regular educational programmes.
6. The teacher should keep in view that special needs can arise from physiological, intellectual, social and economic reasons.
7. The learner should be given importance as an individual rather than as a disabled or as a scheduled caste or scheduled tribe or a girl.
8. Educational adjustment has several dimensions like curriculum decision, class-room organisation, special teaching techniques and aids etc.
9. A teacher should be sensitive to the needs of socially disadvantaged learners.
10. The teacher should have a close link with parents to ensure regular attendance.
11. The teacher should make the parents aware of the special educational and other facilities in the school and the neighbourhood and impress upon them to make use of them.
12. The teacher should find out specific areas of deficiency in learning.
13. The teachers should take all possible steps to develop self-concept and positive image among such learners.
14. Special incentives be provided to such students.
15. The teacher's own example in his behaviour towards students belonging to these castes is the most effective and powerful way to build up a congenial climate.
16. The school staff should ensure non-discrimination between the children of Scheduled Castes, Scheduled Tribes and other communities.
17. The school staff should avoid the use of the caste names or derogatory words while calling roll calls or naming children.
18. Teachers should provide equal opportunities to all the children to participate in the curricular and co-curricular activities of the school, including games.
19. Frequent meetings between the staff, school teachers and parents of

Scheduled Castes and Scheduled Tribes children should be arranged. The details of the schemes for promoting education amongst Scheduled Castes and Scheduled Tribes should be explained to the parents at these meetings. It should be impressed upon them that they must continue the education of their children.

20. Special attention should be paid to motivating parents to educate girls.
21. Teaches should suggest to illiterate parents the advantages gained by attending functional literacy classes in the adult education centre.

Summing Up: For the successful working of Indian democracy and the achievement of national objectives as contained in the Constitution, it is very important to take speedy measures for the promotion of education among the children of the weaker sections.

12

Adult Education

MEANING AND DEFINITION OF ADULT EDUCATION

There is no internationally accepted definition of adult education. UNESCO in '*International Director of Adult Education*' (1952) observed, "In essence, adult education is so closely related to the social, political and cultural conditions, of each country that no uniform or precise definition can be arrived at." However, following definitions of adult education would serve our purpose in explaining the meaning of adult education.

The First International Conference on Adult Education (1949) defined adult education as "Adult education has the task of satisfying the needs and aspirations of adults in all their diversity."

"*Blond's Encyclopaedia of Education*' (1969) states, "Adult education is the provision of learning situations to enable mature men and women to enlarge and interpret their own experience."

According to Liveright and Haygood (1969), "Adult education is the process whereby persons who no longer (or did not) attend school on a regular and full time basis undertake sequential and organised activities within or conscious intention of bringing about changes in information, knowledge understanding or skills, appreciation and attitudes or for the purpose of identifying and solving personal or community problems."

The International Commission on the Development of Education (1972) in their report '*Learning To BC*' (1972) defined adult education as, "The normal culmination of the education process is adult education."

UNESCO in an *International Conference on the Development of Adult Education* (1976) explained the meaning of adult education as, "The term Adult education denotes the entire body of organised educational process, whatever content, level and method, whether formal or otherwise, whether they prolong or replace education in schools, colleges and universities as well as in apprenticeship, whereby persons regarded as adults by the society to which they belong develop their abilities, enrich their knowledge, improve their technical or professional qualifications and bring about changes in their attitudes or behaviour in the two-fold perspective of full personal development and participates in balanced and independent social, economic and cultural development. It is an integral part of life-long education and learning."

A perusal of the above definition indicates that the definition and meaning of adult education is the same as that of education except that it relates to adults. It is a broad and comprehensive definition.

According to Bryson, "Adult education includes all activities and educational purposes carried on in ordinary business of life by people who use only part of their energy to acquire intellectual development."

"Adult education is education given on part-time basis and given, therefore, concurrently with work and the earning of a living." Earnest Baker.

In the words of Morgan and Holmes, "Adult education may be thought as the conscious effort of mature persons to learn something new."

Reense, Fenster and Houle state, "Adult education may be concerned with any or more of three aspects of an individual's life, his work life, his personal life and his life as a citizen."

S.N. Mukerjee defines adult education as to "include all instruction, formal and informal imparted to adults."

'*A Handbook of Adult Education Instructors*' (1980) published by the Ministry stated the meaning of adult education as "Adult education is a package of educational programme for adults outside the formal educational system aiming at providing more information and both knowledge and skills for improving their life-style and also earning capacity."

Summing Up

Adult education may be defined as a package of educational programmes for adults for developing Three's *i.e.*, Reading, Writing, Arithmetic (Literacy), Rights—Responsibilities—Relationships and Recreation.

Nomenclature of Adult Education

Adult Education, Adult Functional Literacy, Basic Education (In the World Context), Community Education, Continuous Education, Fundamental Education, Life Long Education, Non-Formal Education, Professional Upgrading and Social Education. All these terms, by and large, connote the same meaning. In a wider context, all these terms are used to prepare the adult for an appropriate civic, economic, political and social role. In adult education, 'learning', 'working' and 'living' are inseparable. Adult education is not co-terminus with schooling but takes place in work and life situations.

NEED FOR AND OBJECTIVES OF ADULT EDUCATION

Some of the important factors which call for the promotion of adult education are given here.

1. *Development and enrichment of an individual.* Through adult education, deficiencies in earlier formal education must be made good.

2. *Participation in social life.* Adult education should enable every adult

to be able to equip himself or herself to play as full part as he or she wishes to take in social and civic life.

3. *Strengthening national integration.* It can also be a means of creating better understanding.

4. *Development of worthy leisure time activities.* Adult education is needed to enable every adult to have the opportunity of discovering how he or she can most satisfyingly and recreatively use his or her leisure.

5. *Preservation and promotion of culture.* Adult education is needed for the preservation and promotion of culture.

6. *Mutual tolerance.* Adult education is needed to promote international understanding, mutual sympathy and tolerance of different points of view and to put every adult in the way of arriving at the truth.

7. *Adult education and vocational efficiency.* Adult education should enable everyone to study his or her role as a parent and member of a community; as a wage earner and as a responsible citizen. It must also give opportunities for vocational employment.

8. *Adult literacy and economic growth.* Adult literacy, an essential element in overall development, must be closely linked to economic and social priorities and to present and future manpower needs.

9. *Awakening in the people of an appreciation of Five-Year Plans.* One of the essential functions of adult education is to awaken in the people an appreciation of the significance of the country's Five-Year Plans and to enthuse them for participation in it.

10. *Adult education for a changing world.* The development of the modern world, the accession to independence of a large number of countries, the need for the real emancipation of people and for the increasingly active and productive participation in the economic, social and political life of human society, of the hundreds of millions of illiterate adults still existing in the world, make it essential to change national education policies.

11. *Knowledge of the basic skills.* It is an important and traditional function of adult education to bring knowledge to the people especially the knowledge which concerns them deeply, e.g., knowledge of the basic essentials of a healthy life, civic education, etc. As a large part of the Indian population is illiterate, literacy has become one of the most important programmes of social education and is an index of its progress.

12. *Improvement in the quality of leadership and followership.* Men everywhere function in group and a distinctive group is a cluster of people around a leader. The quality of a group is therefore largely a product of its leadership and if the Indian people have to justify their aspirations, this can be done only by improving the quality of leadership in the villages and towns of India. This is a responsibility which adult education alone can shoulder.

13. *Benefits of new knowledge.* Since India has resolved to recover her place in technology in response to the demands of modern times, it is the

function of adult education to serve as a smooth and effective channel between centres of research and the homes and hamlets in which the common people live. It aims to bring down to the people the benefits of new knowledge that is being continually created in laboratories and also the knowledge that is already there, but is not available to them.

14. *Achievement of the objectives of Universal Elementary Education (UEE).* An educated adult is quite sensitive to the importance of promoting UEE of the children under his care and charge.

15. *Accelerating National Development.* The last but not the least significant objective of adult education is to accelerate national development.

The Adult Education Policy Statement (1978) very rightly observed, "Exclusion of a vast majority of the people from the process of education is the most disturbing aspect of educational and social planning. This has been uppermost in the consideration of the Government. While determined effort must be made to universalise elementary education up to the age of 14 years, educational facilities must be extended to adult population to remedy their educational deprivation and to enable them to develop their potentiality. Indeed, universalisation of elementary education and of adult literacy are mutually interdependent."

MAJOR EFFORTS MADE IN INDIA FOR THE PROMOTION OF ADULT EDUCATION

1. Issue of Adult Policy Statement (1978)
2. National Adult Education Programme (1978)
3. National Literacy Mission-NLM (1988)
4. Sarva Shiksha Abhiyan – SSA (Education for All)
5. Grant to Non-Governmental Organisations (NGO's)

Issue of Adult Policy Statement (1978)

The policy statement outlined the philosophy of adult education as the assumptions (a) that illiteracy is a serious impediment to an individual's growth and to the country's socio-economic progress; (b) that education is not co-terminus with schooling but takes place in most work and life situations; (c) that learning, working and living are inseparable and each acquires a meaning only when correlated with the others; (d) that the means by which people are involved in the process of development are at least as important as the ends; and (e) that the illiterate and the poor can rise to their own liberation through literacy, dialogue and action."

National Adult Education Programme

NAEP was launched in October 2, 1978. It was proposed to cover the entire population in the age group 15-35 by the end of 1983-1984.

NATIONAL LITERACY MISSION – NLM (1988)

Components of the NLM

(1) Literacy	(2) Functional Literacy	(3) Awareness	(4) Development and Improvement

Components of the NLM

1. *Literacy*: Making literate 80 million
2. *Functional Literacy*: The Mission has prescribed certain levels in the three Rs to be achieved by the target groups.

Reading Norms: As far as reading is concerned, a person, to be declared a literate, must be able to read aloud a simple passage at a speed of 30 words per minute. While reading silently small paragraph in simple language, a speed of 35 words per minute should be achieved.

The neo-literates must also be able to read and understand road signs, posters, simple instructions and newspapers specially produced for them. Ability to follow simple written messages relating to one's working and living environment is another requisite attribute.

Writing Norms: In respect of writing, the Mission has laid down that a neo-literature should be able to 'copy with understanding at a speed of seven words per minute.' He should be able to take dictation at five words per minute. He should be able to write with proper spacing and alignment. He should also be able to write independently short letters, application and terms of day-to-day use.

Arithmetic Norms: Proficiency in numerals has also been laid down. The new learner must be able to read and write 1 to 100. He should also be able to do 'simple calculations without fraction involving addition, subtraction up to three digits and multiplication and visions by two digits.'

The Mission also expects the neo-literates to have a working knowledge of metric units of weights, measures, currency, distance and area, and units of time. They should also have a broad idea of proportion and interest (without involving fractions) and their use in working and living conditions.

3. *Awareness*: Enabling the adults to be aware of the causes of their deprivation and moving towards amelioration of their condition through organisation, and participation in the process of development;

4. *Development and Improvement*: Acquiring skills to improve the economic status and general well-being; Imbibing the values of national integration, conservation of the environment, women's equality, observance of small family norm, etc.

Strategy of Achieving Objectives

Main features of the strategy are:

1. Increasing motivation of the learner by taking up learner need-based programmes.

2. Securing people's participation through media and communication, creation of local participatory structures, taking out of 'jathas', training of cadres of youth, etc. These efforts are expected to create an environment conducive to learning.

3. Increasing significantly the involvement of Voluntary Agencies.

4. Improving substantially on-going programmes.

5. Launching mass movement by involving educational institutions, teachers, students, youth, military and paramilitary personnel, housewives, ex-servicemen, employers, trade unions, etc.

6. Institutionalising continuing education for post-literacy, particularly through establishment of Jana Shikshan Nilayams and better use of existing institutional facilities.

7. Universalising the outreach by providing facilities for literacy learning, continuing education and vocational training.

8. Undertaking technology demonstration in 40 districts for development, transfer and application of technology pedagogic inputs and thereafter covering more districts after evaluating the results.

Integrated Approach to Literacy

Under the revised NLM scheme, an integrated approach to literacy is being followed since April 2000. The new approach envisages the integration of the activities of basic teaching-learning with post-literacy activities to ensure a smooth transition from TLC to Post-Literacy Programmes (PLP).

Coverage under NLM

The NLM has covered 96.64 million persons under various adult literacy schemes up to December, 2001. At present, out of 593 districts in the country, 160 districts are covered under TLC, 264 under PLC (including 30 under the Rural Functional Literacy Programme) and 152 under the Continuing Education Programme. NLM is now engaged in the task of imparting functional literacy to persons in the 15-35 age group and has set the following medium-term goal for itself.

Goals for Literacy

To achieve a sustainable threshold literacy level of 75 per cent by 2005.

Jan Shikshan Sansthan

The Jan Shikshan Sansthan scheme, which started in 1988, is meant to promote educational, vocational and occupational development of literates, neo-literates,

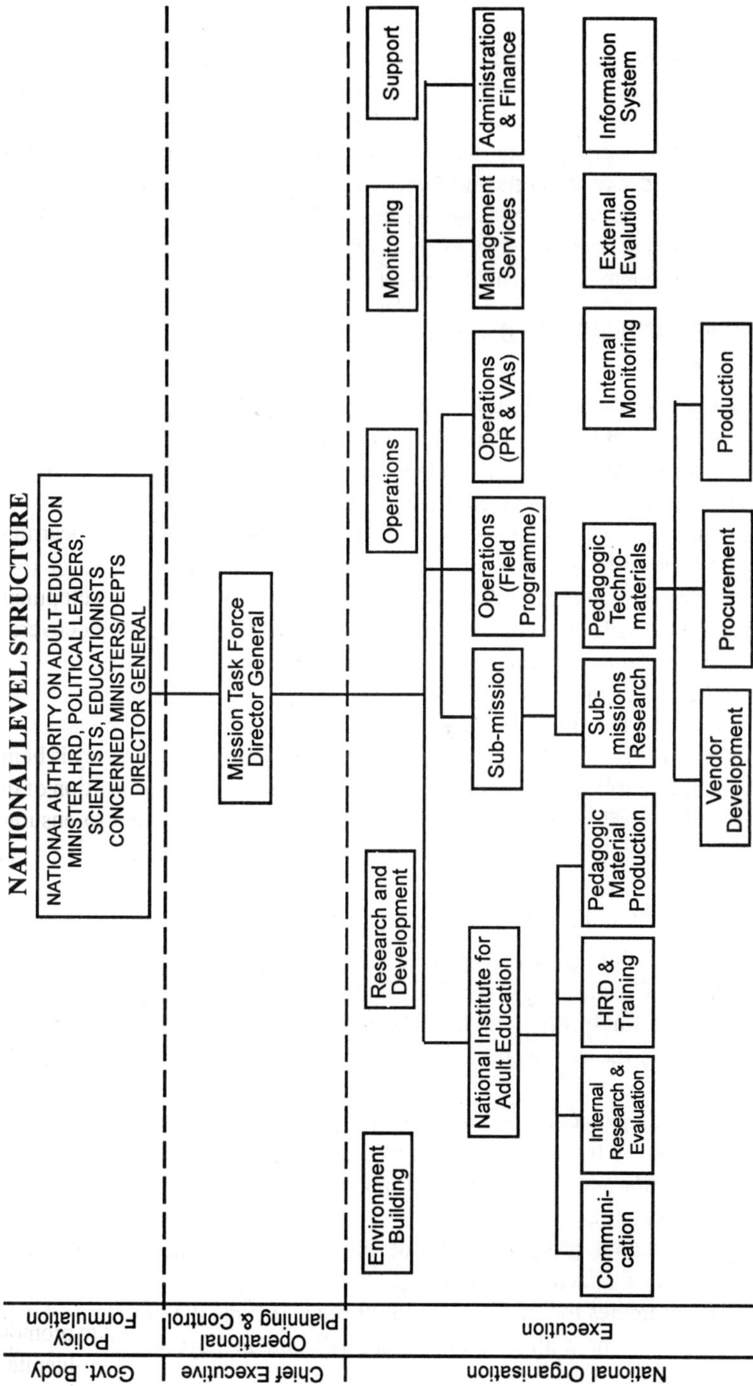

Fig. 12.1: National Level Structure Under NLM

semi-literates and un-lettered persons. These act as Resource Support Agencies especially in regard to organising vocational training and skill development programmes. During the Ninth Plan, the scheme has been strengthened with enhanced funding and a wider scope and area of operation. The focus of the scheme is now shifting from industrial workers in urban areas to the socio-economically backward and educationally disadvantaged groups in urban and rural areas, such as neo-literates, semi-literates, SCs/STs, women and girls, slum dwellers, migrant workers, etc. A total of 108 Jan Shikshan Sansthans have been set up in the country, of which 50 were set up in the Ninth Plan period.

NPE (1986 AND MODIFIED 1992) ON THE SCOPE OF ADULT EDUCATION

The revised National Policy on Education (1992) has set out the scope of adult education in India in Paras 4.12, 4.13 and 4.14. It is to be so planned and implemented that it is "geared to the national goals such as alleviation of poverty, national integration, environmental conservation, observation of the small family norms, promotion of women's equality universalisation of primary education, basic health care, etc. It will also facilitate energisation of the cultural creativity of the people and their active participation in development process." The NPE also observed that the "critical development issue is the continustion of upgradation of skills so as to produce manpower resources of the kind and the number required by the society. Special emphasis will, therefore, be laid on organisation and employment/self-employment and need and interest based vocational and skill training programme."

From above it is quite clear that the scope of adult education is as vast as life itself. In fact, scope of adult education covers all the dimensions of education. Of course, there would be differences in content, approach and methods of adult education which suit the adults.

The scope of adult education, thus, includes the following dimensions:

1. Liquidation of illiteracy, *i.e.*, giving a reasonable mastery of the tools of learning—reading, writing, simple arithmetic and to create an interest in knowledge. The target according to the NPE is the eradication of illiteracy, particularly in the age group 15-35.
2. Providing comprehensive programmes of post-literacy and continuing education for neo-literates and youth who have received primary education with a view to enabling them to retain and upgrade their literary skills.
3. Undertaking programmes for developing a proper sense of rights and duties of citizens in democracy.
4. Programmes for enabling the adults to understand the functions of the Government at all levels *i.e.*, from Village Panchayats to the Central Government.

5. Programmes providing a brief outline of our cultural heritage and activities.
6. Programme related to citizenship training.
7. Programmes related to cooperative movement and values of cooperative work.
8. Programmes related to development of skills in various areas concerning the adult's occupations and vocations.
9. Programmes related to health and sanitation.
10. Programmes related to the development of scientific temperament.
11. Organising recreational activities.
12. Environmental education.
13. Population education.
14. Sex education.
15. AIDS education.
16. Prohibition.
17. International understanding.
18. Latest developments in science and technology which affect them in particular.

Sarva Shiksha Abhiyan: SSA (Education for All). SSA announced on August 15, 2000 contains two components (i) Elementary Education for All (ii) Adult Education.

Adult Education: It includes (i) Attainment of full literacy in age group 15-35 by 2005.

(ii) Special focus on promotion of literacy among women, Scheduled Castes/Tribes and Backward Classes.

Agencies for the Promotion of Adult Education and Continuing Education

(1)	(2)	(3)	(4)
Educational Institutional (i) Schools (ii) Colleges (iii) Universities (iv) Education Boards	Non-Government Organisations	State Directorates of Adult Education	Directorate of Adult Education Government of India

THE ROLE OF SCHOOLS AND UNIVERSITIES IN ADULT EDUCATION

The Role of Schools in Adult Education

From time to time attempts have been made to involve students in adult education programmes but results are not very encouraging primarily because plans in this regard were sporadic, lacked commitment and direction. It is a matter of great concern that we have not made concerted efforts to channelise the energy of the students towards this constructive work.

The Central Board of Secondary Education, Delhi has made a valuable contribution to this area. In pursuance of the objectives of National Literacy Mission (NLM), Government of India, the Central Board of Secondary Education took up a programme from the academic session 1991-92 beginning with classes IX and X as a special measure to remove illiteracy through mass involvement of students. This has been termed as Special Literacy Drive (SALD). The SALD has been made an integral part of the prescribed curriculum and incorporated in work experience as an essential component.

Role of Universities in Adult Education

The Education Commission (1964-66) made significant remarks about the changed role of the universities: "The walls which divide the 'gown' and the 'town' have crumbled and the life of the university and the community can be vitally linked for their mutual enrichment." In this regard it further observed, "Universities in our country must take upon themselves much larger share in the community for educating adults."

The UGC Policy Statement of 1977 clearly underlined this need. In 1982, it revised its guidelines on continuing Adult Education and observed that the universities and colleges should launch a national campaign for eradicating illiteracy which was the first step in rural development. By way of illustration, UGC has suggested the following target groups for adult literacy:

(i) Women in particular.
(ii) Scheduled Castes and Scheduled Tribes.
(iii) School Drop-outs.
(iv) Unemployed and out of school groups.
(v) Workers in the unorganised sectors.

The country's large number of universities and equivalent institutions and colleges are an important part of the voluntary efforts to eradicate illiteracy. Some of the universities like the Gujarat Vidyapith and Rural Institute of Gandhigram have done a considerable amount of work in this area.

In 1986, the Government of India launched a programme involving students under the National Service Scheme (NSS) in adult literacy and education programmes.

ROLE OF VOLUNTARY ORGANISATIONS IN ADULT EDUCATION

The Education Commission 1964-66 recognised the vital role of voluntary agencies in the field of adult education and recommended that they should be given every encouragement, financial and technical. The National Literacy Mission envisages a big role of the voluntary agencies in the adult education programmes. The Ministry of Human Resource Development, Government of India expects that voluntary agencies would play an important role in adult education through the following programmes and accordingly provides financial grant and other help.

1. Running of TLC, PLPs and continuing education programmes.
2. Establishing Jana Shikshan Nilayams (Libraries for Neo-literates).
3. Organising functional literacy component in developmental programmes like health care, women's development, environmental conservation, SC and ST development.
4. Organising vocational and technical programmes leading to development of such skills as may be relevant to the needs of the adults.
5. Undertaking programmes of innovation, experimentation, learner evaluation etc., in this field.
6. Helping in the creation of environment conducive to adult learning through support to mass media, folk and traditional media and Vigyan Jathas etc.
7. Training youth and animators to facilitate implementation of NLM.
8. Taking up varied programmes for women's development and eradication of female illiteracy.
9. Organising conferences, seminars and symposia on adult education.
10. Undertaking publication of literature on adult education.
11. Undertaking such other activities as may be appropriate for the achievement of NAM.

A Word of Caution About Voluntary Agencies. A few years ago, an official evaluation of the Voluntary Agencies/Non-government Organisations working in the field of adult education came up with the disturbing fact that out of the 382 agencies, the work of only 27 could be rated as "entirely satisfactory". The work of 116 other agencies was 'also satisfactory but required improvements to be made." The bonafides of several agencies were found to be doubtful.

Pattern of Grant by the Centre.

(i) Administration cost : 75 per cent and (2) Permanent Costs : 100 per cent.

ILLITERACY AND ITS ERADICATION

Illiteracy is a curse. It is a great hindrance in individual and national development. Adult illiteracy is an important hindrance in the achievement of the aim of UEE.

Table 12.1: Illiteracy Rate in India since Independence

Census year	*Total*	*Males*	*Females*	*Male-Female Gap*
1951	81.67	72.84	91.14	81.7
1961	71.70	59.60	84.65	74.95
1971	65.55	54.04	78.02	76.02
1981	56.43	43.62	70.24	73.38
1991	47.79	35.87	60.71	75.16
2001	34.62	24.15	45.84	78.31

Notes: 1. Illiteracy Rates for 1951, 1961 and 1971 Census relate to population aged 5 years and above. The rates for the 1981, 1991 and 2001 Census related to the population aged 7 years and above. 2. Computed from 2001 Census Report.

Table 12.2: No. of Literates and Illiterates (1991 and 2001)

Literates/Illiterates	*Persons* (Total of Males and Females)	*Males*	*Females*
Literates			
1991	358,402,626	228,983,134	129,419,492
2001	562,010,743	336,969,695	225,041,048
Increase in 2001 over 1991	203,608,117	107,986,561	95,621,556
Illiterates			
1991	328,167,288	128,099,211	200,068,077
2001	296,208,952	106,654,066	189,554,886
Decrease in 2001 over 1991	31,938,536	21,445,145	10,513,191

Observation. In 2001, there were more than 296 million illiterates in India, During the period 1991 and 2001 nearly 203 million people could be made literate. It is, therefore, very difficult to achieve the target of SSA.

Table 12.3: Comparative Data on Adult Literacy Rates : India *vis-à-vis* Select Countries (2000)

Sl. No.	*Country*	*Total(%)*	*Males(%)*	*Females(%)*
1.	Afghanistan	38	51	21
2.	Australia	99	99	99
3.	Bangladesh	41	52	29
4.	Bhutan	47	61	34
5.	Canada	99	99	99
6.	China	85	92	77
7.	Denmark	99	99	99
8.	Egypt	55	67	44
9.	Germany	99	99	99
10.	India	56	69	42
11.	Japan	99	99	99
12.	Myanmar	85	89	81
13.	Nepal	41	59	24
14.	Pakistan	43	58	28
15.	Russian Federation	99	99	99
16.	Sri Lanka	92	94	89
17.	U.K.	99	99	99
18.	U.S.A.	99	99	99

Note: Adult Literacy implies percentage of persons (Males and Females) aged 15 and above who can read and write.
(Source : UNICEF)

CAUSES OF SLOW PROGRESS IN ADULT EDUCATION AND MEASURES FOR THE EXPANSION OF ADULT EDUCATION

Following are the important reasons for slow growth:

1. Apathy of adults towards adult education programmes as they do not seem to be convinced that such programmes can bring about appreciable changes in their earnings.

2. Feeling among the uneducated adults that it is too late to learn to read and write. They feel shy of learning at an advanced age.

3. The problem of earning being so acute that the adults do not have sufficient time or energy to come to the class for receiving instruction. They are too occupied with their own problems and find it extremely hard to get out of this cobweb.

4. The adults are very often indifferent towards adult education. They consider it as useless, sheer waste of money, time and energy.

5. Social customs and traditions put such demands upon the time of adults that they are unable to attend classes regularly.

6. The rural uneducated adults are submerged in superstitions and ignorance.

7. There is a dearth of suitably trained, sincere and selfless workers in the field.

8. Government has also failed to arouse consciousness among the people. People's participation is also conspicuous by its absence.

9. There is a great shortage of appropriate literature an equipment on the subject.

10. The officers and workers lack the spirit of social service. Even its organisation is faulty.

11. The funds earmarked for adult education are too inadequate, and whatever little has been set aside, it is not being utilised profitably.

12. The scheme has been enforced from top to bottom, from the government to the people. It does not originate with the people.

13. There is lack of research in basic vocabulary and methodology for educating the adults.

14. Caste system is proving a great hindrance. People need different centres for various castes. This is not possible.

15. Very little coordination exists among the different agencies engaged in adult education work. Very often there is duplication of work at most of the places.

16. No follow-up work is being taken up by any organisation with the result that in its absence the people lapse into illiteracy again.

17. A large number of the centres exist in name only.

18. Lack of interest in adult education by political parties with the result that they themselves do not organise adult education programmes and take little interest in it.

Measures for the Promotion of Adult Education

1. Giving top priority by the Central and State Governments to adult education.

2. Creation of proper environment in the country for adult education.

3. Involvement of students on a large scale in literacy programmes.

4. Fixing responsibility of industrial establishments—big and small to provide literacy to their workers. Likewise agricultural farms may be made responsible.

5. Making obligatory on the national and state political parties to run a number of literacy centres and on this basis also giving them recognition.

6. Preparing adult literacy booklets in regional languages and including appropriate instructional material.

7. Establishment of reading rooms and libraries for adults at suitable places.

8. Use of electronic media on a large scale.

9. Providing some sort of incentives to neo-literates.

10. Giving functional literacy training to adult education personnel.

11. Fixing flexible timings for adult literacy classes.

12. Monitoring effectively all adult literacy programmes.

13. Ensuring that enrolment data are genuine so that a pragmatic policy is evolved.

14. Cutting down top-heavy bureaucratic establishment and making the optimum use of funds earmarked for adult literacy.

15. Financing only adult literacy centres and not adult education centres involving heavy expenditure. Social education centres in general have failed to generate appropriate environment.

16. Involving Village Panchayats in adult literacy work and making them responsible for giving grant-aid to voluntary organisations. All funds earmarked for this purpose should be put at the disposal of the Village Panchayats. No financial grant to voluntary organisations should be given directly by the Central Government.

Summing Up: A perusal of Table 12.3 clearly illustrates that India is far behind the developing countries in respect of adult education/literacy. It must be remembered that an illiterate population cannot compete with the developed economies of the literate population. Concerted efforts have to be made in India for the liquidation of illiteracy.

13

Quality Control in Higher Education

MEANING OF QUALITY CONTROL IN EDUCATION

Although, quality in education has become the touchstone of education, especially higher education, yet it has not been defined precisely. Terms like quality in higher education, efficiency, effectiveness and standards in education are very bewildering and deny all efforts to define and explain them in a uniform way. It is sometimes stated, "You cannot define these terms but you understand when you observe." Quality or standard of education is not the same as satisfying a customer, for example, with the latest model of a motor car. In the document published by the Higher Education Quality Council, it is observed, "Quality in higher education embraces, but is not synonymous with effectiveness, efficiency and accountability." Sometimes it is said that in the education sector much of the discussion and debate which was hitherto focused on standards has now shifted to quality.

The University Education Commission (1948-49) used the term 'standard' and not 'quality'.

The term 'standard' usually means a basis for measurement or a 'yardstick' to describe a required characteristic or a parameter and this would vary from country to country, from time to time and even from institution to institution over a period of time. However, it is also true that once the standards are set, the institutions and individuals can try to achieve quality so as to attain excellence.

Wider Concept of Quality in Education: The quality in education need to be defined in the wider sense of the overall aim of education as the all round development of the individual and his commitment to social objectives; and viewed in this context, there is no doubt that vigorous efforts will have to be made to improve these to suit the changing needs of the country. It has become increasingly evident that the relevance of education, its significance, its validity for personal aspiration, its link with societal needs and goals, its efficiency and impact are the basic parameters of every educational system.

Narrow View of Quality in Education: According to narrow interpretation, educational standards are judged from examination results. An educational institution that shows high pass percentage is considered to be an institution of great standard or quality.

No Single Measure to Assess the Quality/Standards in Education: Educational output unlike industrial outputs which are tangible and standardised, is extraordinarily an imprecise and slippery connotation. Since outputs vary with variation in institutional objectives, there can be no single measure of outputs and consequently of their quality. Outputs include all the residual learnings, skills, insights attitudes, styles of thinking—all the developed aptitudes and capabilities that a student carries from the educational system beyond what he brought to it, initially from home or elsewhere. Taking students coming out of an educational institution as its outputs, their quality can be considered from the following variable or characteristics.

1. Percentage of passing students in terms of divisions and distinctions secured.
2. The magnitude of wastage and retention.
3. The age earning profiles of the qualified students.
4. Achievement of students in the domain of co-curricular activities lie athletics, dramatics, debates, etc.
5. Admission of students into reputed institutions or professions etc.

Quality of what students learn or more correctly, what they carry with them out of an institution, is largely dependent upon the variables like (i) students—their ability, interest, level of motivation, family background, attitudes, expectancies, etc., (ii) teachers—their qualities and qualifications, and (iii) equipments which students and teaches, are given to work with. Given the same level of other facilities to an identical group of students in two different institutions, one institution significantly excels the other because of its teacher competencies, calibre and professional responsibility.

WHY QUALITY CONTROL IN HIGHER EDUCATION?

Highlighting the importance of the quality in higher education for socio-economic development, Prof. V.N. Rajasekharan Pillai, former Director, NAAL (National Assessment and Accreditation Council) in convocation address of North Maharashtra University, Jalgaon on March 3, 2003 pointed out the need for quality control as given below.

Accountability

Why do we need quality in higher education? The question is answered by the word "accountability". This answer immediately provokes a second question "accountable to whom?" There are several answers to this question because higher education (from whole universities to colleges, departments and individual teachers) is accountable to at least three different groups – society (government), clients (students, employers) and subject (profession, colleagues).

Accountability to Society

There is a popular demand and an economic necessity for more higher education. Society pays for much of this through taxes. Government acts for society in distributing funds to higher education either directly to the universities or indirectly through student grants or loans. Governments have a responsibility to society to ensure that what they 'buy' from higher education is acceptable and provides value for money. Governments all over the world have established agencies concerned with quality and efficiency in higher education.

However, accountability to society is not only a matter of return or investment. Universities and colleges exist to safeguard and transmit a cultural heritage. Society needs assurance that universities are not failing in this duty also. This is also very much a part of quality assurance.

Some institutions are of higher quality than others. How should the available funds be allocated? Should higher levels of funding go to institutions of higher quality? (a reward to encourage all institutions to do better) or to institutions with lower quality in order to raise them, at least to an acceptable threshold standard. The latter option is the one to be more supported in a country like ours where the institutions are deprived of quality for want of support from the state. As the funds to be distributed are finite, the danger is that institutions assessed of having lower quality are deprived of funds, possibly driving quality even lower. Need-based funding has to be there and there should be mechanisms to find out the ground realities causing deterioration of quality. There should be provisions for remedying them. In the case of quality institutions, there should be initiatives for sustaining and promoting them and helping them to achieve much higher levels of quality.

Accountability to Clientle and Subjects

The clients in higher education are the students and the employers of graduates. They desire to have the best possible education available and then to receive certification that particular levels of knowledge and professional competence have been really achieved.

Coming to accountability to the subject, profession and colleagues, we have to ensure that knowledge, skills and attitudes which comprise each subject must not be distorted, suppressed or injured. Teaches are accountable to their professional colleagues that the integrity of their discipline is upheld and that students develop positive attitudes towards their subject and its use in society. (*University News, July 7-13, 2003)*

1. *Quality of the Staff*: This implies—

(a) Acceptable social and financial status of teachers.

(b) A will to reduce inequalities such as relating to gender.

(c) A concern to manage the staff in accordance with the merit principle.

(d) A desire to provide them with the in-service training as they need to fulfill their role in a changing society.

(e) A system of the establishment of incentives and structures to encourage research to work in multidisciplinary teams and thematic projects, thus breaking with the habit of exclusively solitary scientific work.

2. *Quality of Curricula*: This implies—

(a) Taking special care in the definition of the objectives of the training provided in relation to the requirements of the world of work and the needs of the society.

(b) Adaptation of teaching methods to make students more active and to develop an enterprising spirit in them.

(c) Expansion and greater flexibility in training so as to make the full use of the possibilities afforded by information technology (IT).

(d) Internationalisation and networking of curricula, students and teachers.

3. *Quality of the Students who Constitute the Raw Material of Higher Education*: It is dependent upon—

(a) Giving special attention to their problems of access in the light of the criteria related to merit (abilities and motivation).

(b) Adopting proactive policies for the benefit of the disadvantaged.

(c) Undertaking exchanges with secondary education and with the bodies involved in the transition from secondary to higher education to ensure that education is an unbroken chain.

(d) Regulating admissions (Discussed separately)

4. *Quality of Infrastructure*: This implies—

(i) Provision of well-equipped libraries and reading rooms.

(ii) Adequate use and development of Information Technology.

(iii) Provision of guidance and counselling.

(iv) Provision of Co-curricular activities.

(v) University libraries to be greatly improved by:

  (a) larger annual grants;

  (b) the introduction of the open access system;

  (c) longer hours of work;

  (d) better organisation; and

  (e) a well trained staff which should include reference assistants; and

  (f) The laboratories to be improved in buildings, fittings, equipment, workshops and technicians.

5. *Methodology of Teaching*: The University Education Commission (1948-49) made the following recommendations which are still valid to-day—

(1) Lectures to be carefully planned and supplemented by tutorials, library work and written exercise;

(2) No prescribed textbooks for any courses of study;

(3) Attendance at lectures be compulsory for undergraduate students as a present, and that private candidates of only certain categories be allowed to appear for public examinations. An experiment should, however, be made with evening colleges for working people;

(4) Tutorial instruction to be developed in all institutions imparting

university education in the following manner:

(a) Students should report to tutors in groups not exceeding 6 in number;
(b) Tutorials should be made available to under-graduates both pass and honours;
(c) Tutorials should stimulate the mental development of students and should not become mere coaching for examinations;
(d) If tutorials are to succeed, the teaching staff should be improved in quality;

6. *Systematic Evaluation.* This entails inculcating a culture of evaluation within the institution, *i.e.*, a concern for setting up systems for the gathering of relevant, valid, reliable data so as to improve activities and outcomes.

7. *Quality of Regulation.* It involves developing cultures of autonomy, responsibility and accountability.

8. *Research and Innovation.* It is high time that when there is scarcity of financial resources, in no case superfluous and repetitive research should be undertaken. It should be relevant and need-based.

9. *International Collaboration.* Impact and needs of globalisation of education should be given due consideration.

10. *Admission Capacity etc.*

(i) To avoid overcrowding at universities and colleges, the maximum number in the Arts and Science faculties of a teaching university be fixed at 3,000 and in an affiliated college at 1,500;
(ii) The number of working days be substantially increased to ensure a minimum of 180 in the year, exclusive of examination days; with three terms, each of about 11 weeks' duration;
(iii) Expansion of facilities in Higher Education

One of the most important features of educational development in the post independence period has been the very rapid expansion of professional education in engineering, medicine and agriculture and of science courses for the first and second degrees. This was necessitated by the programmes for economic development undertaken in the first three plans. By and large, the expansion has outstripped the facilities available in real terms and has consequently had an adverse effect on standards. At the same time, there has also been rapid expansion in arts and commerce courses at the first degree level. But this has been dictated, not by the enrolment capacity of the institutions or the employment opportunities, but by the pressure of public demand which has increased immensely... In these courses, an attempt has generally been made to manipulate the facilities to meet the demand for higher education rather than to restrict admissions in relation to the facilities available. The effect on standards has been more adverse.

What should be the enrolment policy in higher education during the next twenty years? Our recommendation is that the expansion of facilities in higher education should be planned broadly on the basis of manpower needs and employment opportunities. At present, there is an over-production of this open-door policy; and consequently there is a growing incidence of unemployment amongst them. On the other hand, there is a shortage of professional specialists and there is a consequent need to increase the facilities in professional courses such as agriculture, engineering, medicine, etc., and especially at the post-graduate stage in science and arts.

Selective Admissions: Three main elements needed for operating a programme of selective admissions in higher education are:

1. the determination of the number of places available in an institution in relation to teachers and facilities available to ensure that standards are maintained at an adequate level;
2. prescription of eligibility criteria by the universities; and
3. selection by the institution concerned of the best students from amongst those who are eligible and seek admission.

Quality of Education and Financial Constraints: Monetary inputs are indispensable for qualitative improvement of programmes. But monetary inputs are very often rendered infructuous without the support of non-monetary inputs such as insightful planning and human effort. Therefore, a climate of dedicated and sustained hard work needs to be maintained. Quality of an institution is a function of investment on teaching force as well as on instructional and supporting materials. The appointment of resources varies from institution to institution on the basis of their needs, priorities and programmes. The case studies stressing the hazards of unbalanced resource allocation reported: "If the amount spent on teachers and the amount spent on the tools are seriously out of balance, teachers' productivity and quality of education will suffer."

At a time when education is faced with fiscal stringency and it has to encounter a stiffer and a gloomier future, costs of education have to be weighed against the benefits it accrues. In other words, educational planners and administrators are to be cost and quality conscious.

MAIN FACTORS EXERCISING QUALITY CONTROL IN EDUCATION

(1) Quality of the Staff
(2) Quality of the Curricula
(3) Quality of the Students
(4) Quality of Infrastructure
(5) Methodology of Teaching
(6) Systematic Evaluation
(7) Quality of Regulation
(8) Research and Innovation
(9) Internanational Collaboration
(10) Admission Capacity

ADMINISTRATION AND MANAGEMENT OF HIGHER EDUCATION

The quality of administration and management has a great bearing on the quality of education. The UGC Committee Towards New Educational Management, popularly known as the Gnanam Committee (1987-90) after the name of its Chairman, Professor A. Gnanam, Vice-Chancellor, Bharathidasan University, made the following general recommendations for improving the quality of administration and management of higher education:

(1) Universities are the centres of excellence as also of regional/national development. In the light of current changes and challenges as also the NPE (1986), universities must review their objectives and policies.

(2) The students, teachers, administrators and the society's representatives must be involved in setting the new goals and objectives and fulfilling them.

(3) In deciding the management pattern, it should be recognised that academic administration and management is very different from that in vogue in the governmental or in the corporate system, and it should be based on the principle of participation, decentralisation, autonomy and accountability.

(4) The management pattern of an institution of higher education must necessarily have an in-built flexibility to adapt it quickly to the changing needs of the country and the region it serves and to carry out innovations and experiments.

(5) 'Performance Audit' within the institution must be instituted to apprise the institutions of its own shortcomings and possibilities of improvement.

QUALITY OF HIGHER EDUCATION — NATIONAL ASSESSMENT AND ACCREDITATION COUNCIL (NAAC)

National Assessment and Accreditation Council (NAAC) an autonomous institution of the University Grants Commission (UGC) established in 1994, at Bangalore, has done very useful work in assessing performance of an institution and of its units at the higher education level. It has prepared criteria for assessment of quality education. Naturally this criteria of rating can be used very profitably for institutional improvement and accountability at the higher education level and with some suitable modifications at the school level also. Ratings of institutions serve as incentive for institutional improvement.

Process and Methods Used: NAAC has formulated a three-stage process for assessment and accreditation as given below:

- Preparation of the Self-study Report by the institution/department based on parameters defined by NAAC.
- Validation of the Self-study Report by a team of peers through on-site visit; presentation of detailed quality report to the institution and
- The final decision on assessment and accreditation by the Executive Committee (EC) of NAAC.

Criteria for Assessment: Any assessment and subsequent accreditation is made with reference to a set of parameters so that the standing of an institution can be compared with that of other similar institutions. NAAC has identified the following seven criteria to serve as the basis of its assessment procedures:

— Curricular Aspects
— Teaching-learning and Evaluation
— Research, Consultancy and Extension
— Infrastructure and Learning Resources
— Student Support and Progression
— Organisation and Management
— Healthy Practices

The grade is supplemented by a qualitative report by the team that would highlight the strengths and weaknesses of the institution under various criteria. Institutions which does not attain the minimum 55% points for accreditation, is intimated and notified that the institution is "ASSESSED AND FOUND NOT QUALIFIED FOR ACCREDITATION".

The range of marks of each grade and actual total marks obtained as well as criterion wise are intimated to the institution and notified.

Benefits of the Quality Assessment Programme

Following benefits are claimed for rating institutional performance Rating.

— Helps the institution to know its strengths, weaknesses, opportunities through an informed review.
— Identifies internal areas of planning and resource allocation.
— Enhances collegiality on the campus.
— The outcome of the process provides the funding agencies with objective and systematic database for performance funding.
— Initiate institution into innovative and modern methods of pedagogy.
— Gives the institution a new sense of direction and identity.
— Provides the society with reliable information on the quality of education offered by the institution.
— Provides access to employers to information on standards in recruitment.
— Promotes intra-institutional and inter-institutional interactions.

AUTONOMY IN HIGHER EDUCATION

It is suggested that an increasing number of universities and colleges should be provided autonomy. Following are the main aspects of autonomy.

1. The selection of students;
2. The appointment and promotion of teachers;
3. The determination of courses of study, methods of teaching and the selection of areas and problems of research.

Autonomy for universities is not claimed merely as a matter of right or privilege. The case for it rests on the obvious ground that, without it, universities cannot discharge effectively their principal functions of teaching, research and service to the community and that only an autonomous institution, free from regimentation of ideas and pressure of party power politics can pursue truth fearlessly and build up, in its teachers and students habits of independent thinking and a spirit of enquiry unfettered by the limitations and prejudices.

In considering the question of university autonomy, we must recognise three (somewhat over-lapping) levels, as it were, at which it functions.

1. Autonomy within a university, e.g., autonomy of the departments, college, teachers and students in relation to the university as a whole;
2. Autonomy of a university in relation to the system, e.g., the autonomy of the university in relation to another or in relation to the UGC and the Association of Indian Universities; and
3. Autonomy of the university system as a whole, including the UGC and the Association of Indian Universities in relation to agencies and influences emanating outside that system, the most important of which are the Central and State Governments.

University Finances: University autonomy cannot become real and effective unless adequate provision is made to meet the financial requirements of universities and colleges. While the UGC has been established as an autonomous body to provide the necessary financial resources to the universities without government control or interference. State universities have to depend, for their maintenance grants and matching share, on the funds provided directly by the State Governments. This is an important source through which they can and sometimes do seek to curb the freedom of the universities. This is obviously undesirable.

State Governments should deal with the universities with understanding and imagination and place adequate financial resources at their disposal to enable them to carry out their obligations in an efficient way. It would also be desirable if they seek the advice of the UGC in the matter.

Universities must be free from Government Control: Addressing the 44th Annual Convocation of Delhi University, Dr. L. Mudaliar criticised those who feel that it is their duty to direct, control and otherwise supervise the working of a University and said, "If today it is considered that a university should be treated in the same manner as a department of government or a local body and if a University is to be controlled by the transient personages in authority that rise and fall in a democracy, the future not only of the University but of the country is at stake."

Temple of Learning and University Autonomy: He said, "a University was a temple of learning which the 'iconoclast" could not be allowed to desecrate by introducing methods of control which may find a place in the market-square or the hustings. And yet, the tendency to pay this role among those who believe that they have the democratic authority is great indeed."

Dr. Mudaliar said: "To fix terms of office for the Vice-Chancellor of a University, to determine how he should be selected by a democratic government, to even prescribe condition for his dismissal, to issue directions, controls and various other orders through many a subordinate official of a hierarchy is certainly not the way to allow a university, a temple of learning, to function."

"I do not want to be misunderstood", he added. "There have unfortunately been lapses on the part of some of those who have been in-charge of Universities and who should have known better. Lapses there are in every form of administration and, if anyone were to say there have been no lapses in the political, the economic and the social structures of society, he would be under delusion."

Dr. Mudaliar said: "The fundamental fact has to be realised that as a temple of learning, as far as possible, no hands should desecrate this sacred shrine: no laws should be passed which will make it appear that a University is but a handmaid of the political government of the day."

"In a political democracy, men may come and men may go; fashions may change; slogans may alter and the very objectives of a democratic government, the varied principles that may be laid down by such democracy may vary with the changing moods of democracy. These, however, cannot and should not alter the structure of a temple of learning, and if they do, the future of the country is very much at stake."

QUALITATIVE IMPROVEMENT IN HIGHER EDUCATION — NPE AND PROGRAMME OF ACTION

Significance of Higher Education and the Need for Qualitative Improvement: Higher education provides people with an opportunity to reflect on the critical social, economic, cultural, moral and spiritual issues facing humanity. It contributes to national development through dissemination of specialised knowledge and skills. It is, therefore, a crucial factor for survival. Being at the apex of the educational pyramid, it has also a key role in producing teachers for the educational system.

In the context of the unprecedented explosion of knowledge, higher education has to become dynamic as never before, constantly entering uncharted areas.

Proposed measures:

1. In view of the need to effect an all-round improvement in these institutions, it is proposed that, in the near future, the main emphasis will be on the consolidation of and expansion of facilities in existing institutions.

2. Urgent steps will be taken to protect the system from degradation.

3. In view of mixed experiences with the system of affiliation, autonomous colleges will be helped to develop in large numbers until the affiliating system

is replaced by a freer and more creative association of universities with colleges. Similarly, the creation of autonomous departments, within universities on a selective basis will be encouraged. Autonomy and freedom will be accompanied by accountability.

4. Courses and programmes will be redesigned to meet the demands of specialisation better. Special emphasis will be laid on linguistic competence. There will be increasing flexibility in the combination of courses.

5. State level planning and coordination of higher education will be done through Councils of Higher Education. The UGC and these Councils will develop coordinative methods to keep a watch on standards.

6. Provision will be made for minimum facilities and admission will be regulated according to capacity. A major effort will be directed towards the transformation of teaching methods. Audio-visual aids and electronic equipment will be introduced; development of science and technology, curricula and material, research and teacher orientation will receive attention. This will require preparation of teachers at the beginning of the service as well as continuing education thereafter. Teacher's performance will be assessed systematically. All posts will be filled on the basis of merit.

7. Research in the universities will be provided enhanced support and steps will be taken to ensure in high quality. Suitable mechanisms will be set up by the UGC for coordinating research in the universities, particularly in thrust areas of science and technology, with research undertaken by other agencies. An effort will be made to encourage the setting up of national research facilities within the university system, with proper forms of autonomous management.

8. The open learning system has been initiated in order to augment opportunities for higher education, as an instrument of democratising education and to make it a lifelong process. The flexibility and innovativeness of the open learning system are particularly suited to the diverse requirements of the citizens of our country, including those who had joined the vocational stream.

QUALITATIVE IMPROVEMENT PROGRAMMES FOR HIGHER EDUCATION IN THE TENTH FIVE YEAR PLAN (2002-2007)

All the programmes detailed here are based on the directions contained in the NPE and envisaged in the Programme of Action (1992).

The basic issue of quality improvement would be addressed through the

(i) modernisation of syllabi,
(ii) increased research,
(iii) networking of universities and departments, and
(iv) increased allocation of funds.
(v) networking through local area network (LAN), wide area network (WAN), Information and Library Network (INFLIBNET) would also lead to increased academic activities and research,
(vi) providing autonomy,

(vii) provision of the means to interact across geographical boundaries of institutions,

(viii) improving the infrastructure,

(ix) more rationalised funding of research

(x) *Integrated Multimedia Instructions:* IGNOU has established the Distance Education Council (DEC) to act as the nodal agency for distance education system at the tertiary level. The university has adopted an integrated multimedia instructions strategy consisting of print material and audio-video programmes, supported by counselling sessions at study centres. It manages a dedicated 24-hour satellite TV channel, Gyan Darshan, which beams educational programmes from school to tertiary level 24 hours a day. Preparations are on to launch 40 FM educational radio channels (known as Gyan Vani) under a Memorandum of Understanding with Prasar Bharati. During the Tenth Plan, IGNOU would set up open universities in states where none exist at present, expand the activities of Gyan Darshan and Gyan Vani. The target is to extend the coverage of the open learning system to the backward regions, remote inaccessible areas of the northeast and low female literacy blocks in some of the eastern states.

(xi) *Overseas Contacts in Higher Education:* The Government, in April 2002, constituted the Committee on Promotion of Indian Education Abroad (COPIEA) under the chairmanship of Secretary, Department of Secondary & Higher Education. With the globalisation of the Indian economy, student mobility across national boundaries has increased phenomenally in the higher, technical and management sectors. A large number of foreign educational institutes have also started establishing their presence in India and there is immense potential for Indian educational institutions to set up campuses abroad. The COPIEA will monitor all activities aimed at promoting Indian education abroad and will regulate the operation of foreign educational institutions to safeguard the interests of the students and the larger national interest as well. To this end, a system of registration will be introduced under which institutions will have to furnish information on operations and adhere to certain guidelines relating to publicity, maintenance of standards, charging of fees, granting of degrees etc. The COPIEA would, over a period of time, develop a sectoral policy on foreign direct investment in the education sector.

14

Secondary Education and Its Major Problems: Expansion and Vocationalisation

STRUCTURE AND PROBLEMS OF SECONDARY EDUCATION

See Chapter 2

Expansion of Secondary Education

The Secondary education sector prepares students in the age group 14-18 years for entry into higher education as well as the world of work. The focus in this sector is on reducing disparities, renewal of curricula with emphasis on vocationalisation and employment oriented courses, expansion of the Open Learning System and greater use of new information and communication technologies, particularly computers. The NCERT provides academic and technical support for qualitative improvement.

The Kendriya Vidyalaya Sangathan managed 923 Kendriya Vidyalayas (Central Schools) and Navodaya Vidyalaya Samiti more than 560 institutions in 2004 in predominantly rural areas. The Navodaya Vidyalayas now called Jawahar Navodaya Vidyalayas are fully residential co-educational institutions.

Table 14.1: Expansion of Secondary Education Since 1950-51

Year	*No. of High/Hr.Sec./Inter/Junior Colleges/Pre-degree*	*No. of Students (In Lakhs)*
1950-51	7416	15.0
1960-61	17,257	28.9
1968-69	33,487	61.5
1978-79	46,874	84.1
1988-89	72,635	185.2
1990-91	79,796	249.0
1998-99	1,12,438	277.6
1999-2000	1,16,820	282.1
2001-2002	1,33,000	305.0
2002-2003	1,37,207	332.0

As observed in the Tenth Five Year (2002-2003), "The number is not adequate to accommodate the out-of-school children and the growing number of upper primary school pass outs".

Participation of Private Sector (Including Non-Governmental Organisations-NGOs)

Participation of the private sector has increased. Private organisations currently manage around 51 per cent of Secondary schools and 58 per cent of Higher Secondary schools. Table given below indicates that during 1973-74 to 2001-02, the maximum number of high/higher secondary schools was under private management. The ratio of private managed to government managed varied between 63:37 in 1973-74; 61:39 in 1978-79; 55:45 in 1986-87; 53:47 in 1993-94; 54:46 in 1996-97 and 58:42 in 2001-02.

However, a declining trend in the privately managed schools is observed while Government's share in the management of secondary and higher secondary schools increased to 38.96% in 1996-97 then slightly decreased to 36.16% in 2001-02. Further, the share of private aided high/higher secondary schools receiving annual grant from the government is declining while the percentage of private unaided schools is increasing.

Table 14.2: Percentage of High/Higher Secondary Schools under Different Managements

Year	*Govt.*	*Local Body (LB)*	*Govt. + LB*	*Private Aided*	*Private Un-aided*
1973-74	26.54	10.85	37.39	57.02	5.59
1978-79	30.44	8.71	39.15	57.30	3.55
1986-87	37.49	7.73	45.22	44.79	9.99
1993-94	37.76	9.29	47.05	37.78	15.17
1996-97	38.96	6.74	45.70	36.20	18.10
2001-02*	36.16	6.29	42.45	33.99	23.56

* Provisional

National and State Open Schools

In order to meet the educational needs of those who have not been able to enrol themselves in the formal system opportunities have been provided through the National and State Open Schools, utilising contact centres and multimedia packages.

VOCATIONALISATION OF SECONDARY EDUCATION

Meaning of Vocationalisation

UNESCO, in its recommendation of 1974 defined it as a "Comprehensive term embracing those aspects of the educational process involving, in addition to general education, the study of technologies and related sciences and the acquisition of practical skills, attitudes, understanding and knowledge relating to occupations in the various sectors of economic and social life."

Need for Vocationalisation of Education

It is increasingly being realised that the great need of the hour is to divert our "Single track" education system of the academic type into a double track or multi-track education education to provide diversified vocational courses which really prepare higher secondary students for life, make our education job-oriented and productive. The country's education system is to be re-organised in terms of job-orientation, work experience and development of skills and attitudes that will make for self-employment rather than search for the job. As Rabindranath Tagore has put it "A man may be eminent in book-learning but his education remains incomplete till he has not learnt to put his hand to good and efficient purpose". Mahatma Gandhi also stressed the importance of working with head and hand together. It is high time that we make our education really terminal so that a large majority of our students are prepared for and directed to different walks of life.

The ratio of enrolment in vocational courses at the secondary stage is only about 10 per cent in India as compared with 20% in China, 25% in France, 29% in Italy, 60% in Russia, 65% in U.K. and 80% or more in Switzerland, Denmark and Germany. In this connection, it is of importance to note that the introduction of practical subjects in secondary schools so as to divert the students into different walks of life was recommended as early as 1882 by the Hunter Commission. The report of Abbot Wood in 1937 advocated for a planned and systematic vocational education in this country. The system of basic education as propounded by Mahatma Gandhi in 1937 made education Craft-centred. The Secondary Education Commission 1952-53 recommended the establishment of multi-lateral or multi-purpose schools to provide for diversified courses at the secondary stage. The Education Commission 1964-66 also laid a great stress on vocationalisation of education, especially at the secondary school level to meet the needs of Industry, Agriculture and Trade. The report of the Review Committee on the Curriculum, for the Ten Years School, popularly known as Ishwar Bhai Patel Committee (1977) recommended a compulsory introduction of socially useful productive work. The Plus 2 Committee Report entitled '*Learning To Do—Towards the Learning and Working Society*' on Higher Secondary Education with special reference to vocationalisation, under the Chairmanship of Malcom S. Adiseshiah (1978) recommended the introduction of socially useful productive work at the school stage and also made important recommendations for the voctionalisation of the higher secondary education. The report pleaded very strongly to give serious thought to the effective implementation of this very important aspect of education, i.e., relating education to productivity.

The rate of unemployment has continued to increase with the rapid expansion of educational facilities. The maladjustment between the supply and demand of educated persons is likely to assume unmanageable proportions unless effective steps are from now onwards. The discontent and frustration among our educated youth is clearly visible in their very irrational acts like tearing degree certificates in the University convocation functions.

The Plus 2 Committee or the Adiseshiah Report (1978) outlined the philosophy of vocationalisation as, "In a country where industrial and agricultural production is growing, where the application of science and technology opens up diverse fields of activity, where commerce and trade and a large variety of public services are expanding rapidly, there must be an adequate supply of personnel for the higher administrative and professional levels, but there is a crucial middle level of manpower trained in certain specific competencies without which neither production can be increased nor services improve. If health services have to function and benefit the common man, the doctor alone can achieve nothing, unless the drugs, and instruments are manufactured and hospital facilities established to reach every nook and corner of the country. This focuses or attention on the variety and number of technical people manning of the productive medical enterprises on the one hand, and a host of paramedical and technical people who make it possible for a hospital to function from those who take the X-ray or conduct pathological tests to operation theatre technicians, physiotherapists, orthopaedic assistants, and so on. In agriculture, commerce and the string of cultural and welfare services, this middle-level personnel is of the utmost importance for the very existence of a modern society. Deficiencies, either in number or in training of personnel for these vocations, lead to poor maintenance of equipment, material and services, to frustration for the users and high infructuous costs to the country.

In India, although agriculture is and will remain for decades to be the mainstay of our economy, we have in the past been concerned mainly with industry-cum-oriented vocations. Facilities and services in rural areas have remained generally backward so that the city-trained doctors, engineers and even technicians do not find it sufficiently attractive to settle and serve in the rural areas. Special attention, therefore, has to be given to raising the facilities and quality of life in the rural area, which implies development of particularly those vocations which have the potential of better utilization of rural agricultural resources from the servicing of tractors, tube-wells or other machinery to vocations such as those based on dairy/fruit/vegetable/ horticulture/medical plant/products, or those connected with rural health/ educational/cultural services. Therefore, in a sense, vocational education has the potential of enabling us to really move towards equitable sharing of benefits of economic development towards social justice and socialism."

The National Policy on Education, 1986 as modified in 1992 has pointed out the importance and philosophy of vocationalisation in these words, "The introduction of systematic, well planned and rigorously implemented programmes of vocational education is crucial in the proposed educational reorganisation. These elements are meant to develop a healthy attitude amongst students towards work and life, to enhance individual employability, to reduce the mis-match between the demand and supply of skilled manpower, and to provide an alternative for those intending to pursue higher education without particular interest or purpose. Efforts will be made to provide children at the higher secondary level with generic vocational courses which cut across several occupational fields and which are not occupation specific."

MERITS OF VOCATIONALISATION OF EDUCATION

1. *Education related to productivity*—Vocational education contributes to the achievement of society's goal of self-sufficiency in agriculture and industry by developing suitable skills.

2. *Preparation of individuals for jobs*—It prepares the individual to realize his own potential within the framework of economic development to which the individual contributes.

3. *Employment potentialities*—Education does not produce jobs but vocationalised education makes it more timely for an individual to get a job or to be his own master either starting a new productive activity or a service which may satisfy a felt need of the community.

4. *Broadening of horizon*—It leads to an understanding of the scientific and technological aspects of contemporary civilisation in such a way that they comprehend their environment critically and constructively.

5. *Dignity of labour*—Vocationalisation of education provides useful experience for the development of dignity of labour.

6. *Maximum utilisation of the material resources of the country*—Due to lack of trained technical know how our resources have remained unutilized. Vocationalisation of education provides suitable opportunities.

Centrally Sponsored Scheme of Vocationalisation of Secondary Education

A Centrally sponsored scheme of vocationalisation of higher secondary education was introduced in February 1988 with the following objects:

1. To enhance individual employability.
2. To reduce the mismatch between demand and supply of skilled manpower.
3. To provide an alternative for those who pursue higher education without particular interest or purpose.

Major steps taken in Vocationalisation of Education

1. A Joint Council for Vocational Educational (JVC) was set up in April 1990 for policy formulation and coordination at the national level.
2. In 1993, Pandit Sunderlal Sharma Central Institute of Vocational Education (SSCIVE) was set up at Bhopal to provide technical and academic support to the programme in the country.
3. Nearly 60 vocational courses have been notified under the Apprenticeship Act.
4. Collaborative arrangements have been made with the Ministry of Railways.

TARGETS SET AND ACHIEVED IN NPE, 1986 AND 1992

Target set in NPE, 1986—It is proposed that vocational courses cover 10 per cent of higher secondary students by 1990 and 25 per cent by 1995. Steps will be taken to see that a substantial majority of the products of vocational courses are employed or self-employed. Review of the courses offered would be regularly undertaken. Government will also review its recruitment policy to encourage diversification at the secondary level."

Targets Set in NPE, 1992—"It is proposed that vocational courses cover 10 per cent of higher secondary students by 1995 and 25 per cent. by 2000. Steps will be taken to see that a substantial majority of the products of vocational courses are employed or become self-employed. Review of the courses offered would be regularly undertaken. Government will also review its recruitment policy to encourage diversification at the secondary level.

Present Position—At present only 10 per cent of the students are opting out for the vocational courses against a target of 25 per cent by 2005. Thus the situation is of great concern.

Problems of Vocationalisation

1. General Indifference to vocational pursuits.
2. Vocational courses as dumping ground.
3. Inadequate content of vocational courses.
4. Lack of equipment.
5. Lack of trained vocational teachers.
6. Non-determination of equivalance of vocational degrees.
7. Limited choice of vocational courses.
8. Inadequate guidance and counselling facilities.
9. Lack of research.
10. Lack of systematic vocational set up.
11. Evaluation difficulties.

Suggestions for Accelerating Vocationalisation of Secondary Education

1. *Vocational institutions not to be regarded as dumping ground for drop-outs and educationally backward pupils*—It is extremely important that our attitude towards schools should undergo a revolutionary change. We should form right type of attitude towards drop-outs, who go in for vocational institutions.

2. *Vocational courses should be terminal in character*—At the end of a course, the students should be prepared for career or independent work. The knowledge imparted should be theoretical as well as practical. The courses should produce semi-skilled and skilled workers for lower level and middle level requirements.

3. *Vocational courses for drop-outs*—In our country it is estimated that out of 100 students who join class I, only 50 reach class VIII and only 16 class XII. It is, therefore, suggested that part-time courses should be organised

for these drop-outs. Separate courses should be devised for girls in accordance with their requirements.

4. *Provision for further training and re-training to persons opting for vocational courses*—Provision for further training and re-training to persons opting for vocational courses will have to be assured so that they may have the chance for advance studies and higher specialisation if they have the capacity and will to do it.

5. *Training of village worker for agriculture extension programme*—Short refresher courses to increase food production and to give a new outlook to agriculture be organised for such workers.

6. *Compulsory introduction of work experience in all primary and secondary schools*—Establishment of school complex consisting of a group of schools to provide work experience to the pupils individually as well as in groups will be very useful. Proper care should be taken to see that it does not meet the fate of basic education.

7. *Pre-occupational education and vocational guidance*—There should be provision not only to provide vocational advice but there should also be provision for aptitude and psychological testing wherever possible.

8. *Placement or organised transfer from vocational schools to industries, or enterprises*—A separate statewise agency should be set up for this purpose.

9. *Part-time vocational courses for self-employed persons*—There is a great need to organise courses for the agriculturist who works on the family farm. A careful study of the local needs should be made before the selection of various courses. A few central places in the district should be selected for such courses.

10. *Provision for on-the-job training*—Provision for on-the-job training should be made with the help of nearby industries or enterprises, both of private and public sector.

11. *Provision of building equipment*—Adequate building and proper equipment are essential for the implementation of any educational programme and vocational education is no exception to it. A central place in each district be selected for vocational schools with hostel accommodation.

12. *Training of vocational teachers*—All progressive and industrialised countries attach great importance to this training programme. In India also we have to give due attention to this aspect.

13. *Adequate preparation: more challenging task*—It will be necessary to prepare suitable textbooks and other reading material for various courses to be selected in different vocational schools.

14. *Freeships and stipends to vocational trainees*—In order to encourage more young boys and girls to take up vocational courses, freeships and stipends will be very necessary. The existing Apprenticeship Scheme will have to be strengthened.

15. *Very low fees for vocational courses*—Vocational courses of all types

should be provided without charging any fees or nominal fees at all levels.

16. *Vocational education to become people's movement*—The Government may take the lead but the cooperation of the State Government as well as other non-governmental agencies is very essential.

17. *Study of manpower needs*—It is widely felt that in India the expansion of vocational and technical education should be done with caution and with regard to the development of organised, industries and needs of the society.

18. *District and state vocational committees*—District and state vocational committees having representatives of productive activities and services, trade and commerce, administration, planning and educational institutions would be most useful not only in deciding upon the vocations for which facilities should be provided from year to year, but also in deciding on the content of the vocational courses and more than this, the manner of facilitating training in these vocations by the cooperative participation of the above mentioned agencies.

19. *School industry link*—Through proper legislation, the government could consider involving large public undertakings and workshops, such as those belonging to the reailways to take positive steps to adopt higher secondary schools for teaching and training in certain fields so that the costs of vocationalization do not mount, at least in part, owning to the duplication of facilities. The laboratories and workshops of these institutions should be made available during the vacations and during holidays.

Needless to say that vocational programmes in most cases will have to be run by sharing the facilities of professional institutions also, besides part-time staff. It is in sense a partnership programme between education and other sectors of the economy and the services between the school and the factory or the farm.

20. *Need for systematic supervision and effective administration of vocational education programmes*—A separate department should be established at the State level for the administration and supervision of vocational education.

21. *Problems related to reorientation and training*—The introduction of vocational courses has created enormous problems of training of teachers. As a matter of fact only bonafide vocational experts can impart vocational education effectively. Ways and means will have to be devised so that such trained vocational experts come forward for working in educational institutions. Proper qualifications will have to be prescribed for teachers teaching vocational subjects.

22. *Problems related to evaluation*—Suitable evaluation tools will have to be developed immediately to assess the performance of the students in the vocational courses. Subjective element will have to be reduced to the minimum.

23. *Redesigning of Teacher Training Courses*—The teachers training colleges and departments are required to recast their curriculum so that it is in accordance with the new requirements.

24. *Problems related to the determination of equivalence of diplomas/ certificates and degrees*—A student will not go in for a vocational course unless he is sure that a particular course will lead him to a specific job. This points to the need of a more centralised system for identifying the course which are acceptable to the organised sector and whose equivalence is already determined.

Similarly, proper arrangements will have to be made for those students who wish to go in for higher education after completing a two-year vocational course.

25. *Problems related to research*—So far we have been guided by the subjective opinion of a few educational experts who dominate and whose opinions carry considerable weight. Our educational programmes, by and large, have not been based on try-outs and surveys. It is very much surprising that no authentic survey has been conducted to assess the reactions of the students who are directly involved in the new scheme of secondary and higher secondary education. It is very imperative that suitable techniques of educational research are evolved and used to find out the reactions not only of the students who are studying under the new pattern but also of their parents and teachers. This would provide pragmatic guidelines for formulating scheme of educational reforms.

26. *Easy loans*—Adequate provision will have to be made for a system of easy loans so that vocationally trained students are motivated to set up their own business.

27. *Co-ordination with the finance department*—It has generally been observed that there is no proper co-ordination between the educational administrators and the officials of the Finance Department of the states with the result that there is an undue delay in getting financial sanctions for the requisite staff, equipment, etc. Suitable ways and means will have to be devised so that the officials of the Finance department appreciate the urgency and significance of educational reforms in their real perspective and shed their traditional attitude of putting unnecessary obstacles in clearing schemes of educational reforms.

To the above may be added the following recommendations made by the Ramamurti Committee (1990).

28. *Work benches and practice schools*—In order that the process of vocational education is enriched by a meaningful combination of teaching of theory and practice and effective linkages are established with the 'world of work', 'work benches' and 'practice schools' should be identified, accredited and involved 'work benches' and 'practice schools' are work situations selected for the purpose of giving vocational training and direct experience to students within production units or developmental activities of the official agencies. This arrangement offers a more effective educational strategy for providing vocational experience to students than what can be arranged within the four walls of the 'classroom'.

Table 14.3: Number of Schools, Sections, and Enrolment Capacity in States/UTs under the Scheme of Vocationalisation of Secondary Education (2001-2002)

S.No.	*States/UTs*	*No. of Schools*	*No. of Sections*	*Enrolment Capacity*
1	*2*	*3*	*4*	*5*
1.	Andhra Pradesh	668	1880	94000
2.	Arunachal Pradesh	4	4	200
3.	Assam	225	510	25500
4.	Bihar	251	752	37600
5.	Chhattisgarh	—	—	—
6.	Delhi	38	93	4650
7.	Goa	43	106	5300
8.	Gujarat	364	1032	51600
9.	Haryana	170	876	43350
10.	Himachal Pradesh	40	82	4100
11.	Jammu & Kashmii	38	38	1900
12.	Jharkhand	—	—	—
13.	Karnataka	564	1427	71350
14.	Kerala	363	1008	50400
15.	Madhya Pradesh	465	1307	65350
16.	Maharashtra	1141	3480	17400
17.	Manipur	19	57	2850
18.	Meghalaya	10	20	1000
19.	Mizoram	17	51	2550
20.	Nagaland	8	16	800
21.	Orissa	231	924	46200
22.	Punjab	282	846	42300
23.	Rajasthan	155	465	23250
24.	Sikkim	7	9	450
25.	Tamil Nadu	700	2140	107000
26.	Tripura	12	12	600
27.	Uttar Pradesh	910	2350	117500
28.	Uttaranchal	—	—	—
29.	West Bengal	39	39	1950
30.	Andaman & Nicobar	3	3	150
31.	Chandigarh	17	58	2900
32.	Dadra & Nagara Haveli	2	2	100
33.	Daman & Diu	2	5	250
34.	Lakshadweep	—	—	—
35.	Pondicherry	12	16	800
	Total	**6800**	**19599**	**979950**

15

Development of Teacher Education in India

MEANING OF TEACHER EDUCATION

Dictionary of Education (1973), defines teacher education as "All formal and informal activities and experiences that help to qualify a person to assume the responsibility as a member of the educational profession and to discharge his responsibility most effectively."

Encyclopedia of Educational Research (1941), Walter S. Monroe qualifies, teacher education as, "The total education experiences which contribute to the preparation of a person but the term is completely employed to designate the programme for courses and other experiences offered by an educational institute for the announced purposes of preparing persons for teaching and other educational service and for contribution to their growth in competency for such service. Such teacher education programmes are offered in teacher colleges, normal schools and colleges and universities."

NEED AND SIGNIFICANCE OF TEACHER EDUCATION

The contention that teachers are born, not made, can be true only in a few rare cases. It is also not contended that training, by itself, is sure to make a good teacher. But it is generally observed that a teacher with training becomes more mature and confident to perform his task more efficiently. Proper training and education enables the teacher to have a knowledge of how children grow, develop and learn, how they can be taught best and how their innate capacities can be brought out and developed. Teacher education is needed for kindling the initiative of the teacher, for keeping it alive, for removing the evils of 'hit and miss' process, for according a professional status to the teaching profession and above all for making the optimum use of time and energy of the teacher and the taught.

It has been aptly remarked, "If you educate a boy, you educate one individual. If you educate a girl you educate the whole family and if you educate a teacher, you educate the whole community."

The Education Commission (1964-66) said, "A sound programme of professional education of teachers is essential for the qualitative improvement of education. Investment in teacher education can yield very rich dividends because the financial resources required are small when measures against the resulting improvements in the education of millions."

OBJECTIVES OF TEACHER EDUCATION: GENERAL AND SPECIFIC STAGEWISE

The National Council for Teacher Education has suggested the following:

The General Objectives

The general objectives of teacher education as derived from the context, concerns and scope and applicable to various stages/levels may be as follows:

- To develop a critical awareness among the teachers and teacher educators regarding the realities of Indian life.
- To promote such capabilities in them as may be necessary for the realization of national values and goals as enshrined in the Constitution of India.
- To enable them to act as agents of modernization, social change and development and transmittance of the national and cultural heritage.
- To cultivate rational thinking and scientific temper.
- To promote among them the managerial and organizational skills as required in the contemporary Indian educational contexts.
- To develop among them the capabilities needed for performing their role in a dynamic society in order to meet the challenges of continuity and change.
- To make them aware of the environmental and ecological problems and enable them to find out their suitable solutions.
- To develop interest capacity for involvement in community life and draw its resources for the welfare of the school for meaningful education.
- To develop competencies and skills needed for becoming an effective teacher.
- To enable them to impart knowledge and reconstruct experiences.
- To inculcate positive attitudes towards students.
- To develop the capacities to organise supplementary educational activities.
- To develop interest and skills for undertaking action research/research.
- To inculcate among the teachers a sense of value judgement, value commitment and value transmission.
- To enable teachers to develop aesthetic sense among students.
- To foster their interest in in-service education/life-long learning.
- To sensitise pupil teachers towards the promotion of patriotic feelings, national integration, world peace and protection of human rights.
- To plan and organise for capacity building with a view to enabling

them to look into the students' needs in physical education and helping them in this regard.

- While the objectives of stages specific curriculum have commonality with the general objectives, each stage has specific objectives of its own.

The Specific Objectives of Pre-School Teacher Education Curriculum

- To sensitise pupil-teachers towards physical, mental, moral, social, aesthetic and linguistic development of children.
- To enable pupil-teachers to help in inculcating useful social habits for the development of children.
- To acquire knowledge for understanding the psychological make up of children.
- To cultivate social sensitivity, affection for children and respect for their uniqueness.
- To be able to organise different types of activities for the development of children individually and collectively.
- To acquaint them with the principles of child care and child health.
- To empower pupil-teachers for promoting creativity, inventiveness and developing imagination among children.
- To enable them to select prepare and use different kinds of teaching aids and resource materials for the children.
- To develop skills and competencies in making learning a joyful activity for children.

The Specific Objectives of Elementary Teacher Education Curriculum

- To equip teachers with sufficient theoretical and practical knowledge and skills.
- To develop a proper understanding of the psychological and sociological principles implicit in the elementary education.
- To empower teachers for promoting all round development of children.
- To generate the capacities for greater motivation, aspiration and a sense of value commitment.
- To enable teachers to manage learning resources and organise experiences for children at this stage with the focus on the minimum levels of learning.
- To enable teachers to foster problem-solving ability among pupils.
- To acquaint them with methods and techniques of handling children with special needs.
- To develop among them the capacity to solve the social educational activities for this group of pupils.
- To enable pupil-teachers to organise necessary skills so as to develop

curiosity, imagination and self-confidence among children.

- To enable them to perform their varied roles in the educational system as well as in society.
- To develop communication skills.
- To foster the desire for life-long learning.
- To motivate them to undertake action research and employ innovative practices.
- To enable them to use community resources as educational inputs.

The Specific Objectives of Secondary Teacher Education

- To develop among teachers a clear understanding of the psychology of their students.
- To enable them to understand the process of socialisation.
- To develop in them an understanding of the principles of pedagogy, curriculum development, its transaction and evaluation.
- To enable them to make pedagogical analysis of the subjects they are to teach at the secondary stage.
- To develop the skills for guidance and counselling.
- To enable them to foster creative thinking among pupils for the reconstruction of knowledge.
- To acquaint them with the factors and forces (within the school and outside) affecting educational system and class room situation.
- To acquaint them with educational needs of special groups of pupils.
- To enable them to utilise community resources as educational inputs.
- To develop communication skills and to use the modern information technology.
- To enable them to undertake action research and use innovative practices.
- To foster in them a desire for life-long learning.

The Specific Objectives of Senior Secondary Teacher Education

Academic Stream. In addition to the objectives enunciated for secondary teachers education it may also include the following:

- To promote academic interests and values among teachers.
- To develop knowledge of the subject, clarify its objectives, evolve a suitable methodology of instruction and sharpen the communication skills.
- To develop in them reading and reference skills.
- To develop them to develop love for knowledge among students.
- To develop skills for curriculum development and transaction.
- To enable them to use and develop various types of tests.
- To enable them to reconstruct knowledge and experience under new contexts.

Vocational Stream. In addition to the objectives of secondary teachers education, the following objectives may also be included.

- To make them understand the philosophy and social relevance of vocational education.
- To develop a sense of workmanship and dignity of labour.
- To impart knowledge and develop skills necessary for teaching vocational subjects.
- To give them relevant information for attaining success in a vocation of their choice.
- To develop faith in the efficiency of vocational education.

Broadly speaking there are two types of teachers education–per-service and in-service teacher education.

Types of Teacher Education and Institutions

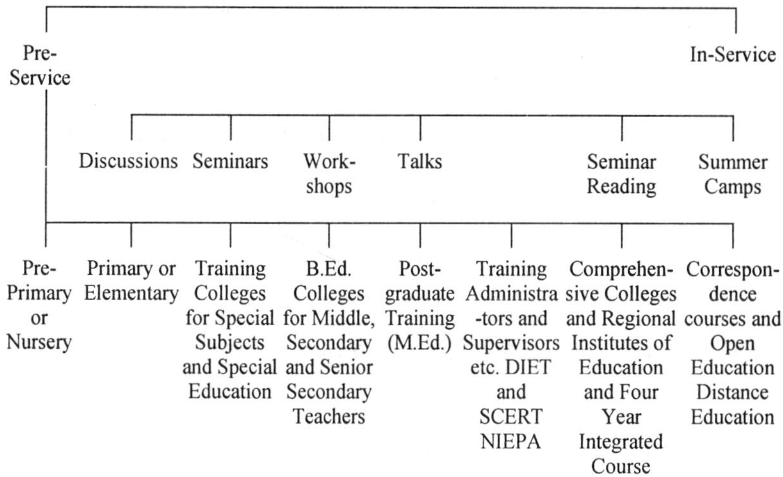

1. *Pre-primary or nursery teacher education institutions*—Catering to the needs of teachers for Kindergarten, Montessori, Bal Vihars etc., minimum qualifications for admission to this course is secondary, higher secondary and the duration of the course in one year. Many institutions impart training for two years.
2. *Training schools for elementary teachers*—In general the course lasts for two years and the minimum qualifications for entrance is secondary. The present trend is to prescribe higher secondary as the minimum qualification for entrance. The duration of the course is 2 years.

   The Delhi University has started an integrated teachers' training course for three years in some colleges. The Degree imparted in B.Ed. Elementary Education.
3. *Secondary training schools*—These schools provide teachers for the

middle and junior secondary schools. However, these training schools are gradually disappearing.

4. *Training colleges or colleges of education*—The minimum qualification for entrance is graduation with usually 45% minimum marks. The duration of the course is one year. Degree awarded are B.T. or L.T. or B.Ed. These colleges provide teachers for secondary and senior secondary schools.
5. *Institutes of advanced studies in education*—These provide opportunities to take up Master of Education and M.Phil courses.
6. *Training colleges for special subjects*—These are separate colleges for preparing teachers in certain subjects like physical education, home science, craft, languages, etc.
7. *Training colleges for special education*—These colleges prepare teachers for teaching students with various types of handicaps—the deaf and the dumb, etc.

Comprehensive Colleges of Education

The idea was suggested by the Indian Education Commission (1964-66) and the objective of a comprehensive college of education is to break the isolation of teacher education. A comprehensive college of educational runs as many levels of teacher training as possible, for example, elementary teacher training, language teachers training, physical education teacher training, B. Ed. etc. A few such colleges exist in Maharastra.

Regional Colleges of Education (RCEs) to Regional Institutes of Education (RIEs)

The Regional Colleges of Education (RCEs) started by National Council of Education Research and Training (NCERT) have been converted into the Regional Institutes of Education (RIEs).

The Five Regional Institutes of Education are located at Ajmer, Bhopal, Bhubaneshwar, Mysore and Shillong.

The Regional Institutes of Education (RIEs) located at Ajmer, Bhopal, Bhubaneswar and Mysore cater to educational needs (pre-service and in-service education) of teachers in the States and UTs under their jurisdiction. To a limited extent, pre-service professional training to prepare school teachers for teaching Science and Mathematics and teachers educators of elementary Teacher Training Institutions is also offered by the RIEs. They act as Regional Resource Institutions for school education and teacher education, extend required assistance in implementing the policies of the States/UTs and assist in implementation, monitoring and evaluation of the Centrally Sponsored Schemes. The RIE Ajmer looks after teacher education and other educational requirements of the States of Delhi, Haryana, Himachal Pradesh, Jammu and Kashmir, Punjab, Rajasthan, Uttar Pradesh, Uttaranchal and the UT of

Chandigarh. The RIE Bhopal has within its pale the States of Chattisgarh, Goa, Gujarat, Madhya Pradesh, Maharashtra and UTs of Dadra and Nagar Haveli and Daman and Diu. The States of Arunachal Pradesh, Assam, Bihar, Kharkan, Manipur, Meghalaya, Mizoram, Nagaland, Orissa, Sikkim, Tripura, West Bengal and the UT of Andaman and Nicobar Islands are covered by the RIE Bhubaneswar. The States of Andhra Pradesh, Karnataka,, Kerala and Tamil Nadu and UTs of Pondicherry and Laskhadweep are covered by the RIE Mysore.

The RIE (NE-RIE) set up at Shillong caters to the educational needs of North-Eastern States i.e., Assam, Arunachal Pradesh, Meghalaya, Mizoram, Manipur, Nagaland, Sikkim and Tripura. This was the last institution set up.

States Institutes of Education

A chain of State Institutes of Education for elementary school teachers was started in 1964. At present there are 30 State Institutions in the country. U.P. is the only State with two such institutions; at Allahabad and Luknow. The main purposes and functions of these institutes are to:

1. Provide various training courses for supervisors of elementary schools or elementary teacher educators.
2. Organise conferences and seminars to senior State education officers
3. Provide, conduct and supervise extension services to training institutions for elementary teachers.
4. Organize research in elementary education and teachers education.
5. Provide correspondence courses for teachers.
6. Assist the State Departments of Education in the planning and implementation of various educational plans at the elementary stages of education.

Colleges of Teacher Education (CTE) and Institutes of Advanced Studies in Education (IASE).

As envisaged in the NPE and Programme of Action (1986), the Centrally-sponsored scheme of Restructuring and Reorganisation of Teacher Education was taken up in 1987 to create a viable institutional structure, academic and technical resource base for orientation, training and continuous upgrading of knowledge, competence and pedagogical skills for school teachers in the country. Under the scheme Eighty six CTE have been set up by upgrading existing Secondary Teacher Education (STEIs) offering B.Ed. courses and 38 IASE by upgrading Colleges and University Departments of Education offering M.Ed. Courses.

Table 15.1: Number of Teachers Training Institutes (Elementary) and Teacher Training/Education Colleges Since 1950-51

Year	*Teacher Training Schools*	*Teacher Training Colleges*
1951	182	128
1961	317	272
1971	427	469
1981	480	627
1991	833	872
2001	1023	1089

State of Teacher Education

From time to time, a great concern has been expressed regarding the quality of teacher education in India. Some efforts have also been made to improve the quality but result has not been quite rewarding.

In *'New Era in Teacher Education'* (1966), Dr. G. Chaurasia drew a very dim picture of teacher education in India. He stated, "Teachers colleges are merrily existing in a dream world. They dream any intellectual contact with other university discipline; their theory is pedantic and a poor imitation of foreign concepts and beliefs. They have scanty respect for schools; their familiarity with educational practices is pedestrian. The sheer weight of deadwood and routine performances drain away all the energy of staff and students in the training colleges."

The NCERT document entitled '*Teacher Education—A Curriculum*' (1978) has made an important observation regarding improvement in all aspects of teacher education that "a fundamental change be effected in all aspects of teacher education, i.e., objectives, structures, staffing pattern, administrative machinery and control of teacher education in the country."

Prof. R.P. Singh struck a very pessimistic note in *'The Teacher in India'* (1984) when he observed, "No matter what the Education Commission may have to say about improving their quality of produce, they, I think, will go on with their ageless practices unmindful of the 'revolutionary changes' in school and society'.

He further observed, "To conclude, the training colleges, at various levels, are operating on the periphery of the problems Indian education faces today and hardly, if ever, touch upon the major issues that constitute the hard-core of our education... Numerous studies have shown that teachers themselves are the bitterest critics of teacher education programmes. They call them irrelevant, lacking in vision and meaningful substance".

Prof. Uday Shanker has observed in *'Education of Indian Teachers'* (1984) that "in such a short time how could one expect to inculcate in the trainee a 'teacher personality' with proper outlook, attitude, teaching skills and faith in the profession".

'The Challenge of Education' (1985) describes the deteriorating situation

of teacher education as "...but unfortunately, the process of updating the curricula of teacher education has been very slow. Much of teacher education is irrelevant even to contemporary requirements, leave alone those of the future."

The National Commission on School Teachers (1983-85) lamented: "What obtains now in the majority of our Teachers Colleges and Training Institutions are woefully inadequate and in the context of the changing needs of India today."

Major Drawbacks and Problems of the Present System of Teacher Education:

1. Faulty methods of selection because of political, social and personal influences.
2. Inadequacy of one-year B.Ed. Course.
3. Lop-sided curriculum.
4. Obsolete and irrelevant methodology of teaching.
5. Neglect of study of education as a discipline.
6. Inadequate training in practical skills.
7. Insufficient time and attention paid to the actual practice teaching.
8. Isolation between the Colleges of Education and the schools.
9. Insufficient training in the art of communicating with the community.
10. Meagre training in the art of organising co-curricular activities.
11. Ineffective supervision of the teaching practice by the supervisors.
12. Faulty methods of assessment of trainee's work.
13. Less qualified teacher educators.
14. Lack of physical facilities.
15. Shorter working hours.
16. Dearth of the use of new technology of teaching.

Revitalizing and Modernization of Pre-Service Teacher Education

The National Commission on School Teachers (1983-85) suggested the following measures:

1. Recruitment before Training where possible.
2. Effective Selection Procedures.
3. Four-year Integrated Course.
4. Restructuring the Curriculum.
5. Study of Education as a Discipline.
6. Due emphasis on Practical Skills.
7. Systematic Internship or Practice of Teaching.
8. Comprehensive Content-cum-Methodology.
9. Use of Technology in the Training of Teachers.
10. Adequate Physical Facilities.
11. Appointment of competent Teacher Educators.
12. Increased Working Hours.

Suggestive Programme for Revitalizing Pre-Service Teacher Education in India

The NCERT working Group for preparing a scheme for Revitalization and Modernisation of Pre-service Education (1986) made the following important recommendations:

1. The national accrediting agency should appoint expert committees to inspect teacher training institutions and on the basis of their reports decide about the recognition of the institution.

2. The candidates passing from an institution or a course not recognised by the national accrediting agency should not be appointed as teachers at the primary or secondary level.

3. After completing the course of studies at a recognised teacher training institution, a candidate should be required to undergo internship in teaching for a period of six months under a trained registered teacher at a recognised secondary/primary school. On satisfactory completion of the internship, he should be granted a teacher's licence and registered as a teacher.

4. No person should be employed as a teacher unless he possess a valid teacher's licence. A teacher's licence may be invalidated if at any time a teacher is found guilty of gross misconduct, corrupt practices, criminal offences or serious neglect of his duties as teacher.

5. The Central and State Governments should make studies to determine the requirement of teachers subjectwise and levelwise during each five year plan period. The number of teachers to be trained in each state during the five year period should be fixed on the basis of manpower study.

6. Admission to the teacher training institutions in a state should be made on the basis of results of a common entrance test given by a state agency. The entrance test should be quite comprehensive.

7. The teacher-pupil ratio in a teacher training institution should be 1:10, subject to minimum of 10 teacher educators. There should be at least one teacher educator in each school subject and at least three in pedagogical subjects. There should be at least two teacher educators in Science Methodology; one in Physical Science and one in Biological Science.

8. Every teacher training institution should have a good library with at least 5000 books in all subject areas. It should have adequate reading room space where at least one fourth of the student strength can study at a time. It should also subscribe to a minimum of five professional journals.

9. Every teacher training institution should have a good Science Methods Labcratory with necessary equipment and apparatus for conducting all experiments in sciences upto higher secondary level. Necessary tools and materials should be available to prepare models and teaching aids in science.

10. There should be a separate laboratory for educational technology where

trainees can do practical work for resource material development for teaching different schools subjects.

11. Every teacher training institution should have adequate hardware and software in educational technology and trainees should be provided practical work in the use of educational technology under micro and mini-teaching sessions.

12. Every teacher training institution should have facilities for practical work in art, music and other aspects of culture. Every student should do some practical work in art and culture.

13. Every teacher training institution should provide practical work in games and physical education in groups for at least two hours a week for each group.

14. Every teacher training institution should have facility for organising practical work in some locally relevant socially useful productive work.

15. The State Government should provide full financial support to all teacher training institutions in the State so as to provide the minimum facilities as outlined above.

16. The four-year integrated programme of teacher education is a better model of teacher education. Such institutions can be started by amalgamating the facilities of an arts and science college and one-year B.Ed. college existing in the same town.

17. The minimum qualifications for a teacher educator in a teacher training college or university department of education in the methodology subject should be Master's degree in the concerned subject together with Master's degree in Philosophy. Psychology or Sociology together with Master's degree in Education. In addition, he should have M.Phil/Ph.D. in Education.

18. The minimum instruction in time in one-year B.Ed. Course should be 36 weeks after the last date for admission. Out of the 36 weeks instruction at the college, not more than 4 weeks should be spent in teaching practice. No candidate should be allowed to appear at the B.Ed. degree examination unless he has completed 36 weeks instruction at college.

19. The teacher training institution should be regarded as non-vocational departments so that the services of the staff should be utilised for conducting entrance tests and annual examinations.

IN-SERVICE EDUCATION OF TEACHERS

Importance and Need of In-Service Teacher Education

Gurudev Rabindra Nath Tagore has very aptly stated: "The teacher can never truly teach, unless he is still learning himself. A lamp can never light another lamp unless it continues to burn its own flame."

The Report of University Education Commission (1948-49) appointed by the Government of India contains these observations, "It is extraordinary that our school teachers learn all of whoever subject they teach before reaching the age of twenty-four or twenty-five and then all their further education is left to experience which in most cases is another name for stagnation. We must realise that experience needs to be supplemented by experiment before reaching its fullness and that a teacher, to keep alive and fresh, should become a learner from time to time. Constant out-pouring needs constant intaking: practice must be reinforced by theory and the old must be constantly tested by the new."

The teacher must catch the spirit of Thomas Arnold, an eminent teacher at Rugbby who said, "I prefer that my students should drink from a running stream rather than a stagnant pool."

NCTE has stressed the importance of in-service education of teachers on account of the following considerations:

(1) The in-service teacher education programmes are essential in view of obsolescence as well as explosion of knowledge and are necessitated to acquire and execute new and different roles. Advances in the fields of curriculum, evaluation, audio-visual aids, telecommunication, etc., demand updating and orientation of teachers. An innovation at a macro level would invariably fail if teachers are not equipped and properly oriented to implement that innovation. In the Indian context the developments, such as, the 10+2+3 scheme, the making of science compulsory up to the class 10 standard, new practices to evaluation the internal assessment, question banks, continuous and comprehensive evaluation and grading, introduction of new topics like environmental education, population education, computer education, etc., demand continuous in-service training of teachers.

(2) The National Commission on Teachers recommended that promotion (upward mobility) of teachers would also depend upon the completion of certain number of in-service programmes. This stipulation itself demands regular in-service programmes of teachers.

(3) In-service programmes need to be built around 'transformational objectives', i.e., increasing motivational level, enriching self-concept, developing climate of enquiry and making teachers reflective practitioners. The thrust of transformational objectives is to develop such qualities in teachers as would enable them to become receptive, innovative and dynamic.

(4) Due to advances in tele-communication and open market policies the world is gradually becoming a global village. Globalisation and liberalisation are becoming key words. Teachers and teacher educators, therefore, would be required to be conversant with international trends and develop competencies in internationalism, multi-culturalism and multi-racialism.

The Department of Education in England has stated this as follows: "The hall-mark of good teacher is that he himself is always learning and always developing his knowledge and understanding of children and young people. In short, a teacher should be a person who, because of his attitude of knowledge, to ideas, to his fellows and to life generally is better educated today, than he was yesterday and will tomorrow be better educated than he is today."

Meaning of In-Service Teacher Education

The term is self-explanatory. It refers to the education a teacher receives after he has entered the teaching profession and after he has had his education in a teachers' college. It includes all the programmes, educational, social or others, in which the teacher takes a vital part, all the extra education which he receives at different institutions by way of refresher and other professional courses, and all the travel and visits which he undertakes. All these things enlarge his experiences and vision.

The Commission on Teacher Education in USA explained this clearly as: "The continued education of teachers means much more than making up in preparation. It means continuous growth in the capacity to teach. It means broadened understanding of human development and human living. And now more than at any previous periods in school history it means growth in one's capacity to work with others, with classroom teachers and principals in a variety of activities with the administration, with the parents and community leaders and with children of different age groups."

Aims of In-Service Teacher Education and Training of Teachers (INSET)

1. To maintain the knowledge and skills of teachers.
2. To give teachers the opportunity to enlarge and improve their knowledge and educational capacities in all fields of their work.
3. To make teachers ready and able to understand and face in time new situations coming up in society and to prepare their students for the new economic, social or cultural challenges.
4. To enable teachers to gain additional qualifications and to develop their special talents and dispositions.
5. To raise the cultural and professional standard of the teaching force as a whole and strengthen its innovative vigour and creativity.

Institutions for In-Service Education

1. State Institutes of Education and District Institutes of Education.
2. State Institutes of Science.
3. State Institutes of English.
4. Extension Services Departments.
5. State Directorates of Education.
6. Voluntary Organisations.
7. NCERT (National Council of Educational Research and Training).

8. NCTE (National Council for Teacher Education).
9. UGC (University Grants Commission).
10. NIEPA (National Institute of Educational Planning and Administration).
11. Professional Organisations of Teachers.
12. International Educational Organisations.
13. Indira Gandhi National Open University.
14. State Boards of Education.

Programmes for In-Service Education—Programmes for in-service teacher education are: (1) Seminars, (2) Extension Lectures, (3) Refresher Courses, (4) Workshops, (5) Study Groups, (6) Conferences, (7) Experimenting, (8) Professional Writings, (9) Discussions and Debates, and (10) Educational Tours and Exchange Programmes.

Shortcoming and Inadequacies of In-Service Education Programmes

The Working Group on In-Service Education of Teachers 1986 (NCERT) pointed out the following shortcomings of in-service teacher education (INSET):

(a) Inadequate understanding of the importance of in-service teacher education. INSET not only helps to update the teacher continuously but also remedies inadequacies of the existing pre-service education. In the process of providing in-service education, teacher educators gain experience relevant to pre-service education of teachers.

(b) Absence of a national system of in-service education. This has resulted in inadequate and unsystematised service to teachers.

(c) Lack of attention to methodology of in-service education. In the absence of specific infrastructure including manpower for in-service education, suitable methodologies for communication with small groups have not evolved.

(d) Unsystematic selection of participants and resource persons. Lack of advance planning and communication regarding content and objectives affects the deputation of suitable participants from various institutions. It can also affect the quality of resource input.

(e) Ineffective follow-up. Contact with teacher participants of in-service programmes is usually not maintained. Institutions and groups do not follow up the functioning of their trainees.

(f) Poor coordination and monitoring of in-service education programme. Agencies are not identified at the State/Central level to monitor the total efforts in the area. There is adhocism both in planning and implementation.

(g) Limited opportunities for training of in-service education personnel. Opportunities for renewal and interaction with colleges are equally important for those who are responsible for planning and implementing in-service education.

(h) Absence of research base for making in-service education more effective and inadequacy of research in INSET. It is the result of poor recognition given in the area which in turn impinges upon its development along suitable lines.

(i) Inadequate infrastructures for INSET at the State and national levels. To make the programme of in-service teacher education really effective, these shortcomings need to be rectified. In-service education needs of a large number of teachers cannot be met without a well developed appropriate infrastructure.

The National Commission on School Teachers 1983-85 pointed out the following inadequacies:

(1) There is today an absence of clear-cut policies and priorities for in-service education.
(2) There has been no systematic identification of needs.
(3) The content and quality of programmes offered are generally poor.
(4) Strategies for training are vague and half-hearted.
(5) Not much emphasis appears to have been placed on solving the practical problems of teachers or meeting their educational needs.
(6) In-service courses rarely result in the development of a corps of instructional material that can be used by participants and other teachers.
(7) Hardly any use is made of new media and technologies.
(8) Administrative support for innovations is lacking as headmasters, and supervisors are not often involved in programmes where teachers are being trained in the use of new methodologies.
(9) The phenomenon of routine transfers finds trained personnel not placed in positions where they should use their training maximally.

Suggestions for Improving In-Service Education

1. *Need for Expanding Facilities*—It has been observed that so far thousands of teachers especially those belonging to private institutions have not been actively involved in the Extension Services Programmes because of inadequate facilities. There is, therefore, a great need for expanding the programme of in-service education.
2. *Co-operation of Various Agencies*—The various agencies like the Extension Services Department, State Institutes of Education, State Department of Education, and State Boards of School Education need to co-ordinate their activities so that there is no over-lapping.
3. *Role of Inspectors*—It is the duty of the heads of institutions to encourage their staff to take part in the programmes of in-service education. The education officers like-wise should also encourage their participation and should ensure that all teachers attend these programmes.
4. *Well-planned Programmes*—The programmes of in-service education should be well-planned and organised properly.
5. *Resource Persons*—Well-qualified and experienced teachers should act as resource persons. They should be drawn from the staff of the Colleges of Education and the State Departments of Education. They must have something new to give to the teachers. The purpose of in-service programmes is not mere repetition of pre-service courses,

but it is to break new ground in content, organization, teaching and evaluation processes.

6. *Follow-up Programmes*—One important weakness of the present day extension service programme is that follow-up work is almost missing. Thus it is not known how far the participants benefit from the programme. Some way should be found out to ensure proper follow-up.
7. *Research*—These programmes should be backed by the findings of research. School teachers should be encouraged to take small research projects and report their findings to others.
8. *Incentive to Teachers*—There is need for providing some incentive to teachers who attend the courses of longer duration and during the holidays. Attendance at these longer courses should entitle them to some credit towards their professional degree such as B.Ed. or M.Ed., which they want to take up at a later stage. This practice is followed in U.S.A.
9. *Subject Teachers' Associations*—As suggested by the Kothari Commission, Subject Teachers' Associations should be formed at the city, district, state and all-India level on the different school subjects. This will stimulate initiative and experimentation and assist in the revision and upgrading of curricula through the provision of better teaching materials and the use of improved techniques of teaching and evaluation. The State Education Department should assist the subject teachers associations to hold periodical seminars and conferences and to conduct journals of their own.
10. *Subject Experts*—In order to provide guidance to teacher in the techniques of teaching various subjects, subject experts should be appointed at the district level.

Role of DIETs in improving in service education of elementary teachers

The NPE 1986 has visualised that for improving teacher education, a network of DIETs would be formed in the country.

Functions of DIETs

1. Providing pre-service education to prospective elementary teachers.
2. Organising in-service education programmes, for elementary teachers.
3. Providing training and continuing education to Non-formal and adult education instructors and supervisors.
4. Training and orientation of heads of institutions in institutional planning and management.
5. Providing academic support to school complexes and District Boards of Education.
6. Conducting action research and experimental work.
7. Serving evaluation centres for primary and upper primary schools as well as Non-formal and adult education programmes.
8. Providing consultancy and advice.

Out of 599 Districts in the country, 498 DIETs had been set up by 2005.

A Six-step Model for In-service Education

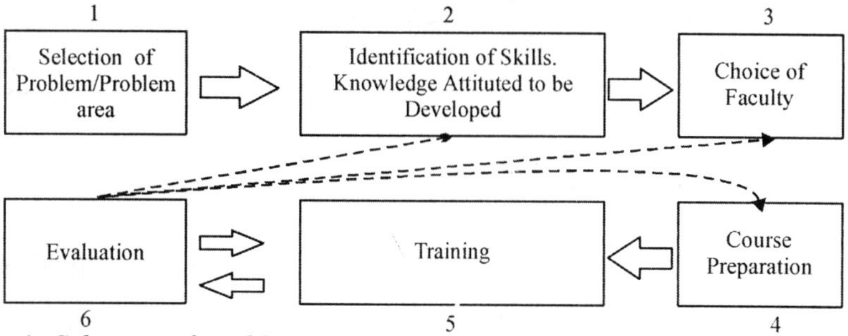

1. *Selection of Problem or Problem Area*—Choice of problem/problem area can involve field survey, study of literature, consultation, group discussions, etc.

2. *Identification of Skills*—It is necessary for evaluation.

3. *Choice of Faculty*—Success of the programme will depend greatly on the suitability of the course faculty.

4. *Evaluation*—This will involve among other things.
   (i) definition of goals/objectives related to serial number 2;
   (ii) definition of tasks/activities to be arranged; and
   (iii) choice of methodology including preparation of instructional materials.

5. *Training*—This will involve the preparation of the course progress and daily time table.

6. *Course Preparation*—It can involve the use of questionnaires and other tools relevant to assessing the relevance and effectiveness of this course.

National Council for Teacher Education (NCTE)

The National Council for Teacher Education (NCTE) which had been in existence for the last more than two decades was given a statutory recognition by a gazette notification issued on August 17, 1995 (Notification No. 484) by the Ministry of Human Resource Development (Department of Education). This was done in pursuance of the National Council for Teacher Education Act, 1993 (No. 73 of 1993). This Act has been enacted with a view to achieving planned and coordinated development of the Teacher Education system throughout the country, the regulation and proper maintenance of norms and standards in the teacher education system and for matters connected therewith. According to the Act "Teacher Education" includes programmes of education, research or training of persons for equipping them to teach at pre-primary, primary, secondary and senior secondary stages in schools, and includes non-formal education, part-time education, adult education and correspondence education. It is further provided in the Act that every institution offering or intending to offer a course or training in Teacher Education on or after 17th

August 1995 is to seek recognition in accordance with this Act by making an application to the respective Regional Committee of the NCTE. Further, any institution which has been recognised under the Act has to seek permission to start any new course or training in Teacher Education by making an application to the Regional Committee of the NCTE.

Territorial Jurisdiction of Regional Committees

I. Eastern

Arunachal Pradesh, Assam, Bihar, Manipur, Meghalaya, Mizoram, Nagaland, Orissa, Sikkim, West Bengal, Tripura, A & N Islands.

Address—Regional Director, Eastern Regional Committee (NCTE), Jana Shiksha Bhawan, Unit-V, Bhubaneshwar-751001.

II. Western

Goa, Gujarat, Madhya Pradesh, Maharashtra, D & N Haveli, Daman & Diu.

Address—Regional Director, Western Regional Committee (NCTE), Manas Bhawan (Near A.I.R.), Shyamia Hills, Bhopal-462002.

III. Northern

Haryana, Himachal Pradesh, Punjab, Rajasthan, Uttar Pradesh, Chandigarh, Delhi.

Address—Regional Director, Northern Regional Committee (NCTE), Directorate Adult Education Campus. Gopi Nath Marg, Panch Batti, Jaipur-302001.

IV. Southern

Andhra Pradesh, Karnataka, Kerala, Tamil Nadu. Laksha Dweep, Pondicherry.

Address—Regional Director, Southern Regional Committee (NCTE), No. 66, 6th Main, 4th Block, Rajaji Nagar, Bangalore-560010.

Functions of National Council for Teacher Education

According to the Act 1993, the NCTE performs the following functions:

1. Undertaking surveys and studies relating to various aspects of teacher-education and publishing the results.
2. Making recommendations to the Central and State Govt. Universities, the U.G.C. and other institutions in the preparation of plans and programmes in the field of teacher-education.
3. Coordinating and monitoring teacher-education and its development in the country.
4. Preparing guidelines with regard to minimum qualifications for the candidates to be employed as teacher-educators at different levels.
5. Developing norms for various courses or training in teacher-

education, including minimum eligibility criterion for admission.

6. Preparing guidelines and specified requirements for starting new courses and programmes under teacher-education.
7. Developing guidelines for general teacher-education programme.
8. Promoting innovations and research studies.
9. Supervising the teacher-education programmes and providing financial assistance.
10. Enforcing accountability of teacher-development programmes in the country.
11. Preventing commercialization in Teacher-education and maintaining quality and standard of teacher-education.
12. Preparing programmes for in service teacher-education for orienting teachers for latest developments.
13. Establishing international relations in the area of teacher-education.
14. Preventing B.Ed. correspondence courses which are lowering the standard and quality of teacher-education and commercialising the teacher-education.
15. Preparing Code of professional ethics for teachers.
16. Developing curriculum of Teacher-education.
17. Developing methodology of teaching and techniques of evaluation procedures, continuing and Non-formal education.
18. Improving role of teacher in social and vocational areas.

Policy Regarding Correspondence Courses

The NCTE has laid down clearly that correspondence programme leading to B.Ed. degree can be offered only to clear the backlog of untrained teachers for the present and that not more than 500 students can be enrolled by an institution in a year.

The other conditions laid down include that teachers seeking admission should have put in three-year service in a recognised school and that the duration of the programme will be for two years, with contact programme during two consecutive summer vacations—the intervening period taking care of correspondence lessons.

The NCTE has also categorically disapproved charging capitation fee from students. Commercialisation has been defined as the total receipts (including those from students per year) exceeding recurring expenditure of the programme by more than 10 per cent.

In order to help teachers already working in the system to keep abreast of the latest development in education, the NCTE has proposed that they should compulsorily undergo in-service teacher training programmes at least once in five years and accumulate credits. Such programmes are to be conducted by the existing institutions including DIETs and University Departments of Education.

It also urged that the expertise of Open Universities including the IGNOU should be fully utilised for offering in-service teacher training programmes as this would go a long way in making the programme easily accessible.

Curriculum Framework for Teacher Education. In 1996, NCTE prepared and circulated a curriculum framework for teacher education at various levels. The framework outlined concerns that teacher education should take note of, objectives of teacher education and several related issues.

Norms for Opening Different Types of Teacher Education Courses—The NCTE has prescribed norms for starting different types of institutions in the field of teacher education.

Need for More Vigilance

It is observed that NCTE has not been quite effective in checking the mushroom growth of teacher education institution. It is, therefore, very necessary that it takes stringent measures in this direction.